Praise for LOVE IS A HAMMER

"You will want everyone you know to read this book." —Bill McKeown, *Concept-Therapy Instructor, Life Coach, McKeown Seminars*

"It's rare that a book can transform you as you read it…a true nugget of spiritual principle is creatively revealed with every turn of the page!" —Dr. Marco Vespa, *SHIFT Wellness Studio, Denver, Colorado*

"LOVE IS A HAMMER'S message of healing, wellness, and wisdom resonates in a real way that holds that deep and timeless quality of articulated truth. What are you ready to learn?"—Pat Wells, M.A., *Licensed Professional Counselor & Advanced Clinical Hypnotherapist,* Author of *Memories of Mama* and *Self-Care for Tough Times*

"WOW! Spellbinding! I couldn't put it down. Intense human drama laced with metaphysical truths. I felt like the Captain was speaking directly to me!"—Dr. Mike Fitzgerald, *National Speaker, Chiropractor, Zone Healing Center Totowa, New Jersey*

"Brilliantly achieved.... A biographical adventure story depicting what we need more to see. Certainly can be read on many levels, a book with impact to grab the young & old!" —Michael Batrano, *CEO of Kaleidoscope P & D*

"LOVE IS A HAMMER is a journey in consciousness. I couldn't put it down! I am a fan of Hurst Peacock's brilliant ability to create a story that stimulates the mind and encompasses age-old principles to assist anyone during times of change and transition. This is a must read! Peacock is a brilliant writer, an up and coming new bestselling author whose time has come!" —Catherine Franklin B.S., D.C., *Morning Radio Host, Atlanta, GA*

"Every once in a great while there comes a book or an idea that is revolutionary and ahead of its time. *Love is a Hammer* is one of those books." —David Frost, D.C., *Zone Specialist, Frost Chiropractic Health Center*

"For those who identified with *The Shack* and want an even more emotional connection to that which lies beyond the obviousness of life as we know it, this is a must-read."—Amanda Alvord, *Author* of *The Frog Prince Finale*

"Hurst Peacock has a great understanding of Dr. Fleet as a man and an excellent understanding of Dr. Fleet's teachings on Life. He is the right person to portray Dr. Fleet to the world."—Dr. Peter Goldman, *Chiropractor, expert practitioner and teacher of Dr. Fleet's healing principles*

"Truly Amazing! LOVE IS A HAMMER is an exhilarating journey and an uncanny way of utilizing fiction and non-fiction to teach profound universal laws. Simply Brilliant!"—Dr. Nicholas T. Tedder, *Upper Cervical Specialist, International Speaker,* Author of *Wake Up America: Is Your Health Care Failing YOU?*

"LOVE IS A HAMMER is a must have for anyone seeking a better understanding of this journey called LIFE. Hurst Peacock does an amazing job of teaching deep spiritual truth in a simple, entertaining and yet profound way. You are sure to learn something new each time you read it. I am definitely hoping for a sequel!" —Dr. Jason A. Lupkes, *Life Coach, Concept-Therapy Instructor, Chiropractor, Zone Healing Center St. Cloud, MN*

"Hurst Peacock has a natural talent for spinning a good yarn while dropping in some powerful life lessons. This charming story is absolutely FULL of Physical, Mental and Spiritual Gems." —Dr. Nick Balovich, *Concept-Therapy Instructor, Chiropractor, Virginia Beach, VA*

Love is a Hammer

HURST PEACOCK

Love is a Hammer — First Edition © Hurst Peacock 2010

ISBN: 978-0-615-34215-3

This book was printed in the United States of America

C.T.P., LLC
814 Terrace Acres Drive
Auburn, Alabama 36830

Acknowledgements

I would like to thank Warren McKenney, George Fleet, Bill McKeown, Barbara Lynn, and Opal Downs for the anecdotal stories, first-hand accounts, and general information about the real Dr. Thurman Fleet.

I would like to thank the Concept-Therapy Institute for granting permission to directly quote Dr. Fleet's copyrighted material in this book and to sample his voice recordings on the corresponding soundtrack.

Thanks to all my teachers for inspiration and knowledge.

Thanks to you for reading and passing it on.

CHAPTER ONE
GO

E leven—twelve—thirteen—fourteen," Dawn whispered as she climbed the steps leading up to the courthouse.

Mom frowned slightly. "Honey, let's try to go up without counting." Dawn stopped whispering and looked down, but I could see that she kept moving her lips, obviously continuing her mental count. Mom noticed too, and her frown increased a bit.

I tried to change the subject. "I don't understand why Dawn and I couldn't just stay at the house," I said. "There's plenty of unpacking to do."

"First of all," Mom sighed, "that house is our new *home*. You can use that word to describe it. Second of all, once my new job starts next week and you kids start school in the fall, we won't see each other as much as we used to. I would like to spend time with my children while I can. Is that too much to ask?"

She waited until I mumbled 'no' and then continued, "We only have a couple of errands and then we can get something to eat together. Trust me, that unpacking isn't going anywhere. It'll still be there when we get home."

"*Home* is in California," I muttered as we pulled open the heavy door and walked inside.

"Don't start, Raymond." Mom's voice was subdued because we were now inside the building, but there was flint in her tone and I retreated to silence. Anyway, I got what I wanted: she forgot about Dawn.

We found the line for the Driver's License Registration and waited for what seemed like forever. The floor was a faded yellow tile and the walls had been painted a putrid green. The whole place smelled like a combination of stale cigarette smoke and bleach. There were no benches or any place to sit; I guess they didn't want people to fall asleep while they languished in the indefinite purgatory of government provided service. The whole scene was too depressing for me, so I asked Mom if I could take Dawn outside to wait.

We sat down on the steps by the side of the front door and people-watched. Parked at the curb by the bottom of the steps was a brown four-door sedan with "Kendall County" and a sheriff's star logo surrounding a picture of the state of Texas painted on the side. "Texas," I muttered, "of all the places we could move, we had to move to Mayberry, Texas."

"It's not Mayberry, Ray, it's Boerne," said Dawn as she drew a tic-tac-toe grid on the granite steps with a white rock. She pronounced it *born.*

"I know it isn't Mayberry—I was being sarcastic. And it's pronounced *BUR-nee*, you nerd."

"Whatever. You know we had to move here because Mom got a job here. You're the nerd. In fact, you're a creep."

She started a game of tic-tac-toe with an X in the middle square and we played for a few minutes, me letting her win, until she nudged my leg with her elbow. I looked up and she nodded toward an old man approaching the courthouse steps. He was dressed entirely in white: suit, shirt, hat, and shoes. Except for his black tie, he looked like an ivory statue. He wore thick, wire-rimmed glasses and was smoking a cigarette that looked like he had rolled it himself.

"That's our next-door neighbor," Dawn whispered as the old man began to climb the steps, "I met him with Mom yesterday while you were gone to the store."

"Of course it is," I responded back dryly, "not only did we have to move to Texas, we had to move in next to Colonel Sanders."

"Shhhh," she hissed as she pinched my leg. "He'll hear you." She giggled a little despite herself.

"At his age I doubt he hears very much at all," I whispered back.

Even though the man had to be well into his seventies, he didn't seem tentative or unsteady climbing the steps like many old people. At the top of the stairs he stubbed out his cigarette in one of those cement ashtrays with sand in the top that you find in places like banks and courthouses, and then he turned toward us.

"Well, hello, Dawn!" His strong, resonant voice surprised me. "Fancy meeting you here!" He looked at me and stuck out his hand. "This must be your big brother."

"Hi, I'm Raymond Tolouthe." I took his hand and saw a flicker in his eyes as we shook. It was as if my touch had sparked a kind of strange recognition or memory of something. It lasted barely a second and then his eyes revealed only good-natured frivolity again.

"Very pleased to meet you, Raymond. My name is Thurman Fleet, but folks usually call me 'The Captain.'" His lips parted in a half grin. "I was glad to have someone move in next door to me. That house has been vacant too long."

After a slight pause he asked, "Well, what do you think of your new surroundings?" His accent was definitely southern, but different than the native Texas accents we were getting used to.

"Um, I'm not really sure yet, to be honest," I fumbled. Convention demanded that I give a polite, vaguely positive response to someone I just met, but I had a strange compulsion to tell this stranger everything. The tone of his question suggested that he already knew exactly what I thought.

"Well, I think you're pretty sure you don't like the change.

I'm guessing you don't like things to change in general, do you?" The Captain squinted and peered at me with his dark eyes. I felt myself flush, and any urge I had felt to open up to the man vanished. I didn't much like a total stranger guessing that about me, next-door neighbor or not.

"No sir, you're right about that," Dawn piped up, "he doesn't like *anything* to change."

"It's been my experience that people who don't like change also don't like to take risks, and they usually take a long time to accept new situations and new people." The Captain scratched his chin and I could hear the rasp of his fingers on his goatee. "Frankly, those types are usually kind of suspicious."

"Yep, that's him," said Dawn brightly. I suppressed the urge to cheerfully kick her down the white marble steps of the courthouse.

"So, since it takes a while to accept a new person, I'm guessing you've had enough of me for one day—HA!" The man's laugh was a single, loud, staccato bark.

I was having none of it though. I mumbled some semi-polite reply, mostly because Mom was just coming out through the courthouse door, but I didn't feel neighborly toward our new neighbor. The Captain tipped his hat and greeted Mom, said goodbye to Dawn, and disappeared inside the building.

"Well, I see you met Mr. Fleet." Mom beamed a little too enthusiastically. "That's how it is in a small town. You run into people you know everywhere you go."

"Yeah, it's great Mom," but she missed the sarcasm and continued to babble about eating out, unpacking, and the local color. She didn't even notice Dawn counting her steps on the way down.

That night after all the boxes had been unpacked and Dawn was in bed, I made myself a peanut butter and mayo sandwich—my personal favorite—and sat down in front of the TV. The ten o'clock news was featuring some woman calling for Nixon's impeachment for "flouting the constitution and betraying public trust." The news anchor identified her as a representative from Texas. Maybe this wasn't the most backward place in the universe after all if the citizens of this great state had seen fit to send a black woman to represent them in Washington.

Still, I missed California badly. We'd moved to San Francisco when I was only three, so I didn't remember living anyplace else. I had to admit that Boerne wasn't what I had expected Texas to be like. On one hand, it was every bit as hot as I thought it would be. On the other hand, I had pictured it flat and dusty, with huge cacti and tumbleweeds dotting a mostly barren landscape. Boerne was nestled in rolling hills and had lots of green. It actually bore a vague resemblance to some areas around San Francisco.

While I was contemplating the geography of our new hometown, Mom came in and sat down next to me on the couch. "We need to talk," she said softly.

"Okay, but I'm not sure I have a whole lot to say."

"Then you can mostly listen." She paused, gathering her thoughts. "I know that this move is not your idea of a great time. I know you're going to be getting the short end of the stick, but I need to talk to you on an adult level about why we needed to move away from your father. You'll be turning eighteen soon and with everything we've all been through lately I figure you're mature enough to hear it."

She paused uncomfortably, struggling with how to begin. Finally she said, "As much as I always tried to avoid fighting in front of you kids, and as much as we tried to keep certain… things…from you, I know you two have known for a long time that your father and I have been having big trouble." She looked at me for a long time for some acknowledgement and I finally allowed her a small nod.

"Your father was always a good-hearted man, and he still

is." She took a pillow from the couch and smoothed it out on her lap. "It's what attracted me to him in the first place. He was in law school when I met him and I was an undergraduate. I was struck by how truly sensitive he was to other people and their feelings. Many of the law students were in it for money or prestige, but he really wanted to help people. By the time he finished law school I had fallen deeply in love with him, and I had no doubt that I would be with him for the rest of my life."

"Mom, I really don't want to h—"

"Ray, *I* need to say it."

Suddenly I didn't see my Mom as much as I saw a scared and overwhelmed woman struggling with a difficult situation. I nodded, and she continued, "You have to remember that back then there was no such thing as women's lib. Unless you had the guts to really go against the grain, your career choices as a woman were pretty much limited to being a teacher, a librarian, a secretary, or a nurse." She kept smoothing out that pillow. I wondered if she was as nervous telling me all this as I was hearing it.

"Unlike your father, I have never been comfortable bucking convention. None of those traditional career choices appealed to me, and we were confident that Sid was going to make enough money for both of us, so I dropped out to get married. I was twenty." It was the first time since we left that she'd spoken his name. "By twenty-two we had you, your father was doing well at his career, and I was completely happy with my life as a wife and mother.

"After a few years, though, things started to change. Your father still had a good heart. He does even now—most of the time, anyway—but he started growing disillusioned. He had thought he was going to change the world, or at least the legal profession. Of course, that was an unreasonable expectation, and I think the disappointment ended up changing him. I think he lost some faith in the human spirit, or himself—or something. He began to act so…defeated." Her eyes were big and full. I could see tears brimming at the surface, but she kept going.

"Anyway, he started drinking too much. When he was drunk, he wasn't the same person, not at all. All the kindness he gave away when he was sober disappeared and was replaced by an anger and bitterness that I wouldn't have thought he was capable of." The tears finally spilled over. "He never hurt me physically," her voice hitched in a sob, "but he was so sad and *angry*."

We had no Kleenex, so I went into the kitchen and grabbed a couple of paper towels for Mom. "Thanks," she mumbled as she dabbed her eyes and her nose. When she had collected herself again she went on.

"Well, like any situation like this it started out with a few benders that I thought were just blowing off steam and eventually it became a regular pattern." She looked at me and smiled nervously, as though she were ashamed. "You were just a little kid when it started; not even in first grade yet, and your father was always careful to not get really drunk until you had gone to bed. I had hoped that having Dawn would get him to change, but it didn't. It just got worse. Eventually, the man I married just wasn't around much anymore. I tried several things to turn it around over the years——the most recent being when I got us all into church." I winced involuntarily at that, but she didn't notice and kept going, "But no mater what I tried, nothing helped."

The TV flickered blue on her face in the otherwise dark room. We sat there for a moment watching Walter Cronkite, backed by images of long gas lines, talk about OPEC lifting the oil embargo. "The hardest thing about all of this has been knowing what would be best for you kids. Everyone tells you that you shouldn't get divorced, that kids shouldn't see their parents split up." She paused to take a deep breath and I could hear her lungs stuttering involuntarily as they drew in air. "But I finally couldn't take it anymore. It brought out the worst in him *and* me, and I had to go. I had to *let* it go. Especially when Dawn started to…"

She held in the sobs and they vibrated her body like small bombs going off inside her chest, finally subsiding and resolving into steady weeping. We sat there for a while, her crying, me silent and holding her hand, and watched the rest of the evening news.

∞

"Are you okay?" Delia called from the kitchen. "Did you say something?" Thurman's wife stuck her head around the corner into the bedroom. "Are you having nightmares again?"

"No," Thurman mumbled as he looked around the room, struggling to re-orient himself to his surroundings. He could still feel toxic mustard gas searing his lungs, and he quickly scanned the small bedroom for any signs of the hollow-eyed German infantrymen that had just menaced him in his sleep.

"No, Deddo, I just sneezed," he repeated, knowing that she would recognize the lie.

Delia raised an eyebrow. "Well, come eat some breakfast, then. You're getting skinny."

Fleet fell back onto the sweat-drenched pillow. Ten years of dreams. Always about killing or dying. Sometimes the dreams reacquainted him with the faces of men he had killed, or that had died under his command. Sometimes he found himself hopelessly surrounded by German soldiers resembling the Grim Reaper, with blank spaces where their eyes should be. Sometimes the dreams would be so bizarre and frightening that he wouldn't remember them at all. They didn't come every night, but much more often than he wanted. And the headaches. Blinding sharp pains like nails driving through his eyes that lasted for hours, and on more than one occasion, days at a time.

Above his dresser hung a large wooden frame that held his military medals pinned neatly to a black matte. George Thurman Fleet had entered World War I at age nineteen, armed with the powerful weapon of the ignorance of youth. Ready to sacrifice his own life for a cause, he had had no idea what it was like to have to take another's life for that cause, or to watch men serving under his command lose theirs. But he found out.

The young Captain had returned home to his family with shrapnel in his body courtesy of the German Kaiser. He had suffered severely damaged lungs thanks to the war's innovations in chemical weapons, and he was indebted to the horror of warfare in general for a badly wounded spirit. Due to his physical injuries and emotional trauma, military doctors ordered disability retirement consisting of light activity only. Fleet found he could not comply with that recommendation.

Ever since the war he had felt a more or less constant impulse that he found impossible to explain to anyone, even Delia. A terrible pressure had built up inside him that had to find some outlet. The dreams were part of that feeling, but not all of it—not by a long shot. It was something deeper and more subconscious, compelling him toward an unknown destination and forcing him to seek unknowable answers to questions that he couldn't articulate. He didn't know where, or for what, or to whom; all he knew was that he had to go.

He would find some temporary channel for the relentless energy—a job or other creative endeavor—and the pressure would lessen for a while, but it always came back, and he would change jobs or move to another city to give himself some outlet for the impulse. Most recently he had declined a huge promotion. Thurman could have been the regional sales manager for a company that sold display cases to grocery stores. He enjoyed sales work and he had been the company's top salesman. He could have accepted the lucrative bonus and attractive compensation package that they had offered him.

Instead, he had resigned from the company and loaded his whole family, including two young daughters and his mother-in-law, into his car to embark on a nine-month trip across the United States and Canada, living off his military disability pay.

The smell of coffee and bacon wafted into the bedroom along with Delia's voice, "Thurman, breakfast is almost ready. Come on in here with me. You need to eat and I don't like to eat by myself."

"Okay, Deddo, give me a minute and I'll be right there." He pushed his nightmares aside, knowing they would almost surely be there for him when he closed his eyes in sleep again. He walked slowly to the bathroom and washed his hands. Once, twice, three, four, five times he washed, focusing mostly on his right hand, completing the entire process of soaping, scrubbing, rinsing, drying, and then starting all over again. He then quickly shaved and pulled on some clothes.

Delia sat waiting for him at their tiny kitchen table. "Thurman," she said when he sat down, "I know you aren't going to be happy about this, but I made an appointment for you to be examined at Station today."

"You did what?"

She fidgeted with her apron. "You have an appointment at Station Military Hospital at three o'clock today, and I expect you to be there on time."

Thurman sighed with mild consternation, "Deddo, I've been examined a dozen times. There's nothing those doctors can do for me. They're just going to tell me the same thing they did the last time."

"I don't care." Delia continued to fiddle with her apron strings, but her voice was firm. "Your headaches have been getting worse over the last year, and your nightmares too." She didn't mention the compulsive hand washing or the psychological instability that the army doctors had told her that her husband was likely to exhibit for the rest of his life. "You are my husband. I am concerned about your health, and it's been a long time since your last exam. You will go." Delia rarely made demands, but when she did they were non-negotiable.

"Okay, I'll go. May I eat my breakfast now?"

"Be my guest."

Captain Thurman Fleet walked though the lobby of the military hospital feeling like he'd been horse-kicked in the chest. He had arrived on time, joked with the nurses, submitted to all the poking, prodding, X-rays, and answered all the questions with the expectation of a routine medical encounter: annoying, but unremarkable. He had been completely unprepared for the head military physician calling him into his private office, pouring him a glass of bourbon, and telling him to get his affairs in order because he had, at most, a year to live.

Shrapnel lodged in the network of blood vessels supplying Thurman's brain was shifting, which explained the recent increase in his headaches. The doctor described how the sharp mass would continue to work its way around the network of blood vessels until it would finally sever one of them, or it would begin to lacerate the brain stem itself. Due to the size and position of the shrapnel, the doctor said, it was unquestionably inoperable.

Thurman had stumbled through the rest of the conversation, not really hearing the head physician's sympathies or instructions. He wandered out of the hospital in a daze, feeling physically and emotionally numb.

"Death," he muttered, "why death? Why is so much of my life about death?" He was oblivious to his surroundings. His body guided itself automatically along the correct course to his house, but he was aware only of putting one foot in front of the other and of the complete vacuum in his soul.

He became vaguely aware that he was walking past St. Joseph's Downtown Church of San Antonio. God was bullshit. No God could sanction what he experienced in that Hell on Earth that pundits were calling the Great War. No God could take a man and put him through that torture only to survive long enough to start a family and then give him a death sentence anyway. Life was a very little bit more than constant suffering and death. There was no God, and if he did somehow manage to exist, he was one cruel son-of-a-bitch.

Something pierced Fleet's veil of thought and he stopped abruptly, eyes staring into the street. In the gutter lay a disemboweled squirrel, killed by traffic and thrown to the side of the road. Its eyes stared woodenly; wide-open, yet seeing nothing, like the glass eyes of a wax sculpture. The pressure of the tire had completely ruptured the animal's body cavity, and its intestines spilled out from the massive wound. Thurman's heart began to pound. He felt dizzy and his legs collapsed under him; he half sat, half fell onto the curb. A roaring in his ears drowned out the street noise. He thought he would simply faint and escape to the welcome shelter of unconsciousness; instead his mind departed on a journey back towards insanity.

The hot Texas sun was gone. He could no longer hear the passing traffic or see the streets of San Antonio. He was standing at attention before the Division Commander under the command tent for the infantry units deployed to a battlefront in France.

"Company officers," barked the Major General, "as you all know, the Krauts crossed the Marne three days ago. We know that they are gathering soldiers for a final offensive, and we need to know how they are distributing those troops." The tall commander paced back and forth before a line of eight officers representing the five Army platoons amassed at Berzy-le-Sec.

"I need volunteers to cross over No Man's Land and map the concentrations of enemy troops."

Silence. Lieutenant Jameson finally spoke up, "But sir, there's constant fire across the lines, and even if someone managed to avoid the machine guns, there are land mines everywhere in that field. How would anyone get through?"

The General allowed several more seconds of silence, and then he addressed them all. "The Lieutenant is right. This is a highly dangerous mission and there is a great possibility that one or more of you will die attempting to complete it. However, the information is important enough that we have to give it a try. The Huns are going to be launching an all out blitz, and we've got to know which direction they are likely to attack from. We'll lose many more lives if we try defending ourselves blind."

He looked into each man's eyes as he walked slowly along the line. "All officers willing to take on this mission, please step forward."

By the time Thurman realized his feet were moving it was too late to stop them.

"Captain, what is your name?"

"Fleet, sir."

"How old are you Fleet? You barely look old enough to shave, much less to have become a Captain in the United States Army."

"I'm twenty-two, sir."

"Goddamn, Fleet! I know that war speeds up the promotion process, but I know soldiers ten years older than you that still don't have silver bars on their shoulders. What makes you such a prodigy?"

"I'm not a prodigy, sir. I just make it a policy to do my best to try to keep my men alive."

"This time keep *yourself* alive, soldier. It looks like you are the only one with the guts to volunteer for this mission, and we need the information. See Sergeant Hall for briefing, and good luck, son."

Belly in the dirt, rifle cradled in his arms, machine gun fire screaming above his head, Captain Fleet crawled across the patch of earth designated as No Man's Land. To avoid sniper fire he had to make the exhausting journey under cover of night, checking constantly for land mines. The pace was painfully slow, and the crawl was exhausting.

Death was all around. Thurman Fleet lived in a circus of death. He had stabbed men with bayonets. He had riddled fellow human beings with bullets. He had blown them up with grenades. He had watched friends get caught in the wire and try to struggle free, tearing flesh and torturing themselves before finally being shot by enemy fire. He had seen men's guts spill out on the ground, eyeballs pop out of their skulls, and seen them choke to death after inhaling poisonous gas.

Perhaps that was the impulse behind his volunteering for this latest death-mission. Maybe he would get killed himself and finally have some measure of peace. If not, at least he would be occupied for a while by the all-consuming task of trying to keep himself alive. Anything that interrupted his reflection on the carnage was welcome.

If exhausting himself into oblivion was his motivation, accepting this mission had proven to be an excellent way to do so. Having already mapped enemy troop concentrations, Fleet was on his way back to American lines to deliver the intelligence. He was so fatigued he could barely keep moving, but he continued to crawl. Daylight would come soon, and he knew that he was as good as dead crawling across an open field without the dark to cover him.

He was cresting a small hill when an artillery shell exploded on the other side of it, blowing him backward into an abandoned enemy foxhole. He landed facedown in the hole, gasping for breath, the wind knocked out of him by the blast.

Due to the adrenaline rush that the explosion had released, he didn't yet feel the shrapnel that had entered his body in a dozen places. He also couldn't see that the mist in the pitch-black foxhole he now occupied was tinged green, indicating some lingering remnants of mustard gas.

He planted his arms in the mud, pushed himself up to a kneeling position, and took a deep breath that was like breathing in flames. His lungs burned, his eyes watered, and he stumbled blindly around in the hole on his knees, coughing uncontrollably and trying to escape the gas.

Once he regained control of his breathing, he groped around blindly for his rifle. His right hand squished through something like soft mud, filling the hole with a stench so foul it made him gag. He finally had the presence of mind to locate the waterproof package of matches in his belt. He lit a match and immediately wished he hadn't. His right arm was covered in human carrion from fingertip to elbow. The foul odor filling the foxhole emanated from a gaping hole in the decaying abdomen of an enemy soldier. The corpse's eyes stared blankly, intestines protruding from the body cavity, just like—

The squirrel. All of a sudden, Thurman Fleet was back in San Antonio, sitting on the curb with traffic whizzing by, looking into the gutter at a dead squirrel. He collected himself and stood up. He noticed that a few passersby were looking at him with a mixture of concern and suspicion. It occurred to him that they might have thought he was having an emotional breakdown over a rodent traffic casualty, and he giggled briefly and crazily at the thought.

He started out towards home again. An awareness began to grow in him as he walked, dimly at first, then more clearly as he went along. Even through the terrible emotional trauma he suffered in the war, and even though he had experienced and would continue to experience all of the typical human emotions associated with receiving a terminal diagnosis, he was still aware of something else, something beyond his emotions. It was the familiar relentless impulse to *seek* that had harassed him for a decade.

He wouldn't have been able to explain it to anyone else, nor did he really understand it himself, but he began to realize that no matter what he went through he always felt this force underneath it all, like a tumor growing inside him. It seemed more real than his emotions, more significant than the circumstances that he found himself in at any given time, as if it was the ultimate purpose that all the other events in his life somehow served.

A deep part of him understood that even this latest unexpected turn of events was part of the plan. He felt that he was approaching some kind of significant milestone on his involuntary journey, and the resolve to confront the impulse responsible for the wandering and discover where it was leading him began to grow.

By the time he reached home, he knew what he was going to tell his wife.

"Delia," he called as he closed the door. When she didn't answer immediately, "*Delia!*"

"What is it?" she answered from the kitchen. "Is something wrong?"

"Start packing. It's time to go."

∞

I got up and went into the kitchen. There was already a half-eaten breakfast plate on the counter. Dawn must have gone outside already to play and explore. Mom was sitting at the table in her fuzzy robe reading a newspaper and munching on toast.

"Where'd you get that?" We had only been here five days; I knew we hadn't already subscribed to any newspaper.

"Oh, good morning." She looked up at me and stifled

a yawn. "The previous renters must have left it—it's three years old."

"Pretty hard up for news, aren't you? Reading a three-year-old paper."

"Yeah, but look." She folded it back and showed me a picture of a bunch of old men wearing military hats and armbands. "See?"

I didn't see anything of interest. "Right here," she pointed to the guy standing third from the left in the back row. "It's our next door neighbor!"

"Oh great," I moaned. "I've met him one time and I've already had enough of that guy."

"Ray! You better be nice to that man. He's been friendly to us, and according to the time line here he lost his wife four years ago, so I know he's lonely. Besides, this article is about these men being inducted as lifetime members in the Legion of Valor." She tapped her index finger on the table. "Do you know what that means?"

"I'm sure you're about to tell me."

She did. "The Legion of Valor is an organization that honors soldiers who have been decorated with only the highest medals awarded by the U.S. military," she read. "Only soldiers awarded the Medal of Honor, the Distinguished Service Cross, the Navy Cross, or the Air Force Cross are eligible for membership."

"I thought you were anti-war, Mom." I pulled out a box of Cheerios from the cabinet and grabbed the milk from the refrigerator.

She ignored me and went right on, "Listen to what it says about Mr. Fleet."

Captain GEORGE T. FLEET received the Distinguished Service Cross for extraordinary heroism for actions amid showers of machine gun bullets and artillery shells of all calibers at Berzy-le-Sec, France, 21 July 1918. He gallantly proceeded to the front lines for vital information needed by the Division Commander and accomplished his mission in spite of the great danger to which he was exposed.

Captain Fleet was inducted into the Legion of Valor in 1919, and is now a lifetime member. After his service in the Army, Fleet practiced for many years as a doctor of chiropractic. He is now retired and currently resides in Texas.

"Wow, he's a retired doctor," she repeated, visibly impressed. "I guess I need to start calling him *Dr.* Fleet when I see him."

I mumbled under my breath, "And all this time I thought he was just the local weirdo."

"What, Raymond?"

"Oh nothing, Mom, just talking to myself about eating these Cheerios."

"Well, eat them and get going. Tomorrow's Friday and I start my job on Monday." She was going to be working with the Red Cross as a fundraiser organizer. "You've got to find some kind of job for the summer or you won't be going anywhere, because there won't be any gas in your car. You know that with what your father is going to send us plus what I'll be making we'll have enough for rent and bills, but no extras. You'll have to generate your own funds."

"I know, I know. I saw some 'Help Wanted' signs around when we were running errands the other day, so I'm going to hit them first."

She folded up the slightly yellowed three-year-old paper with the story of our crazy neighbor and swatted me lightly on the shoulder on her way out of the kitchen. "Go get 'em."

I ate breakfast, showered, put on a shirt and tie, and headed out to my car, which I was lucky to have. Not many teenagers in San Francisco owned their own cars. Doris was a 1963 Volkswagen Beetle, black on white. Dad had given her to me almost two years ago on my sixteenth birthday. She was eleven years old now and had 118,045 showing on the odometer, but she was all mine and I loved her.

I had parked her by the side of the house, and as I made my way around the driveway I saw 'The Captain' tending the vegetable garden that was his entire back yard. He was holding up what I guessed was a seed and studying it like it held the secrets of the universe. What a crazy old bastard.

I drove down our street slowly, taking in as much as I could about our new neighborhood. Our house was at the end of a cul-de-sac, flanked on one side by an empty lot and by Captain Weirdo on the other. We were in an older section of town that wasn't quite a bad neighborhood just yet, but I could tell that if we gave it some time it would get there. There were a few kids in bathing suits playing in the sprinkler and a couple of older boys wandering around, but I didn't see anyone my age.

I drove past Park Hill High School, and I saw Dawn's school, Park Elementary. I kept going past several gas stations with red and yellow flags out. It was Thursday, so by now most of them had already used up their gas until their Friday delivery. My license plate ended in an even number, so I couldn't buy gas until tomorrow anyway. Good thing my Beetle was a gas sipper instead of a guzzler.

I didn't have a whole lot of ground to cover anyway. Boerne was something like eight square miles, so the few places that did have 'Help Wanted' signs were easy to spot. I tried a few places and put in applications, but my hopes of actually getting a job were dampened almost immediately. I learned that the federally mandated minimum wage had just been increased the month before from $1.60 per hour to $2.00 per hour, so the competition for unskilled labor just got tougher, especially for student labor. All three managers I talked to told me they were really looking for someone stable who wouldn't be fouling up the work schedule by taking off work for football games, school dances, or finals.

I was on my way home via a different route and was just about to give up for the day when I spotted another 'Help

Wanted' sign hung on the side of a wooden shack not much larger than a lawn storage shed. **Boerne *Sani-Freeze—Ice Cream, Sundaes, Milkshakes, Hotdogs, Hamburgers*** was painted on the side in large red letters. The shack looked like a stiff breeze would do it in, but it also had a line of people ten deep waiting for service through one of two windows in the front.

I waited until the line cleared out. The guy taking orders was about my age, but huge. I'm not short, about six-foot-one, but this guy was at least six-five. Long black pigtails hung halfway down his chest. He was the only other male in Boerne that I had seen so far with long hair. His massive belt buckle sported a raised emblem of a marijuana leaf, and he wore a t-shirt emblazoned with a rock band I hadn't heard of before—KISS. I stuck out my hand. "Hi, I'm Ray Tolouthe."

"Griffin Smith. Sounds like you ain't from 'round here." His voice was friendly and joking. He exaggerated his Texas accent on purpose, kind of poking fun at it. He took my hand and gave it a good shake.

"Just in from San Francisco. Do you go to the high school?"

Griffin stooped down and leaned both elbows on the window as he talked. "For one more action packed, adventure-filled year. How about you?"

"Yeah, I'll be a senior too. Nice belt buckle."

He grinned. "Anything to ward off the squares."

I liked him more and more. "I'm actually hoping I can get a job somewhere for the summer."

"Well, good luck. As of the last census there were exactly 2,617 official residents of Boerne, Texas, so not many jobs to go around." Griffin lowered his voice and winked. "If there were, I sure as hell wouldn't be working here."

"Are you guys still hiring, like the sign says?"

"Well, kind of—I put the sign out because I know within a couple of weeks it's going to get busier than I can handle by myself, but I haven't officially cleared it with the boss yet. Not that I would wish this job on you." He waved off a fly that buzzed around the window. "Seriously, man, how bad do you need the work?"

"Pretty bad."

"In that case, take it. You really don't have much choice in this town unless you can make it on a paper route budget, which I can't. The owner here is an asshole, but if you stay out of his way and just humor him when you have to, you'll be okay."

"Great—so how do I apply?"

"You just did. As of right now I am the only *Boerne Sani-Freeze* employee that exists, so I am manager, cook, cashier, and janitor, and as manager I just made the executive decision to hire you. I'll call Wilson—that's the owner—and tell him. He'll bitch, as usual, but it'll be alright. I've been telling him for a month that we needed to hire someone else before the really busy season gets cranked up. He's the kind of guy who's going to complain no matter what, so I usually decide it's easier to ask for forgiveness than permission. Come on around back and I'll let you in."

"Right on!"

Griffin called Wilson to tell him that he had hired me. Then he set about showing me how to cook the food, where everything was, how to mix the ice cream, make the sundaes, and check customers out. Basically he just took care of customers and taught me different aspects of the job as each opportunity presented itself.

We had been at it for a couple of hours when Wilson pulled into the back driving a red MG convertible. He got out looking red faced and angry. I could tell right away that he had one of those demeanors that dictated that he wasn't happy unless he was miserable, and he usually did his best to do everyone around him the same favor. He fairly glowed in a pair of white shoes, yellow slacks, a blue shirt and a loud plaid sport jacket. He looked to be about forty-five or fifty, bald on top, wearing a pencil-thin mustache and oversized, teardrop sunglasses.

He burst in the back door as we were refilling the ice in the soda machine. "Griff! *Griffin!*"

"Hey, Wilson," drawled Griffin without looking up from what he was doing.

"Don't 'Hey Wilson' me. We've got rats again. I saw one run out from under the building and go under the dumpster when I pulled up. Have you been putting out the poison like I told you?"

"Nope." Griffin's voice was perfectly calm as he slowly and methodically scooped the ice.

"Why in the blue blazes of hell not?"

"For the same reasons I told you that we couldn't put it out to begin with." Griffin talked to him in a patient tone that someone might use with an older person who was maybe a little senile. "Number one, we can't put it out inside the building because doing that would break about fifty health codes. Number two, we can't put it out under the building where the rats congregate because if one of them died down there, we wouldn't be able to get it out and it would stink up the entire parking lot and drive away customers. Number three—"

"Oh all right, forget it," Wilson spat, "but there has to be something we can do about them."

"Not really," Griff tried one more time, "this barn of a building you got here is going to attract rats and other scavengers; it's just too flimsy to keep them from smelling the food when it's out during the day. But they can't get to anything or really do any harm, because everything's all locked in the freezer at night and the building's built up off the ground, so they can't get in that way. We're not violating any health regulations, and every restaurant in the world attracts scavengers to their dumpster. Just don't worry about it."

"*Don't worry about it,*" Wilson mimicked Griffin viciously. "I'm glad you punk-assed kids have it all figured out, since it's my butt on the line with the health department."

He seemed to notice me for the first time. "So kid, I hear you want a job."

"Yes sir."

"Well, Griffin thinks he has hired you, but he doesn't have the authority to do so, do you Griff?" Griffin ignored him and stepped up to the window to wait on a customer.

Wilson kept looking at me, but he addressed Griff again, "Jesus Christ on a popsicle-stick, Griffin, did you have to hire another longhair? You two are going to chase off all the respectable citizens around here." He rounded on Griffin. "And I thought I told you not to wear that fucking reefer belt buckle up here again. If you do it again, you're fired."

"Sure thing, Wilson," Griffin patronized him in a drawling monotone.

He turned back to me, "Okay kid, I don't have time to stand around here chewing the fat. Do what Griffin tells you to do, keep your nose clean, and don't steal from me, or I swear I'll take it to the cops. I have everything inventoried, and I check revenue against inventory twice a month. If you steal, you will get caught."

"Yes sir."

"The pay is a buck thirty-five an hour. You get paid twice a month, on the first and the fifteenth." He started to leave.

"Sir," I said as he started to walk past me toward the back of the shack.

"Yeah, kid, what is it?"

"A dollar thirty five an hour is below minimum wage."

Time stopped in the shack. Tension engulfed the small enclosure like a tsunami falling on the shoreline of a doomed Japanese village. Griffin started waving his hands and shaking his head 'No' at me from behind Wilson, but I wasn't backing down. I could deal with the fact that the guy was an asshole, and it really wasn't about the money. What he was doing was against the law. It wasn't right.

Wilson squared back up to me and looked me up and down slowly. "Well, Griffin, it looks like you have managed to hire a lawyer here. A longhaired, hippie-liberal, freedom-fighting lawyer. Are you a lawyer, kid?"

I shook my head.

"I didn't think so. Well kid, let me explain some life truths to you. This is my business. You weren't around when I started it and you didn't take any of the risk in opening it. In fact, you've got no stake in this place at all." He got up in my face as he talked until he was just a couple of inches away from my chin. "So the bottom line is that you can take whatever I am willing to pay you and like it, or you can take a big fat zero and shove it straight up your hippie, longhaired ass!"

I looked down into his stupid mid-life crisis teardrop sunglasses and responded, "Just a question, sir. What do you think the Texas Department of Labor would shove up *your* ass if they knew you were violating the minimum wage law?"

Now Griffin was wild-eyed and pleading with me from behind Wilson with his gestures to shut up. Wilson began to smile an ugly smile. "Is that what you want, you fucking creepy longhair? You want your buddy Griffin here out of a job?" His sneer grew as he saw the realization dawning on my face that I would have to sacrifice the only friend I had started to make in Boerne to take this fight further.

"See, you're not as smart as you think you are, kid. You call the DOL, they call me, and I claim restaurant status. You do realize that wait-staff pay is an exception to the minimum wage law, don't you? Of course, this isn't the kind of place that the exception really applies to, where you get tips to supplement your base pay, but chances are thirty to one that the DOL never investigates. Even if they do, I claim ignorance, they give me a slap on the wrist, and nothing happens. I then have to let Griffin here go because I can no longer afford to pay the two dollars per hour that the Federal Fucking Government now dictates that I have to pay, you still have no job, I have to come back here and work this place myself because I can't afford labor costs, and everybody loses."

I knew he was probably right, and in that moment I was so angry and frustrated I thought for a second I might deck the asshole—cops, jail, lawsuits be damned. My face flushed red and angry. I turned and walked out with Wilson gloating behind me, "That's right kid, get the fuck out and don't come back, not even as a customer."

I was still fuming when I got home. I slammed the front door and paced through the house. Luckily, Mom and Dawn were out somewhere. I changed clothes and went out back to jump rope to burn off some steam.

As I exercised, I thought about Wilson. I thought about him knowing that he could take advantage of people who needed a job, and how the Labor Department probably really wouldn't do anything to him. He probably wasn't afraid of the Health Department at all; he had probably just been looking for an excuse to be an asshole to Griffin. I bet he plays golf on the weekends with someone in the county office, or he plays cards with the sheriff on Friday nights. I thought about all the Wilsons across the country and how they managed to screw honest, decent people on a regular basis. I thought about how our nation's corruption extended all the way up the social ladder to Nixon. What can you really expect from a country where the President himself is a common criminal?

I continued to immerse myself in the unfairness of our system while swinging the rope in a steady rhythm, hypnotizing myself. I was so engrossed in my thoughts that I tripped and almost busted my ass when the Captain spoke from behind me.

"Raymond, how are you today?" he fairly yelled. My

initial shock quickly turned into more irritation, as if I wasn't angry enough already. I knew Mom would have a fit if I were rude to our neighbor, so I tried to hide my annoyance.

"Doing fine, sir, how are you?"

He ignored my question. "Are you now? You looked kind of upset."

I wasn't about share my day with Captain Crazy. "No sir, just exercising." He stood there in khaki old-man pants and a black gardening shirt. I looked him over, from his wide-brimmed gardening hat to his waterproof galoshes and tried to change the subject. "Been working in your garden?"

"Ah, that I have, Raymond. I saw you out here in the yard, and I thought I would come over and ask you something." His eyes squinted at me again like they did that first day we met at the courthouse, like they could see into my mind and tell exactly what I was thinking. "I have several projects that I need completed around my house this summer. Gardening is one of them, but I have a few others: home repairs, painting, and a little distribution project I need help with. I was wondering if you might be in the market for a summer job."

"Well, sir, I don't know. I, uh, I applied for several jobs today already, and I would hate to accept your offer and then get a call back from one of these other places." In the space of a few seconds I had decided that I would rather walk everywhere I went and have zero disposable income than spend my summer with this bizarre old man, when something very strange happened.

"I guess you know that minimum wage just went up to two dollars an hour," he intoned slowly, with his dark eyes looking right into my brain, "so I couldn't pay you any less than that. It wouldn't be *right* to do that, would it?"

I suddenly felt like I was under water, or that everything was happening in slow motion. As if I was standing outside myself, I heard my voice say, "No sir, it wouldn't."

"And I'm sure you wouldn't stay in a situation that wasn't *right*, would you? Why, you'd get right up and go."

I answered in a daze, as though the words were liquid streams flowing from my mouth, "That's right, sir, I had to go."

The Captain smiled, "Great. We're agreed then. I will see you Monday morning at seven o'clock sharp. Just knock on the back door." He turned and walked back to his house while I stood there wondering what the hell had just happened.

CHAPTER TWO
HEALED

Delia looked out the window just in time to see Thurman kneel over a tomato plant with an almost religious reverence. His garden was his church and his vegetables were his congregation; there was no doubt about that. She was glad that he had been able to find a new outlet for his energy, but she was very worried about his health.

Not his physical health. He had admitted the terminal diagnosis he had been given after she had insisted that he tell her the whole truth, but that didn't shock her; she had already intuited that much. Nor did she accept that the military doctor's prognosis would come to pass. Delia Fleet believed in the power of prayer, and she was determined that her prayers were going to induce a different outcome for her husband and her family. She didn't know how, or through what form help would come, but she believed with every fiber of her being that it would come.

No, she was concerned about Thurman's mental health and emotional stability. He had changed so much in some ways since he came back from the war. He had always been vigorous and charismatic, which was, she supposed, why men almost old enough to be his father followed him without hesitation into battle. And he was still a very magnetic personality, as evidenced by his post-war sales success. People had always instinctively liked and respected Thurman Fleet, and that hadn't changed, war or no war.

But he absolutely could not find peace and contentment for any significant period of time, and that worried her. They had moved to Corpus Christi seven months earlier. Immediately after Thurman had received his fatal prognosis, he insisted that they move to a coastal town to introduce his damaged lungs to the therapeutic benefits of salt air. Delia knew that mustard gas wasn't the real reason for the move, but she didn't know what the real reason was. That's what scared her: she didn't think Thurman really knew either.

She was afraid that something in that war had disrupted his capacity for stability to the point that he would never settle down. She half-expected him any day to come home and announce that they were moving somewhere else, and she was scared that he would repeat that cycle again and again and again *ad infinitum.*

Thurman came in from the garden holding a full-grown ripe tomato in one hand and a tomato seed in the other. "Deddo, look at this tomato," he purred in wonderment. "I put *this*," he held up the seed, "in the ground. I gave it some water, a little fertilizer, and just left it alone, and it changed into *this*." He held up the tomato with his other hand.

"Yes, Thurman, people have been growing tomatoes that way for thousands of years," she replied in a slightly mocking, patronizing tone.

"Yes, yes, I know we take it for granted," he responded, ignoring the teasing, "but think about the *process*. How does it actually work? What force or intelligence is inside this seed that it is able to direct it to grow a perfectly formed, full-sized tomato? How does it *know*? What is inside this inert seed that comes to life to produce the plant? Or is it really inert? Is there something beyond what we can perceive with our senses that directs the process? There would *have* to be, wouldn't there? Haven't you ever thought about that?"

"No, Thurman, I can honestly say that I have never given it much thought." She turned to go into the kitchen. "As long as a tomato tasted good, I never cared to ponder the process by which it grew."

Thurman followed. He walked over to a calendar on the wall hung from a small nail. A pencil dangled from a string tied to the nail and he used it to make a large 'X' on the calendar.

"You're marking today off a little early, aren't you?" asked Delia. "It's only 3:00."

"Well, unless you think I might die after dinner tonight I think I'm safe marking off another day, don't you?" Thurman had begun to count down the days the doctor felt he had left as a kind of joking defiance. "I think the doctors are full of beans anyway."

Delia looked thoughtful and said, "You know, it is true that you have had fewer nightmares than ever since we moved to Corpus Christi. No real bouts of depression like you had before." She seemed to come to a conclusion. "I think you really are improving, Thurman, in every way except for your headaches." The headaches had unquestionably worsened. His pain had become constant. Sometimes he was less aware of it, and it became integrated into his experience like a sailor at sea who subconsciously compensates for the rise and fall of his ship on the ocean. Sometimes it was violent, crushing, and inescapable. But it was always there.

He absent-mindedly scratched his chin, and his fingers rasped on the half-day growth of whiskers. "Well, it's 1930. With as many advances in science and medicine as we have these days, there's got to be something someone can do about a few headaches, don't you think, Deddo?"

"I do think, Thurman." She checked the cupboard and sighed. "Thurman, I forgot to get flour the last time I was at the store, and we're having fried chicken and biscuits tonight. Do you mind going to get some?"

"Not at all. I think I'll walk over to that new market by the post office. I haven't really explored that part of town yet."

Thurman changed out of his gardening clothes into street attire and began the mile and a half walk to the market. As he walked he thought about what Delia had said. He *was* better, she was right, but he knew she had no idea why. He didn't really understand it either, but he did feel that he was getting closer to that significant milestone that he had sensed that day in San Antonio.

He had, of course, become aware of himself fixating on certain ideas or things with a strange fascination lately, like his near obsession with growing his vegetables. He was enthralled with the contemplation of a force or intelligence that governed their growth.

Thurman hadn't felt the pressure of the familiar driving force nearly as much lately. He guessed it was because he was somehow cooperating with it now in a way that he previously had not. He didn't know how, but he had the feeling that before he was standing still while it pushed and raged against him like water beating against a man standing in a rushing stream, whereas now he was allowing himself to be moved and guided by the water.

He visited the store, bought the flour, and on the way out he saw a sign across the street that he hadn't noticed upon his arrival. It said, "Health With Chiropractic."

"Health with *what?*" he thought. Thurman had never heard of chiropractic and had no idea what the word might mean, but he was intrigued and decided to investigate. He crossed the street and walked into the office.

It looked like some type of medical office. There were half a dozen people in a waiting room and a receptionist sending them back into a treatment room one by one.

Thurman approached the receptionist, a young woman with dark hair, and asked, "Excuse me, Miss, what kind of office is this?"

"This is Dr. Peterson's chiropractic office."

"What is chiropractic? I've never heard of it before. What do you do here?"

"I better let Dr. Peterson explain it to you. I'll tell him that we have a gentleman out here who would like a consultation." She disappeared into the back and reappeared a few minutes later, nodding and saying, "He'll be right with you."

Thurman waited for perhaps ten minutes until the receptionist directed him to a small room with a strange looking examination table. Dr. Peterson turned out to be a large man, mid-forties, with sandy blond hair and a blond mustache. He wore a black tie under a white barber jacket.

"Good afternoon," he welcomed his new patient warmly. "What can I do for you today?"

"Well, I saw your sign and I was wondering if you might be able to help me." Thurman began to relate his situation including the diagnosis and related prognosis. Dr. Peterson listened to the details without comment. By the time he had finished explaining his condition, Thurman had started to wonder if the man really knew what he was doing. He hadn't asked a single question, and Thurman began to get the feeling that he didn't ask because he didn't know enough about his condition to know what to ask.

The doctor immediately confirmed Thurman's suspicions. "Well, Mr. Fleet, I have to say that I don't know much of anything at all about your medical situation," he said with absolute sincerity, "but I can say just as honestly that I know I can help you.

"I'm sure you're wondering how I might be able to help you when I've just told you I'm not familiar with the ramifications of your condition. The answer is that I don't have to know about it because there is an intelligence inside you that knows everything it needs to know about healing your body."

Thurman visibly started in his seat. This man was talking to him about the very concept he had been fixated on regarding his vegetables.

Dr. Peterson pointed to his temple. "If you think about it, most of your life takes place without you being aware of it or knowing how it is happening. There isn't a doctor or laboratory or scientist on this planet that can take beans and cornbread and turn it into heart tissue, but your body can. It's a feat we can't duplicate, and that's because we think with our educated minds, which are limited." The doctor wrote the words *Educated Intelligence* and *Innate Intelligence* on a chalkboard mounted on the wall as he talked.

He turned to face Thurman. "You have another intelligence inside you that is unlimited—the same intelligence that directed your very formation from conception into a perfect baby boy at birth."

He circled the words *Innate Intelligence*. "This intelligence runs your heartbeat, tells your liver what to do, directs your kidneys in removing toxins, regulates blood pressure, tells your body what chemicals to produce for you to sleep or wake up, directs the digestion of food—basically it directs the formation and operation of every cell in your body, without you needing to know how or understand the process. Do you follow me so far?"

Thurman nodded slowly. He felt like he was in a weird play where he was both an actor and a spectator. His ending up in this office was no coincidence, and he was acutely aware of the feeling of being guided by something beyond himself.

Dr. Peterson checked Thurman's facial expression carefully as if to make sure his new patient really understood the concept, and then he went on. "Now, if this intelligence is capable of creating your body in the first place, if it is capable of organizing, regulating, and helping your body adapt to the changing conditions that it constantly finds itself in, wouldn't you think it would be capable of healing it if it becomes imbalanced, hurt, or ill?"

Thurman gave another punch–drunk nod, and the doctor nodded back. "You bet it is. In fact, that's what happens any time someone heals. If you cut your finger, you might put peroxide on it and bandage it, but those things don't actually heal anything. The power that created your body is the only thing that can heal it. Those other things—the bandage and antiseptic—try to create the best environment possible for healing to take place, but it is the power inherent in your body that does the healing."

Dr. Peterson now moved to an anatomical chart of the nervous system mounted on the wall next to an X-ray screen and pointed at it. "Your nervous system is the system that your body uses to communicate this Innate Intelligence. If there is some interference that disturbs the normal transmission of nerve impulses throughout the body, it's like a telegraph line that has static in it—the messages are there, but they can't be delivered because of the faulty communication system. Your body can't make the changes it needs to make in order to bring about healing because it has lost contact with the intelligence that created and sustains it. Chiropractic removes the neurological interference and then trusts the Innate Intelligence of the patient to direct the body to heal."

The doctor sat down on a stool next to Thurman and looked him directly in the eyes. "I don't care what your condition is. The power that I am referring to is the same power that created you, me, the entire universe. It's what keeps the planets in orbit, directs your immune system to fight off an infection, and lets birds know that it's time to fly south for the winter. It's in every cell of your body and every atom of everything else that exists. If we turn it loose, I *know* that it will help you."

Thurman nodded and allowed himself to be led through the process of beginning his treatment. He filled out paperwork, the doctor took X-rays, and he waited while they were developed. Then Dr. Peterson brought him back into the treatment room and showed him the X-rays of his spine and how it was causing pressure on his brainstem and interfering with the transmission of neurological impulses from the brain to the rest of the body. Finally, the doctor laid him sideways on the exam table and with the side of one hand, contacted Thurman's neck and gave a quick thrust that was designed to move the bone back into position and relieve nerve interference.

"I know that didn't feel like much," Dr. Peterson said as he helped Thurman up from the treatment table, "but trust me, the effect on your system will be profound. We will need to continue to remove the pressure until your body makes it a permanent change. It may take repeating the process several times to get you all the way well, but soon you will notice your body changing. Come back tomorrow and let me check it again."

Thurman nodded, but he had one parting question. "Doctor, I understand your explanation, but I still don't understand how what we just did is going to help my body deal with shrapnel around my brain."

The doctor smiled and asked a rhetorical question as he guided Thurman out. "Mr. Fleet, I don't know how it's going to do it either, I just have faith that it will. We may never know how it does it, but if it works, do you really care?"

Thurman was amazed. He had had some degree of a constant headache for months before beginning chiropractic treatments. Yet the day after his first session he found himself completely pain-free. He continued to see Dr. Peterson, and the headaches came less and less frequently until they were eventually gone altogether.

But that wasn't the most fascinating result of his treatment. After having received treatments from Dr. Peterson for about three months, one day Thurman noticed a bump on his arm that was irritated and raised. He rubbed it and to his surprise the skin broke easily and a small piece of metal fell out. Thurman examined it realized that it was a piece of shrapnel that had pierced his body during the war. Over the following month his body repeated this process several times in various places—arms, legs, groin, the back of his neck, chest. He would notice a bump or feel an area of irritation, and when he rubbed it the skin would break, and with minimal bleeding or trauma, his body would expel another piece of shrapnel.

The calendar in the kitchen continued to collect X's, and one day in September Thurman flipped the page to the next month and saw the one-year mark circled in red, just three weeks away. The time the military doctors had given him was almost up, and he was feeling better than ever.

He didn't know if the shrapnel around his brain was still there or not, nor did he care. His headaches were gone, he was about to outlive his terminal prognosis, and he had connected with an idea that was to influence the rest of his life, which he was now confident would be a long time.

With a different expectation for his life came a return of the relentless compulsion to search, and Thurman knew that he could not stay in Corpus Christi. He didn't know what his next endeavor would be, but that restless feeling began hounding him again to make another change. He resisted for a time, partly because he didn't know exactly what direction to take, and partly because he knew that another abrupt change was going to be stressful for Delia. Finally he came up with a compromise.

Delia's heart flopped in her chest when he announced that it was time to move again. But it sang *Hallelujah* when he added, "it's time to go back home."

∞

I ate dinner that night with Mom and Dawn, still confused about how I had just agreed to spend the entire summer with the last person in Boerne I wanted to be around. I would rather have to deal with Wilson than the Captain.

Mom grilled me, "So tell me more about working for Dr. Fleet, Ray."

"Nothing to tell yet Mom. I won't start until Monday."

"Don't you even know what you'll be doing for him all summer? Does he want you to work in the garden?"

"I guess. He mentioned gardening, painting, and something about a distribution project he needed help with."

She raised her eyebrows as she chewed a mouthful of beef and then said, "Distribution project, huh? That's curious. I wonder what that means."

"Who knows? He's such a weirdo."

"I don't think he's so weird," countered Dawn. "I think you just don't like him because he knew you were suspicious of people. By the way," she pointed her fork at me, "you're proving him right by being so suspicious of him, you know."

I tore off a piece of my roll and threw it at her. "It's true," she sang, as Mom yelled at us both.

Dawn was ten years old and Mom was pretty worried about her. She had begun to act funny near the end of Mom and Dad's marriage. Mom got a book on kids and divorce, and she told me once that apparently many young children somehow think that divorce is their fault, that they weren't good enough or did something wrong that caused their parents to be unhappy.

I'm certainly no child psychologist, but that explanation did seem to fit Dawn's situation. She did strange things, like if she walked up or down a flight of stairs she had to count them all. She would only drink from a glass that was full or almost full, and after she drank more than a few swallows, she would refill it before she would drink any more. She had a whole list of things she would do every night getting ready for bed, and all of them had to be done in order, sometimes more than once, before she could get in bed and sleep. It was like she thought that she was responsible for Mom and Dad's breakup because she didn't pay enough attention to some sort of detail, so she was going to fix the situation by controlling every detail she could.

Dawn had a really scary episode right before school ended last term. Her teacher had contacted Mom to tell her that Dawn was having a hard time with her work, which was unusual because she had always been an almost perfect student. She had started turning in her assignments late, and when she did turn them in her papers all had holes in them from repeatedly erasing and rewriting her work. We had all gone to the school to have a conference with the teacher, and Dawn and I were supposed to wait outside in the office while they talked. She had been scared stiff that she had done something wrong and was going to get in trouble, and no matter how much Mom had reassured her that they were just going to talk about how they could help her feel more comfortable about school, she was still upset.

While Mom was inside talking to the teacher, Dawn started hyperventilating. I didn't know what was going on—all of a sudden she just started making wheezing noises and holding her hands to her chest. She got up, scared, and tried to make it to the conference room to get Mom, but she was dizzy and fell down before she could get there. The school secretary got Mom, and I yelled for someone to call an ambulance. They ended up taking Dawn to the hospital, and the doctor in the emergency room said it had been a panic attack. He suggested to Mom that she go see a child psychologist, but we were leaving for Texas in a month anyway so she never made an appointment. I kind of wondered if Mom was hoping that Dawn would grow out of it on her own; I knew we didn't have money for a psychologist.

Mom started clearing the table and said, "Well, Ray, I guess we both start work on Monday. And since you are going to be next door, that takes care of the problem of what to do with Dawn while we're both at work. I'm delighted with the arrangement."

"Yeah, Mom, it will have some big advantages," I said with feigned enthusiasm. Mom talking to me the way she did that night after we first moved in had made me aware of just how much she needed support. I didn't want to work for our neighbor, but I did need a job, and the bottom line was that I had been the one that had told him I would do it, so I had no one to blame but myself.

The phone rang. "RRRay? RRRaymond?" It was my father's voice, slurring badly over the phone.

"Dad? Are you okay?"

"Nnno, Ray, I'm not okay...not at allll," he slobbered into the phone. "Your mmmother left me, and took you and your sssister away. How okay do yyyou think I might be?"

I held my hand over the phone and shouted in a whisper, "MOM! It's Dad, and I think he's drunk." She looked like I had just told her that a giant meteor was going to be crashing into the earth in five minutes and destroying all life on the planet, but she took the receiver from me and hissed, "take Dawn outside until I hang up."

Dawn was watching a summer rerun of *Gilligan's Island*. I snapped off the TV, grabbed my keys, and said, "Dawnie, we have a very important errand to run right now." I grabbed her arm and led her toward the door, "Come on!"

"I was watching that," Dawn whined. "You're such a butthole, Ray!"

"I know, but Mom has issued an emergency request for ice cream, and I know just the place to get it from."

On the way to get ice cream I turned up the radio loud so that we didn't have to talk. I knew how Mom had looked when I told her Dad sounded drunk, and I hoped I had disguised my own feelings from Dawn better than Mom had from me. I had never experienced my father drunk like that before. It wasn't that I hadn't believed Mom when she had told me about Dad drinking too much, but they had done such a good job hiding it from us that it had been a pretty big shock experiencing it for myself. I felt strangely betrayed or lied to, like I imagined a man might feel after catching his wife in bed with another guy.

I also felt a little scared. Mom had been right; his whole demeanor was different when he was drunk. The father that had taken me fishing and had coached my little league baseball team was not the same man I had just been on the phone with. I didn't like the guy I had just talked to.

I thought about my parents, both of them, and I realized that I was getting a crash course in learning that my parents were real people, with real problems. They were more than just what I had projected onto them; more than just what they meant to *me*. They had hopes, dreams, plans, disappointments, and problems that had nothing to do with me, or Dawn. They were just regular people like anyone else.

By the time we got to the Boerne Sani-Freeze I was feeling better. Not great, but better. Allowing my parents some individual humanity had siphoned off a lot of the anger and disappointment that I felt towards my Dad. I hoped that Griffin would still be there, because I wanted to apologize for stirring Wilson up.

The shack looked even smaller at night. Griffin was serving a handful of teenagers at the window.

"Well, if it ain't Cesar Chavez," he beamed as we approached, "the labor freedom fighter from San Francisco!"

"Hey Griffin. Sorry about all that, man. I didn't mean to put you in a difficult spot with Wilson."

"Dude, are you kidding? I got *a raise*, man! See, this is what you didn't last long enough to learn about Wilson: he is mostly full of shit. He acted like he wasn't afraid of you going to the Labor Department." This was, by far, the most animated I had seen Griffin in the few hours I had known him. "But he stood around here for half an hour after you left just grilling me about what I knew about you and whether I thought you would really turn him in. He ended up giving me a 30 cent raise—I guess he was afraid that you might have given me some ideas."

"Well, I'm glad that it worked out well for you." I was relieved for Griffin, but I also felt a tad jealous. I had stood up to Wilson about something that Griffin had been unwilling to stand up to him about, and he got a raise, and I got fired.

As if he could read my thoughts, Griffin said, "Hey, man, I'm sorry about you getting fired. I feel great about getting that raise, but I feel bad for you."

Dawn butted in, "Ray, you got fired?" I hadn't told Dawn or Mom about my adventures with Wilson or the Boerne Sani-Freeze, only that our neighbor came over and offered me a job.

"Not really. Griffin, this midget is my sister Dawn." They traded the customary pleasantries, and she ordered a cone. Griffin got her ice cream, and she sat on one of the ancient, moldering picnic tables to eat it while Griffin and I continued to talk at the window.

"So, any chance that one of those other places you applied to might give you a job?" Griffin asked.

"Well, as it turns out, I already have one." I tapped on the window with a stick I had picked up like a magician about to pull a rabbit out of a hat. "My next door neighbor came over when I got home from here and offered me a summer job at full minimum wage."

"Hey, that's great!" Griffin looked genuinely happy. "You sure don't waste any time, do you?"

"Well, it just kind of happened; I didn't really have much to do with it. The guy just came over while I was outside exercising and offered me a job, and I for some reason accepted it."

"Whatta you mean *for some reason?*" Griffin raised an eyebrow. "You did say you were pretty hard up for a job, right? He isn't hiring you to *deliver*, is he?"

It was amusing to me that Griffin, proud wearer of his marijuana belt buckle, was worried about me being a drug runner. "No, nothing like that," I laughed, "the dude just needs me to help with gardening and house repairs. It isn't the work, it's the guy. He's quite strange."

"He must be an older guy if he needs you to help with gardening." Griffin's previous animation was gone. I guessed that he was now just making polite conversation.

"Yeah, he is, but that doesn't bother me. He calls himself 'The Captain,' and he does strange stuff like—what?" Griffin's expression had suddenly changed from one of casual conversation to one of excited recognition.

"Man, no shit!" Griffin exclaimed, "That guy is probably the biggest character that Boerne has to offer."

"Yeah, I can't say I'm all that surprised." I sighed. "I already figured he was a weirdo."

Griffin seemed half-concerned, half-excited that I would be working for the town crazy. "No, man, you have no idea. He isn't just weird in an eccentric, old-man kind of way. He's out there! He's not *a* weirdo, he's *The* Weirdo!"

"What do you mean?"

"Well, you know he was in World War One, right?" I nodded. "So, he comes back from the war all messed up and becomes this spaced out metaphysical guru. He would have these classes where he would hypnotize people and make them bark like a dog and stick pins in their arms and stuff."

"No way!"

"Yep. I heard he actually got arrested one time for hypnotizing this guy and freezing him up to his neck in a block of ice. I think that was in Chicago or New York or someplace. He used to travel around and hold these classes."

"Wait a minute." I remembered the newspaper article Mom showed me. "I read somewhere that he used to be a doctor."

"He did have a chiropractic practice in San Antonio for a while, but his mind-voodoo stuff eventually took over, and he quit his practice."

Griffin leaned forward as he really started to warm to his subject. "Here's something else. He bought a ranch here in Boerne and converted it into some sort of metaphysical retreat. He's retired, but it's still there—out on the south side of town on the way to San Antonio. The story is that people used to go completely without clothes out there." He threw back his head and laughed. "So have fun working for a flaky old perv all summer."

"Thanks," I said. "Just what I needed."

Dawn was finishing her ice cream, and I knew she would be ready to go soon. I ordered something to go for Mom, but Griffin wouldn't take payment.

"I can't charge my best labor organizer. You're better than the union, man." He smiled as he passed Mom's chocolate sundae through the window. "Will I see you around soon?"

"Sure. I'll be working during the day, but I have nothing to do nights but get acquainted with the fabulous night life of Boerne."

"Excellent. I have to be here Thursday through Sunday from eleven to nine. Plenty of time for mayhem."

"All right then. See you soon."

When we got home I handed Mom her ice cream. She took it with a small 'thank you,' and I could tell she had been crying. Her eyes were red and puffy.

"Everything alright, Mom?"

"No," she gave a weak smile, "but no worse than it has been. Thanks for getting Dawn out."

"No problem."

"No, I really mean it, Ray." She looked like she might cry again. "I really don't know what I would do right now if you weren't here to help me."

"Don't mention it, Mom. We're just going to have to stick together."

"Yes," she said softly, "I think we've all got some healing to do, and it looks like we're going to need to do it together."

We stood still for a moment, and then she broke the silence. "Speaking of which," she sighed, "I need to go help Dawn get ready for bed. Her bedtime ritual is getting more elaborate."

I went to bed that night more resolved than ever to make this summer job work, despite what Griffin told me about my new boss. Mom needed me to help take care of business, and I wasn't going to let her down.

The next morning I got up early, quickly ate breakfast, dressed, and went out to the yard to greet Doris. I wanted to get some work done on her before I started my job, got busy, and began neglecting her. She needed a tire rotation, oil change, plug change, and a good wash and wax. I went to the auto parts store to pick up the parts and supplies I needed, and as I pulled back into the driveway, I saw our old war-hero-turned-next-door-nudist hard at work in his garden. I waved as I got out, he waved back, and I soon forgot about him as I set about getting Doris in shape.

I was about an hour into my work when Dawn came out and sat down next to the car. She acted casual, but I knew she wanted something because she didn't say anything for several minutes; she just sat and fidgeted with my tools for what seemed like forever. Finally she asked, "Ray, who was that that called last night?"

"Someone called last night?"

"Come on Ray," she said in a serious tone, "you know what I'm talking about. The phone rang right after dinner and you made me go with you to get ice cream. Who was it that called?"

"It was a private call for Mom, Dawn."

"It was Dad, wasn't it?"

I kept ratcheting the spark plug I was working on for several seconds. As a general rule, I did not lie to Dawn. Not broadcasting something like that was one thing, but answering with a lie in response to a direct question was something else. "Yes."

"Why did you have to take me out of the house then? Why didn't we talk to him?"

"He was upset, Dawn. He wasn't in the right frame of mind to talk to us last night."

"Ray," her voice was trembling a little, like she was close to tears, "when will we go back home to San Francisco? When will we all live together again?"

My heart just about broke. I had no idea that she thought that at some point we would all move back in together again like one big happy family. I scooted over next to her and took her hand.

"Dawnie, Mom and Dad got a divorce. I thought you knew what that meant. That means that they will never live together again."

She started to cry, and I reached out and hugged her close.

"W-w-well, when can we see Dad again?" she sniffled.

"I don't know. Dad's kind of...sick. It's not good for us to be around him right now."

She pushed away from me and almost shouted, "Sick!

What do you mean, sick?" She stood up and started pacing in a tight circle, wringing her hands as she walked. "Ray, if he's sick, he needs us more than ever!"

"No, Dawn, I don't mean that kind of sick, he—"

"I don't care what kind of sick it is!" She stopped pacing and glared at me. "H-h-he *needs* us! W-we've got to help him!" Tears flowed down her face and she looked wild-eyed and scared. She ignored snot dripping freely from her nose, and she started to make little wheezing noises and stuttering her breaths.

"Dawn, are you okay?" In the space of no more than a minute she had gone from being upset, yet normal, to being completely out of control. She was starting to fully hyperventilate now and looked terrified. I put my hand on her back to steady her, and I could feel her heart pounding, which scared the hell out of me. I was afraid she might have a heart attack or something.

"Dawnie, it's going to be all right. Sit down here and I'm going to get Mom! I'll be right back—don't worry!"

I raced to the door and just about knocked it off the hinges getting inside. "Mom! Mom! Dawn's having another attack! Where are you?" I couldn't find her. I followed the sound of running water to the bathroom.

"MOM," I bellowed at the door, "Dawn's having another attack!"

"What?" She sounded confused, but I guess she could hear the fear in my voice because she was already turning the shower off.

"Dawn's having another attack like the one she had at school," I shouted, a little softer this time since I didn't have to compete with the water anymore.

"Oh God," she moaned, "Do we need to call an ambulance?"

"I think we might, Mom. She asked me about someone calling last night—she figured out it was Dad—and she just freaked out. She's hyperventilating and panicking like she did before at the school."

"Okay, go call an ambulance and then go out and stay with her until I get there. I'm just going to throw on some clothes."

I ran to the phone in the kitchen. As I dialed the numbers, I looked out the window at where I had left Dawn and what I saw startled me so much that I almost dropped the receiver on the floor.

Dawn was standing up, holding a tomato, and calmly listening to our next-door neighbor. He had bent down beside her with his hands on his knees and was whispering in her ear. She looked perfectly fine, like nothing had ever happened.

They were standing with their backs to the door and I started toward them slowly. I was trying to get close enough to them to hear what he was telling her. I got within ten feet of them when Mom burst out of the house and slammed the back door. She was barefooted, soaking wet hair, wearing shorts and a t-shirt with no bra, and running full speed toward Dawn. Dawn and the Captain stopped talking and turned around.

"Dawn," said Mom as she knelt down and hugged her, "are you okay?"

"Yes, Mom." Her face was still tear-streaked and she needed to blow her nose, but she was perfectly calm.

"What happened? Ray said you were having another episode like you had at school that time."

"I—I—don't really know, Mom." She looked genuinely confused about what happened. "The last thing I remember is feeling like I was going to faint and then all of a sudden I was talking to Mr. Fleet."

The Captain spoke up then, "She was having a little anxiety spell. I used to have patients who had those sometimes." He might have been the family doctor talking about any common minor symptom, "Nothing to worry about, ma'am."

"Well, thank you so much for calming her down, Mr. Fleet–I'm sorry–*Doctor* Fleet." Mom seemed satisfied that Dawn was really going to be all right. She started wiping Dawn's face with her hand and the Captain pulled out a handkerchief and offered it to her. "Thank you again," she said with a smile.

She finished wiping Dawn's face, stood up, and said, "Well, doctor, we've only been here a week, and already we seem to be indebted to you for everything from saving us from a ride to the hospital to giving my son a summer job. I think we owe you some home cooked meals."

"Well, I don't mind if I do, ma'am," the Captain said with what even I had to admit was considerable charm, "but only if I can contribute some of my vegetables to the menu."

"That sounds fair. Can you give us through the weekend to get everything organized in there?"

"But of course," he chuckled, and then continued in a slightly more serious tone. "Ma'am, about your daughter's anxiety—I have experience in these sorts of things, and I was wondering if you might want me to work with her a little bit over the course of the summer."

I had stayed silent through this whole exchange, but before I could stop myself I blurted out, "No sir, thanks for your help, but we couldn't impose like that."

"Oh, it's no trouble, really." The Captain's eyes stayed steady on Mom's even as his mouth answered me. "It would be good for me to get to work with a patient again."

Mom looked a tad unsure, but nevertheless she said, "Well, if you're sure it's not too much trouble, and as long as Dawn is comfortable with everything, I guess it would be fine."

The Captain looked down at Dawn and said, "Dawn, what do you think? Can we have a few more conversations this summer?"

"Sure," Dawn said without hesitation.

"Alright then, all business settled. Dinner next week at your house, Dawn will visit me a few times a week," the Captain looked at me for the first time during this entire episode, "and Raymond will become my summer work partner, starting Monday. I think I shall celebrate by returning to my garden to weed the cucumbers." He turned to leave with a wave. "Good day, all."

As soon as we got inside, Dawn went to the bathroom and I cornered Mom. "Mom, I need to tell you something. I don't think you want to let Dawn go over to Dr. Fleet's by herself."

"Why not?"

I wasn't about to tell her that he was some kind of warlock that could cast spells on people to get them to agree to summer jobs against their will, or that he could read minds, so I told her what Griffin told me.

"Ray, I'm surprised at you! You know better than to listen to idle gossip and rumors. That man has been nothing but nice to us since we got here—he even offered you a job!"

"Yes, Mom, but what do we really know about him? What if he really is a nudist? Or used to be? What if he really did get arrested for hypnotizing people?"

"Balderdash! He was a doctor in good standing until he retired. If he had been involved in something inappropriate, the licensing board would have pulled his license." She rolled her eyes. "Hypnotized a man and froze him in a block of ice. Of all the silly things."

"But Mom, h—"

"But nothing," she interrupted. "Let's make it real simple. You tell me—how upset was Dawn when you came to get me?" She waited for a response with both eyebrows raised and her head cocked to one side.

"Very."

"And how does she seem now?"

"Fine. But—"

"No! No buts. The last time Dawn did this it took several hours and a Valium to calm her down. Dr. Fleet did it in a few minutes just by talking to her. He obviously knows what he's doing, he's willing to help, and Dawn needs the help. Case closed."

That night after dinner I got Dawn alone in her room and asked her what she and the Captain talked about that had calmed her down so fast.

"I don't really remember," she said almost wistfully, like she wished she were having the conversation all over again.

"Did you guys talk about that tomato you were holding when I went out to get you?"

That seemed to spark a memory. "Yes, but I can't really remember much about it. I remember Mr. Fleet telling me to hold it and imagine that there was something inside it that was directing it to grow and be healthy. And I remember him telling me that the same something was inside me, and that I could trust it to tell my heart how to beat and my lungs how to breathe. He just kept saying, 'Everything's okay, you can trust it Dawn, it's not your fault' over and over again, and I did, and it worked."

"What do you mean it worked? What exactly happened?"

"Well, when he first walked up he touched the back of my head and that helped. I could breathe better just from him doing that." While she talked she folded and re-folded an old cloth napkin that she used as a blanket for one of her stuffed animals. "So that helped me be able to stand up and hold the tomato. Once I held it and he began to talk to me, I stopped feeling afraid. I started to get really calm, and my body went all the way back to normal. I felt like everything was going to be all right, even us moving away from San Francisco and Dad."

I didn't really know what I had expected her to say, but whatever it was, it had nothing to do with meditating on a tomato. Then again, I knew from my own personal experience with the Captain that the tomato probably had very little to do with it. There was something extraordinary about the strange old man. I was in no way sure that it was good, but it definitely was extraordinary.

CHAPTER THREE
SHINE

I would like to see the evidence for that claim, sir," Thurman Fleet demanded loudly as he stood from his chair.

Dr. James Drake, president of The Texas Institute of Chiropractic Sciences, jammed his hands in his pockets as though he were physically overpowering something that threatened to escape. What he was really subduing was his temper. When he answered his problem student's latest challenge he succeeded in keeping his tone even, but danger lurked in his eyes. "Well, class, we have a dissenter among us. Intern Fleet, what is it that you think you know better than the founder of our profession himself, Dr. Daniel D. Palmer?"

"I'm not saying I know anything more than Dr. Palmer, sir," Fleet stood calmly defiant in the middle of a class of thirty students, "but I will not accept extraordinary claims without any evidence to back them up."

"The evidence is in the philosophy, science, and art of chiropractic, sir," Dr. Drake drawled with dramatic effect while giving the intern his most baleful gaze, "and in the results."

The professor's scolding had no effect; although his most problematic student did return to his seat, it was obvious that he was not in the least deterred from his dissention. Drake knew it would only be a matter of time before the young man issued some new challenge.

Dr. Drake knew that Fleet was a retired military war hero who had fought for his life on the battlefields of France, and this was the main reason that he tolerated the man's insolence. Drake respected service to country and he had been fascinated by Fleet's account of his war injuries and near miraculous results with chiropractic. He also felt that there was something unusual about the man. He couldn't put his finger on exactly what it was, but he had a feeling that this chiropractic intern was a unique character.

Although the president of the college appreciated several qualities about Thurman Fleet in theory, the practical application of the man as a student in his institution of higher learning was a different matter. Fleet seemed to be on a quest for something beyond what the college could offer him, and he acted like he held the school personally responsible for not being able to give it to him. He attacked his studies and sometimes his instructors with the restless passion of a wronged man bent on revenge.

And he was completely uncontrollable. He was thirty-six years old, several years older than most of the other students, and his experience in the war left him impervious to a professor's stern looks or harsh words. He had fought and almost died in the World War. What could a college professor possibly say or do to frighten him?

Dr. Drake continued his lesson. "Snakebite. What category of disturbance would that fall under according to Dr. Palmer?" He pointed to a young man in the front row, "Yes, Phillips?"

"Poisons, sir."

"Correct. And what is the proper chiropractic response?"

Phillips fidgeted in his seat. The professor guessed that his student knew that his answer would be unacceptable, but it was apparently the only one he had. He squirmed a moment longer and finally spit it out, "Remove or neutralize the toxin, sir?"

Dr. Drake paced up and down the rows of students. "No!" he thundered, "that is a *medical* response. What is the proper *chiropractic* response?" He nodded to a student a few rows back, "Davis?" Davis had no answer.

Dr. Drake gestured impatiently, "Come now, why do we adjust the spine in the first place? To give a back rub?"

Davis answered, "To remove neurological interference."

Drake responded, "Quite so, but *why?*"

"To allow full expression of Innate Intelligence, sir."

"And how will we allow for full expression of Innate Intelligence in a patient who has had poison introduced into his system via snakebite?"

Drake continued to pace as he instructed the students through his questioning. "We do not remove toxins; that is for the medical men do. And why not? Because merely removing the toxin, while removing the initial cause of the disturbance, still leaves the body in a neurologically subluxated state." He warmed to his conclusion. "The chiropractic doctor must adjust the spine in the areas that correspond to the immune system, so that Innate Intelligence may correct the action of that system relative to the toxin introduced by the snakebite. Further—"

"*Icon! Icon!*" This time Fleet was pointing and shouting at the top of his lungs.

Dr. Drake had heard this tirade before. Almost since he had arrived at the college, Fleet had openly criticized the faculty for expecting students to believe what they were taught based upon authority only. It was nothing new, but this latest outburst had exceeded the professor's patience for this day.

Face scarlet with anger, Drake bellowed, "*Fleet!* In my office, *NOW!*"

Thurman entered the president's office first and stood motionless before his giant mahogany desk. Dr. Drake followed and was yelling even before the door could slam behind him.

"Dammit, Fleet, I wish to God you'd stayed in the Army!" He threw himself in the chair behind the desk. "I have a school to run and classes to teach, and I can't do it with you getting up every five minutes and making an ass of yourself!"

Thurman was unabashed. "Dr. Drake, I simply will not tiptoe around these sacred cows of chiropractic. If you want me to stop challenging what you say, all you need do is provide proof for the claims you are making."

"Fleet, what kind of proof do you want?" Drake almost whined. "Didn't you get here in the first place by being cured by a chiropractor when the medical men all wrote you off to die?" Thurman nodded.

The doctor continued, exasperated, "Damn, son, if you can't even trust your own experience, please tell me, what the hell can *I* say that will give you confidence in your new chosen profession?"

Thurman softened a bit in his expression, "That's just it, sir. I know that the treatment produced a miracle in my body, but I don't know *how*. I want to know—no—I *need* to know how."

"*Nobody knows how Innate Intelligence works, Fleet!*" Drake screamed loud enough to wake the cadavers in the dissection lab. He rose and continued, waving his hands for emphasis, "We know that it directs all living things, we know that it functions via the nervous system, and we know that it isn't able to function fully when the nervous system is compromised." He turned, looking directly at Fleet. "And most importantly, we know that when we remove neurological insults, people heal!" He paused, then implored, "Isn't that enough to know?"

"It isn't enough for me, sir. I think we could know more than we do. I just think we are being lazy with our investigation and taking too much on the authority of others."

Drake stroked his chin and conceded, "Well, that's your opinion, which you are entitled to." He sat down, extracted a pipe from a desk drawer and began to load it with fragrant tobacco. "What you are not entitled to is constantly disrupting my class. No more, Fleet, or you will be pursuing your obsessions somewhere else." He paused and pointed with the stem of his pipe for effect, "I mean it, son. No more."

Thurman turned to leave, but Dr. Drake said, "Ah, Fleet, one more thing." Thurman turned back to face his professor. "I'm told that the student clinic has been getting several requests for a 'Dr.' Fleet. You wouldn't know anything about that, would you?"

"No sir."

"I didn't think so," Drake lit his pipe and talked in spurts between the puffs, "because the only way (puff) that a person would come to the clinic requesting a student by name (puff) and calling them 'doctor' would be if the student treated them (puff) somewhere else and falsely misled them into believing that they were a full-fledged doctor."

He exhaled a thick cloud of pipe smoke at Thurman. "And that would be completely against the rules, wouldn't it *Intern* Fleet?"

"Yes sir."

"Very good. You may go, Fleet."

Thurman left the college president's office and began to make his way back to the main campus. He had been feeling the familiar pressure again. It had abated somewhat after the move back to San Antonio, but it started back up again soon after with a vengeance, and enrolling in chiropractic college seemed only to feed it this time. The maddening impulse was growing stronger by the week, not so much compelling him to find a new channel for his energy, as was the case before, but to exhaust this channel—to run it out to the end, use it up, finish it out, and then go beyond.

He had to know. *What* he had to know, he wasn't sure. He knew that the central idea of chiropractic—the concept of an Innate Intelligence that guides all living things—was an important piece. But he felt deep down that there was more, much more, and he realized after his talk with Dr. Drake that he wasn't going to find it all in chiropractic college. Nevertheless, maybe the old man was right; there was a time and place for everything, and what he was looking for simply demanded more time and a different place. And, he supposed, that wasn't really the college's fault. Perhaps he should declare a truce with The Texas Institute of Chiropractic Sciences.

He saw his clinic partner, Alonzo Woodman, across the school atrium. Woodie waved excitedly as Thurman approached, and as soon as he was within earshot he called, "Heard you tangled up with Drake again. What happened?"

"Same as always," replied Thurman as he fell in step with his friend, "I challenged him in class one too many times, and he got tired of it."

"What did he do?"

"Yelled a lot. Warned me to quit seeing patients outside of school."

"You've been seeing patients outside of school?" Woodie was impressed by Thurman's boldness.

"A few. I have to do *something* to figure out how all this stuff works; if I waited around until they taught us about it here, I'd be too old to practice once I had it all figured out."

"Thurman, don't you have any fear of being expelled?"

"Why should I? If they can't give me decent answers to the honest questions I have, what good is their degree to me?"

"Well, for one thing, it certifies you to practice chiropractic. You are interested in doing that, aren't you?"

"I've already started practicing chiropractic, Woodie," Thurman replied as he held the door for his friend, "and I'm about to practice some more. Are you ready for clinic?"

They checked in to clinic and went to their assigned treatment rooms. In this portion of clinic the assignment was to palpate patients in hospital-type gowns that fastened up the back so that the spine was accessible. No actual treatment was to be administered. The students were only to gain experience in palpating variations in normal spinal anatomy and feeling for spinal distortions.

Thurman's first patient of the day was a woman who was new to the college clinic. She had come in requesting 'Dr.' Fleet on a referral from a friend. She sat still, as instructed, while Thurman carefully palpated each vertebra. He spent several minutes feeling her spine, and then dismissed her to the changing room to change back into her street clothes while he filled out her chart and reviewed her paperwork.

When she returned to the exam room she handed Thurman a five-dollar bill. Confused, he started to protest, but before he could speak the woman said, "Don't say anything; consider this a tip. I consider it money well spent. I have had chronic pain in my head and back for two years, and right now I am completely pain-free. That was the finest treatment of any kind I have ever experienced. I will be referring all of my friends. Thank you, doctor."

Thurman was speechless. He hadn't adjusted her or treated her in any way. He checked her file and discovered that she had never had a chiropractic session before. It dawned on him that she thought the palpation exercise was the actual treatment.

Thurman spent the rest of the day thinking about the woman and her response to his non-treatment. This was a glimmer of the missing element of healing that he had been seeking. He didn't understand it yet, but he knew that it was the next piece in the puzzle that he had been compelled to put together. The phrase "placebo effect" wouldn't be coined for twenty-four more years, but Thurman Fleet had just recognized it, and at least to some degree, intuited its significance.

He knew instantly that he couldn't explore this new facet of healing in the college clinic. Chiropractic would still serve as his method of experimentation, but he needed a better laboratory, one in which he would have complete control and could deal with patients unrestricted. That night Thurman Fleet conceived of the Mason Street Chiropractic Clinic. He simply stopped going to class and started going to his own home office. He would eventually graduate from The Texas Institute of Chiropractic Sciences, but not until years later, and when he did return to the college, he would come as a teacher instead of a student.

At 6:58 a.m. I walked up the stone pathway to the Captain's back door dreading what lay ahead of me. I knocked softly on the door and any hopes I had that the old man might have forgotten that I was coming and either left town or slept-in were immediately dashed.

"Come on in, Raymond," he called from inside. Even though the door muffled his voice, it was still surprisingly strong and vibrant.

I opened the back door and stepped into the Captain's kitchen. There was an old fashioned blue refrigerator with rounded doors and those big steel handles from the 1950s decorated with flower magnets holding pictures, presumably of children and grandchildren. The refrigerator clashed with the cabinets, which were lime green, but what struck me immediately was how clean the kitchen was. I would have expected an old widower like the Captain to build up some grime, but everything was spit-shined and polished. Maybe there was something to that old military discipline. I also noticed a strange chart hung on the wall by the kitchen table. In the middle of the picture it said, *Perfect Digestive Health*, and it had other words emanating out from the center like spokes on a wheel that said things like, *normal weight, liver,* and *bowel movements.*

There was fresh-brewed coffee in the coffee maker on the counter, and it smelled delicious. As always, the Captain seemed to know what I was thinking. "Ray," he called from another room, "pour yourself some coffee and come on in here. I left a cup out for you."

I filled the yellow coffee mug he had left by the pot and followed the sound of his voice to the den where he sat in a green recliner, smoking a cigarette. "Come on in and sit down, Ray," he said, smiling. "Are you ready to get to work?"

"Yes sir. Are we gardening today?"

"No, no gardening today. You aren't ready for that yet. Today we're going to start the process of repairing."

"The process?" I was confused by his choice of words. "How long will it take, and what are we going to fix?"

"Well, how long it will take depends on how fast you can work, and we'll get around to the repairs in a minute. First we need to discuss some ground rules for your employment."

He leaned forward in his seat. "First of all, I have a very particular way that I like to have things done. Some might say my methods are unorthodox, or even irrational, but I need to know that you will be willing to follow my instructions without question."

"Oh boy, here we go," I thought, "I knew this was a bad idea." The Captain saw my expression and responded with his eyes. I can't really explain it, but he interrupted me *emotionally*; I *felt* him somehow calming my suspicions.

He went on to provide the verbal assurance he had already given me silently, "Ray, you can rest assured that I will not ask you to do anything that is illegal, immoral, or that would hurt you or any member of your family, or anyone else you know, for that matter."

As much as I did not want to trust this strange old man, I *knew* that he was telling the truth. I nodded, and he continued, "Many things I will ask you to do will not make sense to you at first, but I need to know that you will comply anyway." I nodded again.

"Good. I noticed that you were here at exactly 6:59 this morning, which is good. The first rule I have is that you must be on time," he said as he stubbed out his cigarette in a green ashtray by his recliner. He paused to light another and then added, "And the second rule is that you must be your best."

"Yes sir, you can count on me," I said earnestly. "I am always on time, and I will do a good job for you no matt—"

"No, Raymond," the old man said in that slow, rich voice that had penetrated my brain the day I agreed to work for him, "you must *be* your *best*, and you must be *on time*. If you will do those two things, we will be able to make all the necessary repairs."

I felt strange again, like I was swimming under the surface of a river of molasses. "Yes sir. On time, be my best."

"*On* time, be your *best*," he repeated, looking pleased.

"Yes sir," I warbled.

"Good!" he thundered sharply, and I came out from under my molasses river. "All right," he boomed, let's get to work!"

For the next four weeks I did minor carpentry and major painting on the Captain's porch and outside walls. I had to admit that overall he wasn't a bad boss, but he wasn't kidding about being strangely particular in his methods. When I hammered nails, he insisted that I be able to drive the nail in hitting it no fewer than five and no more than eight times. If it took more or less than that, he insisted that I pull out the nail and start over in a different spot.

It was, he said, because if it took fewer than five hits it meant that the nail was sinking in a soft spot in the wood, and if it took more than eight it obviously indicated either a brittle spot in the wood or a dull nail. I had to measure boards, cut them, sand them, and then measure them again. If they weren't *exactly* the same length, I had to start over again. When preparing paint I had to stir the paint exactly one hundred times clockwise, then exactly one hundred times counterclockwise, so that it was guaranteed to be uniform on application.

But that's not the craziest part. The entire time I worked the Captain would be talking to me about each little thing I was doing. He would start by having me close my eyes and relax, because he said that I wouldn't do any of the tasks properly unless my body was relaxed. I had to sit, relax, and meditate for ten minutes before I was allowed to do so much as stir a stinking bucket of paint.

Then, as I was stirring, he would coach me about keeping the strokes even and talk to me the whole time about how the paint was evening out and how it would flow perfectly onto the boards, be absorbed by the wood, and provide protection from the rain and sun. He would talk about how everything protected itself against harmful elements in the environment, that doing so was part of the process of each organism adapting, but that sometimes people insulated themselves too much because they were afraid, and their own protective shield held them back from normal growth processes.

I didn't know what to make of these ramblings, but they provided a constant verbal backdrop to my work. I did everything just the way he told me to, got paid at the end of the week, and hung out with Griffin on the weekends. The Captain didn't do anything too weird, and once I got over my initial annoyance at the hyper-meticulous nature of the work, I was able to settle into a routine. I actually got to where I liked it, because I would become so absorbed in the task at hand and start to float away on the waves of the Captain's constant talking that three hours would pass by without me even knowing it. Plus, I already had an appreciation for doing things exactly a certain way; that had always been a part of my personality. The degree to which the Captain took this principle was a little extreme, even for me, but I innately liked it as a general way of doing things.

The Captain was with me all the time during my work except for the hour or two each day he spent in the garden or when he was playing with Dawn. She would come over several times a day to ask for help with something, tell us something, or just because she was bored or lonely, and the Captain never complained. He would play games with her on the porch while I worked, and when they played I noticed that he kept up a constant dialogue with her the same way he did with me. Whatever they were doing, he kept her focused intently on that activity, and he would spin off on tangents that seemed at one and the same time unrelated yet somehow intensely personal and relevant.

As much as I had distrusted the Captain before, I began to feel comfortable with him despite myself. If someone had asked me about it, I would have explained it away as me simply spending so much time with him and getting used to him, but I knew that wasn't the case. That was true, but it was more than that. I still thought he was strange, but I could feel on a deep level that he meant my family and me no harm. It just took a while and the lack of any incidents to prove otherwise for me to actually admit it to myself.

I also could not deny that he was helping Dawn. Even though he had no formal sessions with her, she underwent a significant change in a short time just from the conversations they had while playing games or rocking on the porch. The first indication that Dawn was improving came after I had been working for him for about three weeks. We were at the Captain's house following our usual routine—me working, Dawn and the Captain playing—and he had gone inside to pour himself and Dawn a glass of lemonade. When he came out I could see that he had only poured each glass half full, and he saw me looking at the glass and gave me a wink and a small smile.

This was no feat of ESP or omniscience, just normal observation. The Captain had been over several times for dinner and had observed Dawn's ritual of refusing to drink from a glass that wasn't full. He came out talking to her about lightning bugs or some other topic designed to fascinate a ten-year-old and painted such a vivid verbal picture that she didn't even pay any attention to the lemonade and drank the whole glass.

The amazing thing, though, is that just from that one incident she seemed to be completely free of her previous compulsion. From that day on she drank from a glass normally, and I don't know if she ever even realized that she was doing something differently. I sure never said anything. It was almost like she had a good spell on her, and I was afraid that if I called her attention to it I would break the charm. I also noticed that her other compulsions had greatly lessened in intensity as well, though many of them were still there.

On the Monday morning of the fifth week of my employment, I arrived at the Captain's back door to find a strange note. It said, *"The first stage of repairs are over, now it is time for some gardening. Your garden is a* Hortus Conclusus, *meaning,* Enclosed Garden. *Interestingly, this phrase has also been used throughout history to refer to the Virgin Mary. My garden is a* Hortus Expositus, *an open garden. Come on in and let's get started.*"

I didn't know what the hell he was talking about. We didn't have a garden, enclosed or not, but I had dealt with the Captain enough by this time that I didn't question his nuttiness and just went inside. I poured my coffee and went into the den, as was our normal routine. The Captain sat there in his recliner as usual, but there was also a large chart on the wall that I had never seen before that said, *Evolution of Consciousness* at the top. It was divided into vertical sections labeled, *Electronic Phase, Mineral Phase, Vegetable Phase, Animal Phase, Human Phase, and Cosmic Phase,* with pictures of each phase on the chart. I said hello and then pointed at the chart, "What's this?"

"Oh, that's nothing," he shrugged, "just an old visual aid from when I used to teach. Ready to get started?"

"Sure."

"All right. We're going to be moving into a new phase of your work, starting off by centering and relaxing, just like we always do." His voice was casual, but his eyes were starting to get that squint that I had seen before. I could tell that I was in for some new Captain weirdness, but I assumed the usual position which was me lying on his couch with my eyes closed. He sat in a wooden chair behind me like he usually did and started talking me through the relaxation process.

"Ray, turn your attention to your breathing and begin to relax your body," the Captain started off in his usual slow, subdued tones, but there was an extra resonance to his voice this morning. Almost right away I began to feel that strange sensation of floating that I had experienced when I first agreed to work for him, and then again when I arrived for my first day of work.

He continued in his deeply rich, almost musical voice,

"As your body continues to relax, *remember* what it was like to be *on time*. Remember…remember…remember your experience of being *on time*."

I wondered what he was getting at; I was always on time for work, and everything else, for that matter.

As always, he knew that I was thinking instead of relaxing, "Let your mind rest, Ray," he purred slowly, "don't think, just relax—and *remember*."

I started feeling that underwater feeling again. Time began to slow down and the Captain's voice started melting into my mind in a strange way. Normally when we would have these pre-work sessions I would hear his instructions for relaxation and I would consciously receive them, interpret them, and carry them out, as though I were reading a manual and making a conscious decision to follow through on each instruction. This was more like his voice and my body merged, and my conscious mind was left out. I didn't have to consciously interpret or process what the Captain was saying; responses came automatically from a part of me that was beyond language.

"*Remember* what it was like to be *on time*. *Remember*… *remember*…it's okay to remember, Ray. There's nothing wrong with being *on time*. It's okay."

I drifted deeper and deeper into some other place of consciousness like Alice in Wonderland disappearing down the rabbit hole. I felt like I was in a slow free-fall, like a feather drifting down from high above the earth.

Falling
Falling
Falling

When I finally landed, I was nine years old standing in a church. The entire congregation was swaying to the music from a huge pipe organ. The choir was humming while the preacher was shouting for anyone who wanted to be saved to come up front. Red faced and sweating, he was describing the tortures of eternal damnation in Hell for all those whose sin was not cleansed by acceptance of Jesus.

I knew that I was a sinner and headed for Hell, and I was scared out of my mind. I imagined myself writhing in a lake of flames, roasting alive for all eternity, never able to die and escape the torture. My imagination was so vivid that I could almost smell my own burning flesh and hair, feel the heat from the molten lava, and see the waves of heat and gas rising up out of the pit. Eyes watering from my near hallucination, I wanted to go up front and receive forgiveness. I was desperate to escape the fate of the flames, but I was so frightened that my feet would not obey the commands of my brain to move, and I cried out silently from my inner being with an earnestness that surpassed any emotion that I had felt before or since. My entire emotional world was filed with the pure, simple intention of a child expressed in a single unspoken plea: *"Please forgive me."*

All of a sudden, the church faded into the background of my reality as though it had shifted into a parallel dimension that wasn't quite connected to the one I usually occupied. The white, ornately woodworked ceiling of the church was suddenly gone, and shining down from where it used to be was a Light that dwarfed any entity I had ever experienced. It shone with a brilliance that penetrated my soul, vibrated into my body, and jolted me out of the reality that I usually was aware of. I found myself completely outside the flow of linear space-time.

I was aware that the universe existed *in* me; not the limited configuration of desires and fears that I had conceived of as myself, but what everything IS in essence—pure Consciousness. My experience of the universe in that moment was one of being aware that everything that ever existed or would ever exist was a perfectly ordered symphony——a totally unbroken whole. There was nothing random or coincidental in even the most remote corner of deep space.

Every atom was accounted for and playing its part in a cosmic drama that existed for the Self-revelation of the supreme irony that nothing is real but Consciousness itself.

And as the Light continued to shine on me, the words came. The experience was more than just hearing them with my ears—I *felt* them with my soul, like I was feeling music composed of elements beyond the harmonic frequencies of the physical plane we normally inhabit. The words thundered through my being, *"There is nothing to forgive."*

And then I was back in the Captain's den.

I tried to speak, but the Captain said, "Hold on Ray, let's let you settle back into your normal consciousness for a minute."

He went into the kitchen, and I lay there on the couch bewildered—like a sleepwalker who has just awakened to find himself out of his bed and wandering around out in his front yard. Gradually I came back to myself, and when the Captain returned with a glass of water for me I said, "H-how did you do that?"

"How did I do what, Ray?"

"How did you make me remember that?" I sat up and rubbed my eyes, then took the water. I felt like a massive electric current had coursed through my body; my legs didn't quite feel like they would support me if I stood up. My muscles felt exhausted, like I had just run a marathon.

"Well Ray," the Captain sat down again in the green recliner across from the couch, "I didn't really make you remember it so much as I gave you permission to remember it. You've been repressing that experience for some time, haven't you?"

I nodded as I swallowed a big gulp of water. "How'd you know?"

"We'll talk about that some other time. For now, let's process your experience. Tell me about it."

I paused and took a big breath. I didn't really know how to describe it; a lot of it wasn't really explainable in words.

As usual, the Captain could tell what I was thinking. "I know that some of it may be hard to relate, but do your best. I think it will help us to help you understand what it is all about if you can talk about it, and you need to understand it."

I nodded and gave it my best shot. "Ah, I was nine. My Mom had gotten us into this church because she was hoping that it would help with—something we were having a hard time with—and they scared the crap out of me every time I went. We would go every Sunday, and the preacher would talk about going to hell and what it was like, until I worried about it all the time. Everything I did, said, or felt, seemed like a sin, and I was certain that I was going to burn for all eternity."

The Captain nodded like he had already known what I was going to say. "One Sunday I got so scared that I didn't think I could stand it anymore and something happened—I felt something...I...I—" I couldn't figure out how to describe it.

The Captain interjected, "There was a brilliant light." He said it as a statement, not a question. I nodded.

"And you felt as one with all life." I nodded again.

"And time and space seemed like they didn't exist anymore, and you knew that everything was good." The Captain recited these things matter-of-factly, as though he were checking off a grocery list.

"Yes. How do you know all that?"

"Let's just say I have a little bit of experience in these sorts of things. Was there anything else?"

"Just before it happened I prayed silently for forgiveness, and during the event a voice spoke that said, *there is nothing to forgive.*"

The Captain looked thoughtful for a moment and then said, "Ray, as much as those church people may have scared you, I think they ultimately did you a favor. They increased your longing for a Divine connection on the basis of forgiveness to the point that you reached a kind of critical mass that enabled you to induce that event into your consciousness."

"I guess so. It sure didn't feel like a favor at the time."

He kind of chuckled. "It usually doesn't in these cases. At this point in our collective evolutionary process it usually takes a significant crisis, stressor, or a person intensely concentrating on solving a problem that they feel is of tremendous importance to induce such an event. So naturally, the illuminated person frequently associates their experience with the unpleasant trigger. But as a higher awareness becomes more commonplace, the triggers will become less and less stressful—the next phase of awareness will just happen more naturally."

I looked at him like he was speaking a foreign language. "What?"

The Captain lit another cigarette, completely ignored my request for some kind of context for his last reply, and countered with a question of his own that I was sure he already knew the answer to. "You didn't tell anyone about it, did you?"

"No. I didn't know how, for one thing, and I knew no one would believe me." I finished the water and set the glass on the coffee table by the couch. "And I also figured that it wouldn't go over very well since I knew that what I experienced had nothing to do with what they were teaching about God."

"How does it feel to be able to talk to someone about it and have them believe you?" The Captain puffed blue smoke that circled his head in expanding waves.

"Better."

"Well, we are just beginning the process." The Captain winked. "We've still got repairs to make."

"What do you mean?" I still felt pretty woozy.

"You'll see. Take the rest of the day off; we've done enough for one day. Rest and be back tomorrow morning at the usual time."

"But—"

"No, Ray. Tomorrow."

∞

Dr. Fleet bent over his patient and delivered a precise chiropractic adjustment designed to relieve neurological interference and return the man's body to normal function. He brought the patient up to an upright position and told him to return the following week for another session. "Yes sir, doc," the man beamed, "I haven't felt this good in years. No more indigestion."

"All right, Mr. Thomas, I'll see you next week and we'll keep the power flowing," replied the not-yet doctor.

Thurman waited until the man had checked out and then walked from his study-turned-treatment room into the makeshift waiting area where Delia was acting as receptionist. "Is that it for today, Deddo?"

"Yes, Thurman, that was our last patient for today, and boy was he happy! I think he'll refer several more patients in."

Thurman sighed. "Well, I just hope that I can do them some good when they get here."

"Thurman, you've got to stop with that." Delia took on the tone she used when she scolded her husband. "You've been in practice all of three months. Don't you think you could stand to give it a little more time before you wring your hands in despair? Besides, most of your patients are ecstatic with their results. Can't you focus on the six out of seven who do heal instead of the one that doesn't?"

Delia was right. Most of Thurman's patients experienced the positive responses that he expected from his treatment. However, some were not responsive at all, and these were the cases that monopolized his attention. He might have four patients suffering from the same condition, and he would treat all of them the same way in accordance with the accepted chiropractic protocol. Three might completely heal, yet the fourth might experience no improvement whatsoever, and it drove Thurman to distraction wondering why.

What Delia didn't know was that the strange compulsion to understand that had hounded her husband for over a decade had recently increased to an almost frantic level. He thought about this missing link of healing all the time: during treatment hours, on his off time, when he was with his family—he even dreamed about it. He couldn't ever stop thinking about it, and the internal pressure to understand increased to the point that he began to lie awake most of the night imagining the Innate Intelligence that Dr. Drake had taught about flowing through his patient's bodies like electricity travelling over power lines. He personified it in his imagination and asked it questions in the hope of drawing out some revelation from somewhere inside himself, but no truth came.

"Deddo, I don't mean to sound like I'm complaining. I just don't understand why some patients don't get better when they all are treated the same way for the same condition." He scratched his head. "It doesn't make sense."

"No doctor has a one-hundred-percent success rate, darling," Delia sighed.

Delia loved her husband, but sometimes his intensity overwhelmed her. She had felt intense relief when Thurman had informed her that it was time to return to San Antonio from Corpus Christi, but she was beginning to feel uneasy again. He seemed constantly preoccupied with this unending quest that she didn't understand, obsessed with solving an unsolvable riddle. First it was the vegetables in his garden, then this chiropractic obsession. She was wondering if the rest of his life would be a compulsive search for something beyond his grasp.

She would have felt much more uneasy if she had known what was about to take place. Delia Fleet didn't know it yet, but her husband was teetering on a high wire between two worlds, and she was about to witness him tumbling off into the unknown.

CHAPTER FOUR
LIGHT

As usual, the Captain had been right: I'd been so tired after our short morning session that I slept most of the rest of the day.

And dreamed.

Wild dreams of strange ancient symbols, and my body melting into air like a block of ice being heated into water first and then steam. I dreamed that in place of my two normal eyes, I had one big eye in the center of my forehead. Through that one eye I could somehow see Life from the perspective of all things—living organisms and inanimate objects alike. It was as though I was experiencing all of Life at the same time. Finally I dreamed of a single lighted candle, burning small at first but growing and growing until finally the flame totally engulfed me in a brilliant white light.

I crept up the stone walkway to the Captain's back door the next morning debating with myself about whether I should continue on to the door and knock or turn around and run the other way. I wasn't so sure I wanted to continue down the path that he was leading me. I had a strong feeling that this was not something that I could trifle with or turn back from if the going got rough.

The trouble was, I was already in it up to my eyeballs and I knew it, and to tell you the truth it made me a little angry. I didn't ask for this. I never wanted a light to shine on me and conscript me into involuntary enlightenment. I didn't ask to move next door to the one crazy old man on the planet that could read my mind and bring it up again when I thought I had successfully avoided it. I would have been perfectly happy remaining blissfully ignorant of all of this stuff and living the relatively carefree life that most American teenagers took for granted. In the end I decided that I had no choice but to push my resentment in a corner and move forward.

I knocked on the Captain's door not knowing what to expect. He called me in and told me to get my coffee and come on in the den. He then started chattering about how we were going to need to tie up the tomato plants and spray the lettuce. I noticed that the evolution chart that had been on the wall was gone. I listened to him talk about tomato plants growing best when tied a certain way, and how he knew when it was the right time to harvest cucumbers until I couldn't stand it any more.

I interrupted him mid-sentence, "Excuse me, Captain, what about yesterday?"

He looked like he didn't understand what I was talking about. "We didn't do any gardening yesterday," he said, wide-eyed and innocent.

"I know we didn't do any gardening." My irritation started to boil over. "I was here. I was here when you tricked me into reliving an experience that I tried hard to forget. I was here when you questioned me about it and stirred me up so that I slept all day and all night having crazy dreams about it." The more I talked the louder my voice got until I was almost shouting. "I know we didn't do any gardening yesterday because what we did instead was play around with my head, and now you're acting like nothing happened, *and I don't appreciate it!*"

The Captain looked like he might be repressing a smile, which only made me angrier. He held up both of his hands pressed together at the palms, as if praying, and asked,

"Which of my hands is more important?"

"I don't know," I spat angrily. "What does that have to do with anything? I just told you that I didn't appreciate you—"

"Which one, Ray?" he interrupted in a firm, resonant tone.

"I don't know!" I waved my own hands in impatience, "They're both equally important if you ask me."

The Captain smiled and dropped his hands. "Good. I *was* asking you, and you gave the correct answer."

He picked up a cigarette from the green ashtray by his chair, took a drag, replaced it, and continued with his hands pressed together again, "My hands are like two sides of the same coin. Neither can fulfill its potential without the other working with it."

He dropped his hands. "Your life has more than one aspect as well. There is the aspect of *being*, which includes the experience you intuited, and there is the aspect of *doing*, which includes what action you take relative to your awareness. You have had a relatively rare experience, at least at this point in human evolution, but we can't spend all our time sitting around meditating on our navels and re-hashing it. You do need a conceptual framework for your experience, and we are going to get to that, but it is just as important for you to learn *how to live* or you are going to have problems."

"What do you mean?" I wasn't exactly enthusiastic about the thought of having future problems as a result of something that happened to me when I was nine.

"For now, let's put it this way." The Captain held his hands up again, this time palm down, at the level of his chest.

"People's lives depend on the balance between the possibilities they are aware of and their ability to live up to those possibilities. As long as they maintain a pretty decent balance, everything is fine."

He illustrated a gap by raising his right hand much higher than his left. "But sometimes, people become aware of greater possibilities or ideals, so their awareness is raised. Unless they also understand how to raise their life to match the possibilities they have now become aware of, there is going to be a gap between what they know is possible and what they are actually living, and a gap like that causes problems."

"What kind of problems?" I fidgeted uncomfortably.

"Physical illness, emotional disruptions, mental problems. The human race as a whole is going through a *consciousness gap* experience right now; it's why there is so much illness, unrest, so many wars. In short, it's why we are finding it so hard to live in harmony with each other, our environment, and ourselves. As we become aware of a more realistic picture of what we are as human beings, we will suffer until we close the gap between what we know and how we live."

He leaned forward. "We are at a point in history in which the inductive pursuits of science are catching up with the knowledge that has come deductively through religion and philosophy for quite some time. Science now says that we only *think* we are separate beings living separate lives; in reality we are all connected with each other and with our Source. Which is all good and well except that we don't live that way yet, and we are suffering as a race for our collective hypocrisy."

He got quiet for a moment. "I'll bet you probably know someone close to you who has experienced the consequences of not being able to live up to certain ideals." I noticed that the Captain was giving me that squint again, and I knew that he was somehow picking up on my Dad. I remembered Mom saying that Dad had grown disillusioned and that's what had led to his alcohol problem.

I nodded and he continued, "We need to help you understand the ideal you became aware of so that you don't have similar problems. We've got to close your gap by helping you learn how to live. Without that understanding, all the phenomena in the world isn't worth much—not even revelatory phenomena such as you experienced."

"So how do you propose to teach me how to live?"

"Easy." He smiled and rose from the recliner. "In order to understand how life should be lived on an individual basis, we will start by studying Life in a universal sense. Follow me."

The Captain and I spent each of the next three days tending to his garden. He talked non-stop about each vegetable, telling me how to plant the seeds, what time of the year to plant, how deep the seed holes should be, how long it took to grow to maturity, when to harvest, what bugs to look out for, how to rotate crops—basically everything I never wanted to know about growing a garden.

But interwoven in these constant lectures were ponderings about plants in general. He pointed out that life was flowing through those plants just like it was flowing through us, and the more he talked about plants the more appreciation I began to have for them. I had never really given much thought to the vegetable kingdom, but the Captain changed my perspective in three days time. He pointed out how important vegetation was to the entire ecosystem and he talked about many different types of plants that I had never heard of before, but mostly he talked about how responsive plants were to their environment.

He would say things like, "Ray, if I were to take a potato and put it down in my cellar, even if it was ninety-nine percent dark in there, if there was one little crack letting in just a peep of light, that potato would sprout shoots that would grow in the direction of that light even if it was twenty feet away." Then he'd take off his wide-brimmed hat and mop the sweat off his forehead, give a good dramatic pause, and ask the question that he asked me over and over during our gardening sessions, "Now, how does it know to do that? It doesn't have any eyes. How does it know there is light in that corner?"

And I would give the same answer I always gave, "I don't know."

"Well, let me ask you this, how does any plant know which way to grow? Have you ever thought about that? The seed goes in the ground randomly, yet I have never heard of an example of a plant growing upside down or sideways; they always grow roots-down, leaves-up. How do they know?"

"I don't know, Captain."

And on and on it would go. He would tell me about exotic carnivorous plants like the Venus Fly Trap and the Devil's Noose that trapped insects or even small animals and fed on their flesh. He talked about seeds that propelled themselves through water with projecting filaments so that they looked like insects instead of seeds. He told me about the strange Diatom, or *living crystal*, which he said was the connecting link between the mineral world and the vegetable world because it had properties of both.

As we were finishing up on the third day, he said, "Okay, tomorrow is going to be an inside day. No need for work clothes, but you might not want to plan anything for this weekend—we may have some extra work to do, but if so, don't worry. You'll get good overtime pay."

"An inside day? What does that mean?"

"That means that tomorrow it will be a great time to work on your own internal garden instead of my external one, and in preparation for that work I have a question for you to ponder between now and tomorrow."

I didn't answer right away. I was distracted thinking about that note the Captain had left me on the door that day I remembered. What was it the note had said? Some kind of Latin or Greek words that referred to the Virgin Mary.

Finally I realized he was waiting for acknowledgement, and I said, "Ah, all right, what's the question?"

"The question is this: we've spent lots of time talking about how life expresses through these plants and their different attributes. What do you think their most valuable attribute is? In other words, what can we best learn from them?"

I started to say something, but the Captain stopped me, "No, Ray, don't answer now—sleep on it tonight and let me know what you think tomorrow."

I didn't remember until later that night after the shit had already hit the fan, but during that whole conversation the Captain had been looking at me with his crazy squint again.

When I got home Mom wasn't in from work yet, so I started getting things ready for dinner. Dawn was helping me slice vegetables when a knock came at the front door. "I'll get it," I told her. I opened the door to find a large man wearing a sheriff's uniform standing on our porch.

"Is Janet Tolouthe here?" He was chewing on a toothpick that looked like its natural lifespan had expired a couple of hours ago.

"Um, no sir," I stammered. "She isn't home from work yet."

"Well, give her these papers, and I'll have to get you to sign for them saying that you received them."

"Okay, but what are they about?" I signed the clipboard the man held out for me.

"They are lawsuit papers for unpaid notes. I guess your Mom hasn't paid her bills."

I closed the door and put the papers on top of the refrigerator while Dawn's back was turned. "Who was it?" she asked as she filled up a pot to boil.

"Girl Scouts," I answered, breaking my own rule about not lying to Dawn. "I told them we didn't want any cookies." Just then Mom's green Chevrolet Impala pulled in the driveway and I said, "Hey Dawn, why don't you go take your shower now so that you won't miss *The Waltons* after dinner?"

"I've got plenty of time for that."

"Yeah, but you know how it always sneaks up on you and you miss the beginning." I took her arm and steered her toward the bathroom.

"What do you care?" she mumbled, but she went anyway.

Mom came in and put her stuff down. I waited until I was sure Dawn was in the shower and got the papers down from the refrigerator.

"Someone from the sheriff's office brought these by a little while ago, Mom." I handed her the papers. "Dawn doesn't know."

Mom read the first page and crumpled down in one of the kitchen chairs.

"What is it, Mom? Is everything okay?"

"No, Ray," she mumbled in a flat monotone that scared me, "it isn't. It seems that your father has failed to make payments on several debts this past year, and since both our names were on the notes we are both being sued." She made an ugly face. "Your father finds a way to stay connected even when he's not around, doesn't he?"

"How much do we owe?"

"Does it matter? We barely have enough to get by, and if Sid hasn't been making payments I assume his situation has deteriorated to the point that he can't contribute. It might as well be a million dollars."

Dawn and I had only spoken to Dad a handful of times since we left, and only twice since he called that night drunk. I had already suspected that he was spending more time drinking and less time working, and this turn of events seemed to confirm that theory.

"What are we going to do?"

She sighed and said, "The first thing I am going to do is talk to Mr. Jim and find out what our options are." Mr. Jim was Dad's best friend. They had known each other practically all their lives and had gone to law school together. Mom and Dad were both only children and Mr. Jim was the closest thing to an uncle that we had.

Dawn was still in the shower, so Mom went ahead and dialed Mr. Jim while I finished the vegetable spaghetti. Dawn was a hundred times better since I started working for the Captain and she started hanging out around his house, but she still took forever in the bathroom. Actually, that was probably just a normal girl trait.

I stirred and seasoned while I listened to Mom's end of the conversation.

"Jim? Hey, it's Janet." He obviously asked how she was. "I could be better, Jim. We have a pretty big problem. I got lawsuit notices today—apparently Sid hasn't paid on some of our debt since early last year, and I had no idea."

She paused again, "No, he's not doing well at all. I don't even know if he's working much." She listened again for a few seconds and said, "Would you, Jim? Maybe you can help. M-maybe he'll listen to you." She grabbed a paper towel and dabbed at her eyes.

"Anyway, we have to figure out what to do on our end." Mr. Jim obviously asked her how much the debt was because she said, "It's around $19,000. No, Jim, we have *nothing*—no savings. Sid paid all the bills and kept track of the finances, and I had no idea that he had let so much slide until I was on the way out. He's supposed to be sending child support, and I only hope to God he's able to keep up with that."

She began to cry again, and she had to excuse herself to blow her nose. When she resumed the conversation the first thing she said was, "We can't do that, Jim. We can't go bankrupt. There has to be something else we can do." She paused to wipe away the fresh tears that were now flowing.

"I have no credit history as it is because for all these years Sid has been the only one with income. We put my name on these things in the first place in order to establish some kind of credit history. If I have to start out with that kind of black mark on my record we'll never be able to get any kind of loan, and God knows I can't count on Sid for anything. Raymond graduates next year, and I already don't know how we are going to be able to afford to send him to college." She broke down completely. I took the phone, thanked Mr. Jim for his help, and told him that we would call him back tomorrow. Mom got it together while I was talking on the phone and was relatively calm by the time I hung up. I walked up behind her, patted her on the back, and whispered, "It's going to be all right, Mom. We'll figure something out," though I had absolutely no clue what solution anyone could come up with.

The next morning I arrived at work at the usual time, but I was completely pre-occupied with our family situation. The Captain called for me to get my coffee and come in, and when I went into the den I saw that he had put up that strange chart again.

He squinted at me with those dark eyes from his green faux leather recliner and asked, "Well Raymond, what answer did you come up with?"

I'd completely forgotten to think about the question the Captain had asked me the day before. "Um, I have to be honest, sir, I had something come up, and I haven't thought about it at all."

"Ray," he boomed in his deep voice, "that's why I like you. You are nothing if not honest." He kept squinting and continued, "Do you remember what the question was? We can pick it up and go from here."

"Not exactly, sir."

He pointed to the middle of his chart where it said *Vegetable Phase* and said, "For a few days now we've been observing how Life expresses through these forms we call plants. What can we learn from them, do you think?"

I tried to concentrate on what the Captain was asking me to do, but I was too worried about Mom and the family. I must have been showing obvious signs of distraction, because the Captain brought me back to focus.

"*Ray!*" His voice was controlled and airy like a whisper, but it had the intensity of a shout. "I know you think that where your mind is chasing you right now is more important than where I'm asking you to lead it, but I assure you it isn't."

Seeing that he now had my attention, he went on, "I know all about your family troubles, and we *are* going to solve your problem, but we can't lose sight of the real lesson here." He lit a cigarette, blew a cloud of blue smoke directly upward, and said, "It's opportunities like these that will help you learn to be *on time* more often."

"W—what are you talking about?" I couldn't believe what the Captain had just said. "First of all, how can *you* solve our problem? Second of all, how do you even know we *have* a problem? And last but not least, what the hell are you talking about with me learning to be on time? I'm *always* on time. *I've never been late for anything I was supposed to do for you, ever!*"

The Captain sat calmly peering at me from behind those thick wire-rimmed glasses and finally said, "Not being late for an appointment isn't the same as being *on time*, Ray, although I know it's confusing because we use the terms synonymously in common parlance."

He pointed again to the large chart hung on the wall behind him, this time toward the right side of the chart

labeled *Cosmic Consciousness.* "You experienced a taste of this consciousness, Ray. What was it like?"

My frustration intensified. "I already told you what it was like. The best I could, anyway. Why are you asking me again?"

"Because I am trying to explain what I have been driving at about being on time." He gestured at his bookshelf, "Go get that grey book on the second shelf there. See it?"

I located the book and tried to hand it to him, but he waved me off. "No, you keep it and turn to the very first part of the book, past the table of contents."

"Okay." I flipped through the pages and found the correct section.

"That introduction was written about a man who had an experience like yours. I'm sure you remember asking me how I knew so much about what it felt like?"

I nodded.

"Well, this book helped me a lot in understanding those kinds of things." He pointed at the pages. "This commentary was based upon the man's first-hand account of his experience, and it does as good a job of describing the feeling as any other source I have ever consulted. Take a minute and read it—it's just one page long."

I sat down, still annoyed, and began to read:

The doctor experienced his illuminated state while visiting friends in London. He had spent the evening discussing literature and philosophy, subjects for which he had always had a deep and abiding passion. His head and heart vibrated with the low, steady, pleasant thrum of the human soul engaged in honest contemplation of its own nature, like the purring of a lost cat that has successfully navigated her way home and now sleeps warm by the fire.

He began his journey home that evening in a state of passive, unconscious meditation. His carriage had traveled perhaps a half a mile down the cobblestone road when his consciousness exploded into Light.

His first perception was that a fire colored cloud had engulfed him like the Biblical fish that swallowed Jonah, but he quickly realized that the spectacularly brilliant Light that seemed to simultaneously surround and penetrate his entire being emanated from within himself. He felt a euphoria that he had never before imagined was possible. A Power reverberated deep within him—an ineffable Force that the human mind universally ascribes to some conception of the Divine. Without the slightest trace of uncertainty he instantly knew that all life is manifested as a united expression of this Power. Knowing that he was neither his body nor his mind, he would never again fear physical death. Any concept of sin was forever erased from his consciousness. This true experience of spirituality stood out in sharp relief against the impotence of his former theology, a jumbled laundry bag of mental and emotional constructs he had fashioned to soothe fears of mortality and rationalize the indulgence of the ego.

How long this rapturous state lasted, the doctor could not tell. Time was irrelevant. Space was a non sequitur. The man's consciousness filled past the limits of his mind with an image of immortality reflected in his own soul. He did not cease to be the person he was before, as in the oft-repeated mystical analogy of a drop melting into the ocean. Rather, it was as if the entire ocean entered into a single drop. He felt a sense of joy and peace surpassing all understanding, defying language or even conscious thought. It was an experience that he felt more intensely than he had ever felt any sensation or emotion before.

And then it was over.

I finished reading and looked up at the Captain. He reached out and I handed him the book. "Now," he said, "let's get back to this issue of being on time."

I breathed a small sigh of irritation, but he ignored me and asked, "What do you think? Is that account similar to what you experienced?"

"Yes."

"And while you were in that state, what was your awareness of time?"

All of a sudden I knew where the Captain was going. "It was like I existed outside of time," I responded.

"Yes," he said. "You were no longer *in time*; rather, you were *on time*. You were suspended in an awareness that transcended our normal experience of linear time. You were in a state that was somehow beyond time or above time, or we might say *on time*."

I felt the hairs on the back of my neck prickle as the Captain's words stimulated a faint memory of what it was like to be in that state. "Yes."

"Now, we can't always be in that state, at least not at this point in the evolution of consciousness." He blew some smoke toward the ceiling. "But those who are interested in moving forward need to be aware that all too often we place ourselves *out of time*."

I heard myself repeat, "Out of time?"

He answered back with his own question, "What time is it Ray?"

I looked at my watch and said, "7:13."

"Nope, try again."

I looked at the mini grandfather clock beside the couch and said, "But your own clock says the same thing."

"I'm not asking a clock or a watch, I'm asking *you*. What is the only time it can be, ever?" I shrugged.

"*Now!*" he startled me by shouting. "It is *now*, and it always was and always will be *now*. No matter what the clock or the watch says, the important thing is to be aware that you exist only in the present moment."

He pointed to the *Human Phase* portion of his chart.

"When we are in this normal human consciousness we tend to project our minds into the past or future. Really we always project from the past, usually subconsciously. We focus on memories of emotions from previous experiences and mentally fit them into the circumstances of the present and then expect to recreate the past experience in the future."

He blew some more cigarette smoke and went on, "Let me ask you this: did you come over here yesterday?"

"You know that I did."

"Forget about what *I* know. What do *you* know? Did you come over here yesterday?"

"Yes." I rolled my eyes.

"How do you know?"

I had been standing up while the Captain sat in his usual place in the green recliner, but I could tell we were going to be here a while so I sat down on the couch and answered, "Because I remember doing it. I remember being here."

"*When* do you remember being here?"

"Whenever I think about it."

"Which is always when?"

I finally got it. "Now."

He stubbed out his cigarette and said, "Correct. The truth is that the past doesn't even exist. Not like we think it does, anyway. What we call the past is a particular mental state we call *memory*, which is still experienced in the present. It's nothing more than identifying with an image that has been manifested on the physical plane. The future is nothing but another mental state, also experienced in the present, that involves identifying with an image that we personally *haven't* yet experienced on the physical plane."

"What does that mean, 'identifying with an image?'" I could see the word *Image* on the Captain's chart over on the far left.

"We're going to get to that, sooner than you think," he replied cryptically. "For now, I need to know that you really get what I am saying. The past and future are mental constructs, illusions of the mind. The only time that is real is *NOW*. Understand?"

I nodded.

"Good. Then you can stop putting yourself *out of time* and deal with Life *as it is*, not as it appears to you based upon your memories. You can stop identifying with fear and worry and start living in reality rather than illusion."

I wasn't yet connecting those dots. "Captain, I think I get what you are saying about focusing on the present moment, but I don't understand how that helps my situation or my feelings about it. We really do have a problem and no way to solve it. My focusing on the present isn't going to change that."

He smiled a slow smile and replied, "Ray, you focusing on reality rather than illusion is going to change *everything*."

He got up and went in the kitchen, talking as he went. "First of all, getting acquainted with reality will clarify for you that whatever your situation is, it isn't nearly as bad as you imagine it to be. Most of what we are afraid of is just projection and fantasy and it never even happens. Mark Twain said, 'I've had many troubles in my life, the vast majority of which never happened.'"

He turned on the water from the sink and began speaking louder to make sure I could hear him. "Second of all, Life happens *now*. When you are aware of the present moment, you will be plugged into Life instead of clouded by your own fear-based, limited perceptions, and you will then be able to see clearly how to *act* in any given moment. When you live from the standpoint of your personal illusion you aren't acting, you are *reacting*, and since what you are reacting to is illusory, your responses are similarly mistaken."

He turned the faucet off and brought back two glasses of water, handed one to me, and finished, "It's only when you act instead of reacting that your actions are authentic. When your actions are authentic they are woven into the fabric of Life, just like the rain, the planets spinning in orbit, or the subatomic particles that make up all matter in the universe vibrating perfectly in harmony. When you are living in harmony there is no trouble. There are preferences and desires, but they don't rule your life or your actions any more than any other random events or circumstances. At that point you are not so much living a personal, limited life as you are allowing Life to live through you."

He gestured at the chart with a sweeping motion of his arm. "Other forms automatically participate in the symphony of Life, but humans must *learn* to do so. It's what you must learn. When you learn that, you will have an open garden like me instead of a closed garden like most people."

There was a long silence. "Sorry. I still don't get it."

The Captain threw back his head and laughed. "That's okay Ray," he managed between giggles, "I taught thousands of people over the years and only a relative handful of them ever really got it. But don't worry; I think you'll understand more as I give you some concrete examples. Remember, we're just getting started."

The Captain continued to laugh, and his mirth was contagious. I chuckled a couple of times despite myself. Finally I asked, "So what now?"

His laughter gradually died down. "Well, we start by getting back to my question about the vegetable kingdom. What can we learn from it?"

"I'm afraid I still don't know, Captain."

He shifted out of the way so that I could fully see the chart on the wall behind him. "Let me explain this chart and it will be a little easier for you. Each division on this chart represents a stage in the creative or evolutionary process. Evolution just means an *unfolding*, starting with un-manifested energy. Whatever power is behind everything expresses through forms, and both science and theology agree that creation began with space——pure potential. Then arose sub-atomic particles, then those forms combined to form minerals and chemicals, then vegetables, then animals, then humans, and finally, the forms will have evolved enough that the power that created the universe will be able to express through authentic humans. A few early examples are listed there on the chart." I saw a circle on the chart halfway between the human phase and the cosmic phase that contained some familiar names: Buddha, Jesus, Moses, Krishna, and some others I didn't recognize. "See how the chart reflects that idea?"

I nodded.

"Notice that each phase of evolution has an attribute that is added to the ones before. For example, the electronic stage has only one attribute: the attribute of attraction. The next stage, the mineral/chemical stage retains that attribute, but adds another: the attribute of organization. See?"

"Yes," I nodded again.

"And what does it say is added to the vegetable phase?"

"Adaptation."

"Correct." He took a big gulp of his water and asked, "Now, what does that mean?"

"Well, in biology we learned that this is when life appears. When you have an organism that responds to changes in its environment, assimilates food, removes waste, reproduces, and so on. That's what we mean by adaptation."

The Captain was nodding, "Not bad, Ray, but I am going to amend what you were taught a bit."

He went into another room and wheeled back a small rolling chalkboard, upon which he wrote the word *Life*. Then he produced a gigantic dictionary from his bookshelf and handed it to me. "We're going to have to start from the beginning to get where we're going, so let's get to it. What does that dictionary say the meaning of this word is?"

I looked it up and there were nineteen definitions for the word *life*. "It says a bunch of stuff, Captain. You want it all?"

He shook his head. "No, just the definitions you think are relevant to our discussion."

An organismic state characterized by capacity for metabolism, growth, reaction to stimuli, and reproduction. I shut the dictionary with a clap.

"Not so fast, young man," he said. "Open that book back up. That is a common definition, and it is basically the same one you just gave me, but it isn't the most accurate definition for our purposes."

"All right, how about, *One or more aspects of the process of living?*"

"Nope. Aspects equal illusion. Perceiving reality demands wholeness. We want the truth, the whole truth, and nothing but the truth, so help us God." He smiled at his own joke while I kept looking.

"Um, *A principle or force that is considered to underlie the distinctive quality of animate beings?*"

He nodded, "That's probably as close we'll get in there." He wrote *Principle* and *Force* on the board. "Unless you are consulting a metaphysical book, it is difficult to get a perspective that doesn't involve life being equated with this idea of humans being able to perceive that the form in question is animated."

"Isn't that true?" I asked. "I mean, we don't generally consider inanimate objects to be alive."

"No, we don't, but why not? What is our reasoning behind that perspective?"

"I don't know that there is any *reasoning* behind it," I answered. "It just seems obvious."

The Captain smiled and said, "Ray, always be on guard for things that seem obvious. For example, that couch you are sitting on, is it in motion or is it still?"

"It's still. I haven't seen or felt it move the whole time I've been here."

"And yet any physicist would tell you that it is composed of sub-atomic particles that are constantly moving at a velocity near the speed of light." He waved his hands around to demonstrate constant motion. "The truth is that it is never *not* in motion."

He kept one hand moving back and forth, like waves on the ocean. "The reason that it seems to be still to you is that your outer senses are too crude to perceive the movement. That's why we perceive things the way we do; we often let our senses define things for us. We buy in to the illusion that we are a body because we trust only the sensory vibrations that come in through our outer faculties, and we confuse those experiences with what we really are."

He lit another cigarette. "We define living things only in terms of having similar biological attributes as ourselves, but tell me, since everything that exists is ultimately made up of waves of energy, is there really a good reason to differentiate between forms and objects that way?"

I shrugged.

"Let's put it another way. Suppose I ask you what any physical object is made of—say, a toothpick for example. What would you tell me?"

"Wood?" I said tentatively.

"Of course, quite right," smiled the Captain. "But what is the wood made of?"

"Um—dead plant cells?"

"Right again!" The Captain blew smoke up to the ceiling. "But what are those cells made of?"

"Lots of stuff."

"What kind of stuff?"

"Chemicals—compounds—molecules."

The Captain pointed to the chart and said, "You see

where we are headed, Ray?"

I did. We had backtracked from the vegetable phase on the chart through the mineral/chemical phase and were now at the electronic phase.

I nodded and the Captain continued, "Now, look at what is at the very beginning of the chart."

I read it out loud. "God Unmanifest, Consciousness, Energy, X. What does the X mean?"

He answered my question with another question, "What is energy, Ray?"

"The capacity to do work," I answered automatically.

"Who told you that, Mr. Wizard?" The Captain laughed. "Come on, you're better than that. What kind of definition is that? What does that even mean?"

I blushed and shrugged again.

The Captain affected an expression obviously designed to soothe my embarrassment and said, "Well, don't feel too bad, because the smartest scientists in the world don't know what it is either. No one does. It's an unknown. We can observe it working and make lists of its attributes, but *no one* knows what it is in essence."

He followed up with another question, "Now that we have that one out of the way, let's try an easy one: what is God?"

"I don't believe in God," I replied somewhat bitterly.

He seemed amused by this response and said, "Oh, you do more than believe—you are one of relatively few people who *knows* that the Divine exists. You just don't believe in the concepts they gave you in church about an old man with whiskers sitting on a throne in a heaven up in the clouds with golden streets and everyone wearing white dresses and playing harps. There *is* Divinity; you experienced it. It's just that it is a great omniscient Power in which all forms live and move and have their being, not some all-powerful humanoid monstrosity with common jealousies and anger and hate. Isn't that what you experienced?"

I nodded.

"But that still doesn't answer the question of what the Divine *is* in essence, does it? What is the ultimate essence of that Power?" He waited for my answer.

"I don't know, Captain."

"How right you are!" he yelled almost jubilantly. "Neither does the most pious theologian that has ever lived! None of us know, so you know what?"

"What?"

"I think we should stop acting like we know. I think that we should give this Power some name that denotes that we acknowledge that we cannot comprehend it, what do you think?"

"Um, sure."

"Then I think using a letter variable like we use in algebra is appropriate, don't you?" He pointed at me with one nicotine-stained finger. "I think calling it X gets the point across."

He chuckled, took a deep breath, and delivered a summation. "So here we are, with a power we know is there but we can't define. We know that science calls it energy, theology calls it God, and we call it X. We know that everything in this universe, including our thoughts and emotions, is composed of this X. Nothing exists that isn't ultimately made of this same energy.

"Since everything is ultimately the same in essence, isn't everything equally alive or equally dead, and only expressing this power to a greater or lesser degree depending upon the form that it is expressing through?"

My head was hurting by this time, but I gave the Captain a slow nod.

"All right, we're almost home, so stick with me for just a few more minutes," he soothed. "One more example:

there are many devices in your house that are animated by electricity, right?"

"Yes."

"And yet some of those devices are more complex than others, right?" I nodded. "A light bulb can only turn on and off, whereas a television set can produce phenomena that is much more complex and interesting to us. Yet the same power animates all of them, and if we unplug them we say that they are *dead*, don't we?"

I pulled at the collar of my shirt. I felt like I was suffocating under all these heavy ideas. "Yes."

"So the presence or absence of life doesn't have to do with the form, does it? It has to do with the power that animates the form. And since the same Power animates all forms as well as makes up all forms, the truth is that there is nothing *but* Life, is there? Just energy, or Spirit, or consciousness, or whatever you want to call it constantly changing and interacting with itself in one great harmonious living symphony. *Remember*, Ray?"

I closed my eyes and remembered that feeling of absolute Oneness, and those hairs on the back of my neck stood up again.

The Captain stubbed out another cigarette and waited while I reveled in the pleasure of Cosmic Unity like a dog having his belly scratched.

Finally he snapped me back into my normal state of awareness. "But we can't stay in that consciousness all the time—not yet at least. We must be able to go to the top of the Temple, but we must also be able to go back down into the bottom of the pit, and we must be able to move freely between those two extremes as duty calls."

He took a deep breath and finished, "And so, it is often instructive to examine fragments or parts in order to teach ourselves to live more in harmony with the whole. Consequently, we must return to the original question: what do those vegetables have to offer us in the way of living in harmony with Life?"

I looked at the chart again for help. "Adaptation?" I asked tentatively.

"Very good, Ray," he smiled. "Adaptation is acting in accordance with what *is* rather than trying to force things to be the way we would like them to be. It's a very important step in learning to act authentically. When the plant grows from a seed in the ground and it encounters a rock or a root on its way to the surface of the earth, it doesn't despair, it simply changes course and grows around it. It doesn't complain or worry about it. It doesn't feel angry or afraid; it just acts according to its nature. And so will we. We will adapt to your situation in a way that is congruent with our abilities and circumstances."

"Captain, I appreciate the intention, but unless you have a lot of money stashed around here that you would like to give us, I don't see how you can help us adapt to this situation."

"Why Ray, I thought I had already explained that." He looked genuinely surprised at what I had said. "I have it all. All the money in the world. I told you that mine was an open garden."

"Um, okay, sir." If it hadn't been for my history with the Captain I would have sworn at that moment that I was talking to a very senile old man. I would soon be proven wrong about that.

"And so," he said, "we are going to be working overtime this weekend. We need to leave as soon as possible; we have a very long drive ahead of us."

"Where are we going?"

"The place everyone goes to solve money problems," he said with a mischievous twinkle in his dark eyes. "We are going to Las Vegas."

CHAPTER FIVE
LOVE

⟨⟩

Delia Fleet was terrified. She had taken the children to her mother's house when the episode started. She hadn't wanted them to see their father, and she honestly hadn't known whether she would have the courage to return to the house herself.

But she had gone back, and when she checked on Thurman he had been in the front bedroom writing on the wall in strange symbols that would later be identified by an archaeology professor from the University of Texas as Sanskrit, though Thurman had never even seen the ancient Hindu liturgical language, much less studied it or become fluent in it.

It was obvious to Delia that her husband was having some sort of breakdown, but she didn't know what to do about it or how to help him. She waited for her brother, Calvin Wright, to arrive from work. Calvin and Thurman were close; they had worked together for the Weber Company and Thurman loved and respected Calvin.

She stopped pacing when she heard the front door bang shut. "Cal, thank God you're here!"

"Delia, what's wrong?" Delia hugged Calvin like a drowning woman clinging to a life raft. "Mother said Thurman was having some kind of a breakdown," he said.

"I—I don't know, Cal." She wept uncontrollably from a mixture of stress and relief. "He's been driving himself crazy lately with this obsession with healing and I think he just sn—sn— snapped!" Her voice rose to little girl pitch. "H—he said he was going into the bedroom to figure it out once and for all, and for no one to disturb him under any circumstances."

Calvin patted her hair. "That doesn't sound too bad, Sis. Thurman's an intense personality. He probably just—"

"*Cal*," she almost screamed, "he's been talking to people that aren't there! He's in there right now drawing symbols all over the wall! And sometimes he looks..." She dropped her gaze and her sentence trailed off. She wanted to say something but couldn't quite bring herself to admit it. "Just go see him, you'll understand what I'm talking about. He's just not in his normal mind!"

"Okay, okay. Shhh," Calvin was alarmed at the intensity of his sister's distress, but he didn't let on. He held Delia until she had calmed down enough for him to leave, then he started for the door to the front bedroom. He felt a mysterious dread that grew as he approached, as though he sensed a powerful vibration behind that door that he was in no way prepared to confront. He hesitated at the door for several seconds before turning the knob.

Calvin took one look at Thurman and understood his sister's distress. He was indeed busily covering the walls in exotic-looking symbols with a thick black pen. He looked completely disheveled, and he had shaved off his mustache. His shirttail was pulled out, his shirt was unbuttoned halfway down, his suspenders dangled from his waist, he had one shoe on and one shoe off, and his hair was in complete disarray.

But it was when he turned around and looked Calvin in the eyes that Calvin felt his knees weaken and a sharp jolt in his solar plexus. Thurman's eyes looked *through* Calvin, like he wasn't there, and they burned with a numinous glow that Calvin had never seen before, in anyone.

"Thurman," Calvin croaked, "are you alright?"

"Calvin?" Thurman answered as though they were in a giant throng looking for each other instead of in a small room by themselves. His eyes seemed to finally find Cal. "Hello Calvin. How was work today?"

"Um, it was fine." He slowly circled his brother-in-law, inspecting him as he talked. "Thurman, are you okay?"

"Yes Cal. I've never been better. In fact, right now I am *being my best*." He started gesturing as though conducting a symphony and asked, "Calvin, can you hear the music?"

"No, Thurman, I don't hear anything."

"I didn't think so, but it's a shame." He closed his eyes as if taking in an experience of profound beauty. "The most beautiful music I have ever heard."

Calvin didn't quite know how to proceed. "Thurman, what's this all about?"

Thurman turned the full incendiary force behind his eyes on Calvin and replied, "Cal, I've tuned in to the secret to healing. I understand it now. It's so simple, I can't believe I didn't see it before." Thurman began to laugh, which scared Calvin even more.

He stopped laughing abruptly and stared into space for almost a full minute. Finally he said, as if repeating a question, "What would I do if I were in charge of all life?"

"Thurman, what are you talking about?" asked Calvin, but his brother-in-law ignored him. Whatever Thurman thought he was interacting with could not be seen by human eyes or heard by human ears.

"Well, I sure as hell wouldn't conduct things the way you have been," Thurman said to the wall.

Calvin watched in silence as his brother-in-law had a heated discussion with no one. It was difficult for Calvin to tell for sure, as he was privy to only half the conversation, but the subject matter seemed to revolve around how Thurman would change society if he were in control of it.

"I would take all of the money, all of the gold, and lock it up in the bank. I'd dole it out according to individual merit. The way you've got things set ain't fair, not at all. Al Capone is a murderous son-of-a-bitch, but he's got more money than a king, while little old lady Reed, who loves you and goes to church every Sunday has nothing and can barely feed and clothe herself."

Calvin was alarmed to realize that Thurman thought he was talking to God.

"Good," Thurman nodded, "and the next thing I would do is get the young people off the streets. They are just running wild right now, but I would put them in camps designed to get them doing something constructive."

Calvin slipped out of the room while Thurman was still telling God how he would fix American society in the Year of Our Lord, 1931.

Delia jumped up from her large chair in the living room. "What do you think? What's wrong with him? Is he going to be okay?"

"Sis, I don't know. You were right, he seems pretty disoriented, but I don't think he's a danger to himself or anyone else. I think our best course of action is to just watch him and hope he comes out of it at some point."

"But he's been like that for almost a whole day now, since last night after dinner. How long can we let it go on?"

"Sis, I don't know what choice we have. If we call the doctor, he'll have him committed to the mental ward and we don't want that. Let's just wait and see—Thurman's a strong man, he'll come back out of this. I know he will." Cal tried to sound convincing for Delia's sake, but he was anything but confident.

The next day Thurman's behavior was unchanged.

Delia met Calvin at the door and said, "Calvin Wright, we've got to do something. He isn't any better; in fact, he may be worse."

"Is he still writing on the wall?" Calvin asked.

"No, but he won't come out of the room, he won't eat or drink anything, and he hasn't been to the toilet since the whole thing started. He just wanders around that room talking to people who aren't there." Her eyes were red from crying and her hands were raw from wringing them, but she couldn't stop herself. "And you know what he told me today? I went in to try to get him to come out and eat and he sat down with his head in his hands and said, 'Deddo, if all this energy doesn't stop flowing through me pretty soon I don't know if I can take it.' What does that *mean*, Cal?"

He sighed. "I don't know, Sis." He sunk down in a chair with his head in his hands. After a minute he rose quickly as if he had come to a decision and said, "Drake."

"What?" Delia asked, confused.

"Dr. Drake, Thurman's chiropractic professor. He might be able to help."

"What makes you think he can do anything?" Delia shook her head. "I'm not being argumentative, I just need a reason to hope. How do you think his professor can help?"

"When I was in there last night, Thurman mentioned something about tuning in to the secret of healing. And didn't you say that he had been downright obsessed with chiropractic and healing lately?" Delia nodded. "So I think there's a good chance that this is what precipitated this whole event for Thurman. Drake is an authority on healing; at least for Thurman he is, so maybe he can bring him back to reality."

Dr. Drake agreed to come over immediately to see if he could be of assistance. He arrived shortly thereafter and following the obligatory exchanges of *thank yous* and *don't mention its* he stepped into the front bedroom to confront his most difficult student.

Drake was shocked. He hadn't expected what he was now seeing. Thurman was barefoot with his pants legs rolled up as though he had been wading through knee-deep water. He had a two-day growth of beard and the unkempt shrubbery of his hair hung down over a sweaty brow and eyes framed by dark circles. He stared blankly at the wall and mumbled to himself incoherently while his hands moved in small circles at his sides, seemingly involuntarily.

Dr. Drake quickly composed himself. "Fleet." Then louder, "*Fleet!*" No response. Drake circled around in front of Thurman and waved a hand in front of his face while watching his eyes carefully to see if there was any sign that he was aware of the movement. He snapped his fingers and clapped his hands in front of the younger man's face. Nothing. He turned to leave the room to decide what to do next; Thurman was clearly catatonic.

He was halfway to the door when Thurman said, "I've found it, Dr. Drake. I've found what I was looking for."

Drake turned around and answered cautiously, so as not to drive the man back into wherever it was that he had been retreating to. "What have you found, Fleet?"

Thurman shifted his body, turned his head, and looked through Dr. Drake as he had done with Calvin. It was all the professor could do to keep himself from running out of the house and not stopping until he was home. "I have found the Power, Dr. Drake—what you call Innate Intelligence."

"That's fine, Fleet," Drake soothed after having composed himself. "I'm glad you found what you were looking for. Say, you look a little tired. Why don't we get you something to eat and you can rest, and then you and I will talk about Innate Intelligence tomorrow?"

Thurman smiled. "No sir, I can't eat or rest right now. I don't know how to explain it, but I am very aware that I am not my body and I can't tend to something that isn't real."

Dr. Drake moved closer and touched Thurman on the shoulder. "Well, son, it feels real to me. See?" He held Thurman's arm and grasped it in several places.

"Yes sir, I know that you perceive it to be real, but think about this: the arm that you are touching is nothing but energy. Your own arm is nothing but energy. Energy isn't solid, we only think it is." As Thurman spoke, Dr. Drake began to feel that time seemed to be slowing down. He had a sensation of floating.

Thurman continued to talk about the true nature of what humans collectively perceive to be reality, and to Dr. Drake's astonishment he realized that he could see *through* Thurman's body as though it were clear liquid. His body seemed somehow to flicker in and out of existence, as though he were on the dividing wall between two dimensions, first leaning one way and becoming more a part of one, then the other.

The professor shook his head and rubbed his eyes to clear his vision, yet his former student remained rhythmically transparent. This was more than the doctor could comprehend; his mind shut down like a circuit that blows a fuse to keep from destroying the entire mechanism.

"Fleet, I want you to lie down over here," he instructed in a daze, defaulting to the only thing he knew and had faith in. "I am going to adjust your nervous system. We'll check you and clear any interference as many times as necessary, and you'll return to normal."

Thurman laughed a dry, woody laugh. "Dr. Drake, what if I don't want to return to what you call normal?"

"Fleet, you don't know what you're talking about. You're not in your right mind. Get over here and—"

"What about Nettie?" Thurman interrupted while staring right through the doctor, eyes blazing with an intensity that made his former professor's brain vibrate.

Drake's face flushed in an instant. "What about her, you bastard? You leave her out of this!"

"Didn't she tell you that there were things that the human mind couldn't understand? *There are more things in heaven and earth, Horatio, than are dreamt of in your philosophy.* Didn't she used to quote that to you all the time?" Thurman spoke in his normal masculine pitch, but his words took on the exact cadence of James Drake's mother. She had died in 1912 in Scott City, Kansas, the same year that James graduated from chiropractic school in Davenport, Iowa. Thurman had never met or even heard about the woman, yet he had adopted her speech patterns perfectly.

"Jim, you can't figure it all out," Thurman said. "It's like a mule chasing a carrot on a stick. Every step you take, God moves the carrot one more step."

The doctor's knees failed, and he sank into a chair. The color that had flooded his face seconds before vanished just as quickly. He began to weep and his tongue felt too thick to speak, but he tried anyway, "H—how could you p—possibly know that? She d—didn't say those things to anyone but me, and I n—never told anyone."

"She loved you, Dr. Drake, and she knew that you loved her too."

At this the doctor began to cry even harder. Thurman walked toward him. "And there was nothing you could have done. You couldn't have saved her, even if you had been there. It was her time to transition." He touched the doctor on the shoulder, and the man felt a regret that he had carried for almost twenty years melt away like ice cubes in a glass of tea on a Texas summer afternoon. He stopped crying and began to collect himself.

Thurman walked slowly back to the corner of the room and slipped back into whatever world he had been occupying for the past forty or so hours. He began mumbling to himself again, staring off into space, and Dr. Drake could no longer coax out any response. He had obviously been dismissed, so he withdrew from the room and joined Calvin and Delia in the den.

They heard the bedroom door open and hurried to meet him in the hall. Delia spoke first. "How is he, doctor? Is he going to be okay?"

"Ah, I'm not sure what to tell you, Mrs. Fleet. I-I've never seen anything like this before. I don't know whether he has blown a gasket or what. The one thing that I can tell you is that your husband is in touch with some—" he faltered, grasping for the right word, "—knowledge—that transcends our normal conscious knowledge."

"What the hell does that mean?" Calvin demanded.

Drake sighed. "I don't know myself. I know that he has knowledge of things that there is no way that he could know about through the normal transmission of information. I know that I saw—something—in there that I can't explain."

"Saw what?" asked Calvin, but Delia laid her hand on her brother's arm and quickly changed the subject. "Doctor, what do you think we should do? What *can* we do?"

"Unfortunately for you, I don't think you can do a whole lot," the doctor said as he put on his coat. "I will be back tomorrow to check on him, but I think you just have to wait it out. I don't know why I think this, but I think he is eventually going to come back down to earth and be all right."

They thanked him for his help and saw him out. Delia knew that Calvin was aggravated by Dr. Drake's assessment, but she felt better. The feeling of peace that Thurman had imparted to Dr. Drake had passed on in some degree to her, and she was able to sleep some that night while her husband paced and mumbled to unseen entities.

∞

"You are one crazy old man," I said as I shook my head at the Captain. "I am *not* going to Las Vegas."

He feigned indignant surprise and slight hurt. "Why?" he asked, "don't you like to gamble?"

"I wouldn't know—I've never tried—but I do know that there is no way, *no way*, that my Mom is going to say, *Sure Ray, just hop in the car with our crazy old neighbor and drive a thousand miles to Las Vegas. Gamble away what little money we do have while you're at it.*"

"We've got to work on that attitude of yours," the Captain said as he got up from his recliner. "You've got to be able to see some possibilities instead of dead ends everywhere. And by the way," he winked on his way past me, "it's closer to twelve-hundred miles according to the map." He headed for the front door.

"Where are you going?"

"I'm going to get permission from your Mother. You stay here."

"Yeah, right," I thought as I flopped down on the couch. "That'll happen when pigs fly."

I sat on the couch for a few minutes but quickly tired of just waiting with nothing to do, so I decided to check out the Captain's bookshelf. There were lots of strange books about all kinds of subjects—there was a set titled Phase One, Phase Two, all the way to Phase Seven. There were books on Yoga, vibrational healing, Rosicrucianism, Pyramidology, Zoroastrianism, the Baghavad Gita, the Gnostic Gospels, comparative religious mythology, probably two dozen philosophy books, at least as many botany books, several on quantum mechanics, and a bunch of notebooks, some faded and yellowed with age. I picked up one of the notebooks with the words "Concept-Therapy" scrawled on the front and thumbed through it. In the front it had a bunch of diagrams of stick people with large heads, and toward the back it had a bunch of random essays in the Captain's handwriting.

One passage in particular caught my eye:

On December 17, 1931, I experienced what is known as an illumination. This experience seems to parallel those recorded in Dr. Henry Bucke's book entitled 'Cosmic Consciousness.' This conclusion may be wishful thinking on my part, and yet it may have been a true case of the higher consciousness that I experienced. At any rate, I was suddenly transferred out of my normal consciousness into one much higher, a consciousness that made me feel as One with all of life. I am convinced that there is no use in trying with words to describe such a state. It has to be experienced.

During the seven days that followed, I received a set of orders from a Source that we usually ascribe to the Deity. It seemed that a vision of Life in its entirety was revealed to me. I was conscious of an Entity telling me that Truth had been scattered, that it needed to be put back together again—that it should be brought back, out of the depths, back to this place which seemed to be a higher plane. I looked down into all the world and could see the Truth shining amidst all that was dull and dross. Truth appeared as a glittering jewel amidst all the rubbish of that lower plane.

To go back down there, gather up this Truth and return it safely to the upper plane seemed a Herculean task, something far beyond my abilities, something that I felt I would be unable to do, a job impossible. Revelation upon revelation was disclosed to me. I saw Life in its entirety. The past was shown, the future revealed. It seemed as though I stood and watched Life pass by, in review, from its beginning to its end. At last I became convinced that I should go back— back from whence I had come—and try to find the hidden Truth, try to return it to the upper plane. I was promised the needed help. So I went back into the normal consciousness— the only consciousness I had previously known. It was like returning to the City of the Dead. That was in 1931.

The orders I received during my illumination were accompanied by a visual picture. In brief, the instruction stated that I would be taught a new philosophy of life that I was to communicate to others. I was to obtain teachers and train them, and then secure a place wherein this philosophy could be taught to the world. This illumination ended at midnight on December 24th, 1931. Since that time I seem to have been hypnotized to an idea. That idea was, and is today, Concept-Therapy.

The back door opened as I finished reading the passage and I quickly replaced it on the bookshelf as the Captain walked into the den. "Okay," he said, "go pack in a hurry. We'll drive straight through the night so that it won't take us as long to get there and back, so I figure on maybe four days worth of clothes. We can—"

"What?" I interrupted. I couldn't believe my mother had given permission for this. "Did you tell her where we were going?"

"I told her that you were going to drive me to see a sick friend in Nevada and that you would get overtime pay. Which she was happy about, by the way."

"Captain!" I was shocked. "That's a complete lie!"

"No it isn't." He was the epitome of wide-eyed innocence. "We are going to see the pit boss of the casino. He isn't a friend of mine yet, but he will be when he hands over all the money we are going to win. And then he'll feel sick." The Captain smiled, proud of himself.

I was not amused. "Captain, I can't go under false pretenses like that. What would I tell Mom if something happened?"

"You'd tell her that you had no knowledge of my explanation for the trip. That's why I had you stay here while I talked to her."

"That's another lie," I barked. "I thought you told

me that you wouldn't ask me to do anything that would hurt anyone. Isn't that would you said?"

He took a drag on his cigarette and exhaled a double plume of smoke. "That is what I said, and I meant it," he replied calmly. "No one you know will get hurt. Trust me. Sometimes you have to tell a little lie in order to tell the *Truth*."

Something in the Captain's tone when he said the word *truth* made me go against every hesitation I felt. "Okay," I sighed.

He slapped his thighs with his hands. "Great! My bags are in the hall; you can load them in the car on your way to your house to pack." I went around to the hall and sure enough, he had already packed for the trip.

An hour later we turned onto I-10 to Arizona in the Captain's jet-black 1967 Oldsmobile. I had avoided Mom while packing so that I wouldn't have to tell or confirm a lie. I swear, if I hadn't observed so many unusual things about the Captain so far I would never have agreed to any of this.

He sat in the passenger side and chain-smoked. I glanced at him sideways and said, "So what is our plan when we get out there?"

"I think you know what the plan is, Ray."

"What? Just walk into a casino and win a whole bunch of money?" I was starting to feel irritated again. "Do you realize how many people go to Las Vegas every day with the same plan, and do you realize that almost none of them achieve that outcome? It's a complete sucker's bet."

All he said was, "In our case it isn't a bet." And that was that.

We drove for a while without really talking, just listening to the radio. Finally I broke the silence. "Captain, what is Concept-Therapy?"

"Ah, I see you checked out my book collection."

"Yes," I admitted.

"Well, Concept-Therapy, or *CT* as we used to call it for short, was the name of the series of seminars I used to teach people."

"What were the seminars about?"

He blew a cloud of smoke inside the car and rolled down his window a bit more. "They were about the same thing I am going to teach you—how to live so as to participate in the expansion and evolution of Life. How to be healthier, happier, serve Life—basically how to be a more effective human being."

"Why did you stop teaching? You don't seem like the kind of guy that could just stop doing something like that and retire and play Bingo."

"You're right about that. I stopped because I wanted the work to go on after me. I established a teaching and healing center here in Boerne, and I trained other teams to go out and hold seminars to teach the material. Because I founded the whole thing, as long as I was involved people looked to me to lead the procession, and nobody lives forever. If I wanted it to go on after me I had to withdraw while I was still alive. Other people needed to learn to take control and accept responsibility for continuing the work, and I figured that it was better to start that process while I was still around so that I could still give help and support from the sidelines."

"But wasn't it your whole life's work?"

"No," he chuckled, "it was *Life's* whole work. It wasn't ever about me, it was about playing whatever part I could to lift Life."

I debated about asking the next question for fear that I might offend the Captain, but in the end I went ahead and asked anyway, "So how come I have never heard of Concept-Therapy? If there's a healing center dedicated to it and all these teaching teams across the country, why haven't I heard of it?"

The Captain laughed again and responded with a question, "Ray, do you remember when I asked you whether you ever talked to anyone about your illumination experience or not?"

"Yes, I remember. I didn't."

"Why not?"

I paused as I passed a Volkswagen bus in the slow lane. "You know why. You can't just talk to people about that stuff. They'll think you're crazy or lying."

"Exactly. Human consciousness isn't quite ready for the next phase of awareness to become common knowledge just yet. There will come a time when consciousness has evolved to the point that every person will have some degree of cosmic awareness by the time they reach adulthood, but that time is still a ways off."

He rolled down the window and flicked his cigarette out. "Concept-Therapy's time hasn't come yet, but it will. After I'm gone. Mass consciousness isn't quite ready for it, but it will get there. In your lifetime, if the writings are correct."

"What writings?"

"Never mind. People will begin to understand that they need to change their locus of living from being self-centered to becoming Life-centered."

"What does that mean?" I asked.

"What are you, Ray?"

"What do you mean? I'm an American. I'm a guy. I'm a human being."

He shook his head. "Nope. You're none of those things. Those are your illusions. They're not reality; they are ideas that you have identified with—some inherited and some acquired."

"I'm not a guy?"

"Nope. Remember the evolution of consciousness chart?" I nodded. "What was at the beginning?"

"Energy, God, X."

"Yes. That's what you are. Saying you are a guy is limiting that power to a particular expression. But the expression isn't the power."

He warmed to the subject, "Imagine a movie projector. The pure white light that comes out of the projector is like the energy that creates and sustains all. It contains all frequencies of light and has all the possibilities."

He held his hand up with his palm turned inward and fanned the fingers of his other hand towards it as though they were individual rays of light. "Now, when the light passes through film, it filters out certain frequencies, and the image that is formed as a result is the movie that you see projected on the screen. But the movie is just an illusion, as your life is only an illusion. You identify with ideas and concepts that filter out some of the possibilities that Life contains—those concepts are like the film that the light from the projector passes through—and the resulting phenomena is what you call *your life*."

I gripped the steering wheel tighter. "It sure feels like my life."

He pointed at me. "No, your feelings and experiences are the result of *Life* expressing through a limited channel. Your concepts about yourself as being a separate being apart from the rest of Life further limit the possibilities for it to express through you, just as the film limits the frequencies of light that are able to pass through it."

I tried to get my mind around what the Captain was saying, but it was difficult. "I'm not sure I'm getting you, Captain."

He waved one hand as if to dismiss my statement. "Don't worry about it. This is a whole new way of understanding the experience of Life. It's okay if it takes a little while for it to feel natural to you. In the meantime, ponder this: what do I have in my hand?" He held up one of the unfiltered Pall Malls that he smoked.

"A cigarette."

"Really? I don't think so." He took a matchstick and carefully poked the tobacco out of the paper. He held up a handful of tobacco and paper and said, "Where is the cigarette you saw?"

"It's right there, Captain." I pointed to his hand.

"That's not a cigarette, it's just some tobacco and a bit of paper."

"It *was* a cigarette before you destroyed it."

"I have destroyed nothing," said the Captain with mock indignation. "Everything that was here before is still here. You are confused because you think that there is such a thing as a cigarette, but you are mistaken. *Cigarette* is just a mental construct we collectively use to refer to tobacco and paper arranged in a certain manner that we recognize with our senses. It's a name, a concept, not a thing."

He deposited the former cigarette into the small plastic wastebasket he kept in the car. "Now, if we were inclined to continue this process indefinitely, what point do you think we would eventually reach?"

"I suppose we would be back to the X."

"Yes. It makes up everything in the universe. What we call things, people, or trees are just perceptions. The reality is that everything in the entire universe—including you and I—are nothing but different expressions of Energy, or Consciousness, whatever name you would like to call it. Any differentiation is our perception, not reality."

"So you mean this car we are riding in doesn't exist?"

"It exists for you as your perception, but it does not exist in essence." He must have noticed my slightly disgusted expression, because he looked thoughtful for a moment and tried again. "Think of it this way: remember that all forms have some ability to perceive the universe around them. If they are simple forms, they don't have sensory organs such as so-called 'living' forms have, but they have their own perceptive abilities, as rudimentary as they may be.

"What do you think an electron perceives about, say, the steering wheel you are using?" He paused and added, "Pretending it could form thoughts, of course?"

"I don't think it would perceive anything about a steering wheel," I said. "I think it would only be aware of other electrons whirling around."

"I would say you are exactly right. It wouldn't even have any awareness of the object we call a steering wheel. In its reality a steering wheel wouldn't exist. It would just be aware of other forms like itself, having no idea that they were all part of something much bigger that our particular form of consciousness would perceive and conceptualize as a steering wheel."

The Captain picked a bit of tobacco out of his teeth. "That electron could whirl around a nucleus for a billion years, and it would never know that it was part of something much bigger and more complex. It wouldn't perceive that it was part of an atom, which was part of a molecule, which was part of a chemical, which was part of a compound, which was part of a steering wheel, and on and on and on."

I protested, "But all of those things would, in fact, exist. Just because the electron wasn't aware of them doesn't mean they wouldn't really be there."

He smiled. "Ah, the question of 'reality,' huh, Ray?" He reached over and tuned the radio to a local station, then cranked the volume up pretty loud. It was playing *Bennie and the Jets*. "What do you hear?"

"Elton John?"

He shook his head. "Close, but not exactly; you aren't hearing Elton John, you are hearing music that the man recorded, yes?"

I nodded.

"When you hear it, it evokes thoughts, mental associations, and emotions, right?"

"Yes."

He held up one finger as if to emphasize a point. "Have you ever heard music that really affected you, inspired you, took you to another place entirely?"

"Sure, everyone has, I guess."

"You'd guess wrong." He smiled. "Ever had a dog?"

"Yes, we had a mutt we adopted from the pound for a while. What does that have to do with—"

"Bear with me," he interrupted my protest, "I'm getting there. Was your dog ever around when you were playing music?"

"Sure, sometimes." I paused to pass an eighteen-wheeler. "We played the stereo all the time in the house, and he was always there."

"Did he ever seem like he was anything other than completely indifferent to the music, no matter what you played?"

I started to get the point. "No, he ignored it all."

The Captain smiled. "And it wouldn't matter if you played him the most ingenious works of music that had ever been created. He could listen to Mozart for a thousand years and it wouldn't exist for him because he doesn't have the capacity to *perceive* it."

He reached over and turned the radio down so that we wouldn't have to continue to talk over it. "The dog *hears* the sounds, same as you and I. In fact, he has better hearing for most of the frequencies, so he's hearing more of it than we are; in that sense the music does exist for him.

"But he doesn't *perceive* it. It doesn't mean anything to him. It has no significance, evokes no feelings, induces no higher experiences, it doesn't register with him, and therefore it only exists for him as noise. His reality is that there is no such thing as music, only sounds, and it is quite true that music does not exist for him."

He pointed at the steering wheel again. "Just like the steering wheel doesn't exist for the electron. And despite our assumption that human awareness is the hub around which all consciousness revolves, the very pinnacle of universal reality, it isn't. What is real or unreal to us is no more or less real than what is real or unreal to an electron, a plant, or a dog. It's all an illusion based upon the framework of perception for each particular form."

He took a deep breath and finished, "And it's a good thing that human consciousness has no monopoly on truth, because in normal human consciousness we are only aware of randomness, coincidence, separation—that is the 'reality' that we experience. Just like reality for your dog is that noises exist, but not music. But if we can raise our awareness up a notch, we can become aware of how it all fits together to form a harmonious unity. We can hear the music, so to speak. That's what you were doing when you felt the Oneness—perceiving a higher degree of reality. The universe simply is what it IS. It doesn't change, but our *experience* of the universe changes with wisdom. When you spend enough time realizing that the universe is one unbroken whole, parts have no reality for you. Just like you have no perception of the individual atoms that make up that steering wheel. The only thing that is real to you is the entire wheel. Imagine a person living in an awareness that doesn't separate *anything* from the whole—not even themselves. When you live from that standpoint, you are living from a Life-centered locus, and things are much different."

I didn't have a conversational reply to that discourse, so we rode in silence for a while. Finally I asked the question that I had wanted to ask since I'd read his notebook. "Captain, you had an experience kind of like the one I had, right?"

The smallest hint of a smile tugged at the corner of his mouth and he replied, "Kind of."

"Well—what was yours like?"

"Difficult to explain in words—but you already know that." He laughed. "I guess it's different for everyone who has those kind of experiences, because you filter everything through your own concepts, and a lot of them turn out to be concepts you didn't even know you had."

"Like what?"

"Well, I wouldn't have thought my childish religious concepts were so intact at the time of my experience, but they obviously were because I experienced a God figure that looked just like my boyhood conception of God: a kindly old man with whiskers." He laughed at the memory. "And I went to Heaven, which was just like I thought it to be as a child—golden streets and St. Peter at the gate."

"What do you mean you went to Heaven?"

He lit another cigarette and smoke puffed out of his mouth and nose as he answered. "Human consciousness has gone through two dispensations of knowledge through the ages. We're on the cusp of the third, but we're not quite there yet as a race.

"The first was the age of symbolism, in which humans related to their spirituality obliquely, metaphorically, and relatively unconsciously. People generally held to some version of the belief that everything had a spirit—rocks, trees, air, people."

I called him on his previous statements, "But that's what you believe now."

He shook his head. "No, I don't believe that everything *has* a spirit. I know that everything *is* a harmonious manifestation *of* Spirit. Big difference."

He checked the map against a mile marker. "As I was saying, during the age of symbolism we related to spiritual things metaphorically and mostly unconsciously. We used symbols that carried profound meaning, but we usually were consciously unaware of what the meaning was. We felt it more than we consciously understood it."

"Then we passed into an age of faith, during which we got a little more of an idea of our spiritual nature, but we are still a bit confused about it. We still tend to project our own experiences onto the universe and attempt to make things like us, rather than perceiving Life for what it is."

"Man making God in his own image," I remarked dryly.

"Yes, exactly. Well, remember that I was relatively unprepared for the experience I had, and Spirit can only express through the concepts that you have identified with at any given time. I had relatively undeveloped concepts about spiritual matters; I was still firmly entrenched in the consciousness of symbolism and faith, so my experience was filtered through those undeveloped concepts. I knew that my experience was real, but that I was experiencing it in fantastic terms. Kind of like a dream—the content is very real and important, but you experience it metaphorically or in symbolism."

"So you're saying that you didn't really go to Heaven?"

"My body didn't, but my consciousness did. I experienced paradise in the fantasy of my mind according to my undeveloped concepts, but the spiritual nature of the experience was very real and important."

I thought for a moment and asked, "So what is the third phase?"

"Ah, yes. The third dispensation is knowledge. Not faith, not metaphors, but the real thing—direct experience like you and I had. Humans have traditionally appealed to two authorities for information about the universe and ourselves: science and theology. Science is a relative newcomer, but it's grown up a lot in the last fifty years. Now, instead of telling us that we are alone and isolated within our own skins, science agrees with all the major religious teachings that we are points of consciousness in an infinite sea of awareness. We are all connected to each other and our Source. As this idea grows in mass consciousness, more and more people are going to begin to realize what they really are."

"You mean they will have episodes like we had?"

"Sure. Those experiences are going to become more and more commonplace, but there have always been individuals that have had them. Where do you think all the world religions and great works of art and literature came from?"

He pointed at me. "You do know from your own illumination that the feeling of Oneness that you experienced is beyond words—it has to be experienced to really be understood, but people have always tried to explain it anyway. Those with direct spiritual knowledge had to communicate using the only tools that those to whom they tried to communicate had—symbolism and faith."

"So you're saying that people like Buddha and Moses and Jesus had these kinds of realizations, and their attempts to teach people about them resulted in Buddhism, Judaism, and Christianity," I interjected.

He nodded, "Buddha, Jesus, Moses, Krishna, Zoroaster, Mohammed and others. Artists like Shakespeare, Michelangelo, Mozart, Walt Whitman, inspired philosophers, even a few scientists here and there." He smiled and held up a finger at me. "Imagine what people would think if you told them about your illumination. Even the ones that didn't think you were lying or crazy. Do you think they would be able to conceive of what you experienced or interpret the significance of it in any accurate way?"

I shook my head.

"No, they wouldn't," he agreed, "not without a lot of instruction designed to give them the concepts they would need to understand. Those people back in the times of the founders of our religions were no different. They heard the teachings, but mass consciousness wasn't ready to understand them yet, so they interpreted them incorrectly. They interpreted some teachings literally that were written as metaphors, and some that were literal they took to be allegorical. They misunderstood and therefore misquoted statements, and sometimes less innocently, they manipulated the doctrines to influence their own political or social agenda.

"Only now," he finished, "is mass consciousness poised to gain a higher understanding of those teachings. Quantum physics has demonstrated since the early part of this century that the teachings of the spiritual masters are based in truth, not wishful thinking. Like all new ideas, it takes a while for the idea to permeate mass consciousness and reach critical mass. We are on the cusp of that permeation."

He paused for a minute and added, "But don't think for a minute that people having experiences like we had is an end unto itself. It isn't. The experience is just a signpost. A higher order of living is the real destination." And with that, the Captain sat back in his seat and fell silent.

We drove for a while without talking. I tried to assimilate some of the deep stuff the Captain was telling me, but it was a lot to take in. My mind ended up getting fatigued just thinking about it, and I was glad when he suggested we stop to eat lunch at a roadside diner. After we ate the Captain paid the bill and asked me if I had any money. "A few bucks," I answered, "but I'm not gambling any of it."

"How much did you bring?" The Captain asked through a cloud of post-meal cigarette smoke.

"Let's see." I counted. "It looks like I brought twenty-seven dollars."

He nodded and checked his own wallet. "All right, I have forty-one. That should be enough."

I didn't really want to hear the answer to my next question, but I had to ask it. "So you have credit cards, right?

Or at least some checks?"

"Nope," he replied crisply, "I don't believe in credit. And where we're going, checks wouldn't do us any good."

"So forty-one dollars in cash? That's all you've got?"

"Well, that's more than you brought," he shot back.

"Yeah, but I'm not the one who engineered this crazy trip," I growled. "I told you from the beginning that I'm not gambling any of my family's money! Forty-one dollars won't even get us to Las Vegas and back with hotel charges. Hell, gas is up to 70 cents a gallon; we won't even have enough *gas* money to get back! What do you plan to gamble with, much less get home with?" I was livid that I had allowed myself to be convinced to go on this financial suicide mission.

"Ray, you worry too much," he said peacefully. "When you live in harmony with love, you don't have to worry."

"Love? *Love?* What the hell are you talking about?" I jammed my wallet back into my pocket. "We're sitting here on our way to Las-frigging-Vegas with sixty-some-odd dollars between us with the grand plan that we will simply waltz into a random casino and gamble my family out of debt, and you're talking about love?"

"What is love, Ray?" the Captain asked while giving me his signature squint. "Is it when you feel all weak-kneed sitting next to a pretty girl? Is it when you go on a civil rights protest march? Is it when you feel devoted to a cause, or become immersed in art or music? What *is* love?"

"I don't know," I sighed. "What does that have to do with us right now, Captain?"

His eyes blazed through the smoke and he boomed, "It has *everything* to do with it! Love is the most powerful force in the universe. It is not to be trifled with."

I sat back in my seat. "I'm not trifling with anything. What are you even talking about?"

The Captain leaned forward and put his elbows on the table. His eyes smoldered like a slow fuse burning toward dynamite. "Love is not what people think it is, son. It's as terrible as it is beautiful. It's as confounding as it is comforting. It is the supreme law of the universe in action, and to the degree that you live in harmony with the constructive side of that law you will experience knowledge and power you can't imagine. Not power to exploit for the gratification of selfish desire, mind you." He shook his head. "No, only to serve. In service, the apparent separation between you and Spirit breaks down and you become Life's agent, and everything you need is given freely to you."

His voice slowed and became very deliberate. "But to the degree you align your energies with the opposite expression of Love by pursuing only selfish interests, you will experience the corresponding frustration and sorrow. We all have disappointments, frustrations, perceived failures. Most people blame luck, or other people, or God, or fate for their problems."

He took his elbows off the table and sat straight up, his eyes still burning into my skull. "But it all comes down to how we relate to the Law of Love. You can't break that law, Ray. You can violate it, but even then the law will remain intact and *you* will be broken."

I shuffled the pile of paper strips that used to be my napkin. "That doesn't sound like any description of love I ever heard before."

"That's because you've always heard that love means personal, selfish pleasure through physical or mental connections, but that isn't it at all. Love isn't a feather, tickling your tummy and making you feel all warm inside. It's so much bigger than any individual's pleasure. Love is a hammer, beating and molding the raw material that Life has forged into a perfect, harmonious creation. If you're in harmony with Love you become its agent, and its efforts become your own. Then you swing the hammer with all of its power behind you, building Life up. But Love constantly tears down just as much as it builds up. If your focus remains on serving only your limited life, your personal interests, and your own desires, then you're on your own. You'll still be ruled by the Law of Love, but you'll play the part of the nail instead of the hammer."

He paused and took a deep breath. "Life needs both, by the way. In order to make something new, something old must be destroyed. Life demands balance, and it takes both hammers and nails to build anything." He intensified his squint. "But we must all choose personally, not just contemplate universally. So, Ray, would you rather be the hammer or the nail?"

I rolled my eyes. "The hammer, of course. Listen, that's all well and good to say, but how—"

"You start by paying attention!" The veins on the side of the Captain's neck pulsed and his face turned scarlet. "You *felt* Love, Ray. Real Love. Most people at this point in time will go their entire lives without becoming aware of that power. And yet, you have no idea what I'm talking about when I tell you not to worry."

He sat back in the booth. "Love is a *force*. It isn't just sexual or physical attraction, mental affinity, or emotional resonance, although those are all tiny aspects of it. Real Love is what governs and harmonizes the entirety of creation.

"When a person so attunes himself that he is able to act out of Love, there are no mistakes. No wrong turns. He experiences everything as it should be. That person is equally content to experience death or life, success or failure, comfort or hardship. He no longer experiences events in terms of how they affect him personally; things no longer happen *to* him, he experiences Life happening *through* him. Guided by Love, he feels a pure impulse and simply follows it."

"And I suppose you're such a person?"

"The point, Ray," he pointed at me, "is for *you* to become such a person!" He spoke with an intensity that rendered my sarcasm lame. "I told you this before, but in case you missed the significance of it, I will say it again: visions are *nothing*, signs and wonders are *nothing*, knowledge is *nothing*, philosophy is *nothing*, science is *nothing*, religion is *nothing*, if it doesn't change your life in some way! The only value in any experience is in how it influences the way you live. That's the process of personal evolution."

He took a pen from his shirt pocket, turned over the diner check, and scrawled the word *Love* on the back of it. Directly underneath, he wrote the same letters in the reverse order—*Evol,* and pushed the paper toward me so that I could see it. "Ray," he said as he counted out the tip for the meal, "do you by any chance know anything about the Hungarian language?"

"No. I take Spanish."

He tucked the money under the side of his plate. "Well, Hungarian is somewhat different than most Romance languages. In Hungarian, the suffix *ve* reveals or amplifies the true character of the root word."

He added the letters *ve* to where he had already written *Evol* to make the word *Evolve*. "Life evolves relentlessly, and Love is the energy, the enthusiasm, and the passion of it all. Love and Life are two sides of the same coin—the One that *is* and the One that *does*. Do you see, Ray?"

I was pre-occupied wondering how the Captain knew so much about Hungarian. I responded to the question with a placating nod, but I was obviously distracted and the Captain noticed. He snapped his fingers and raised both eyebrows at me. "*Focus*! This is serious. Things in your life may seem backward sometimes, like me reversing those letters. Things may not seem to fit sometimes, like me using parts of words from different languages to get my point across."

His eyes blazed with intensity again, and I squirmed a bit in my seat. "But rest assured," he finished, "*everything* fits, all the time. Everything is related, even when you can't see the connection."

He stood up to leave. "Even when things don't look good, you can still count on Love. I told you that I was going to teach you how to *live* as an aware human being, and this is your first lesson—we are here on this trip because we are supposed to be here. The same Spirit within that gave us the impulse to go is not going to allow us to fail to fulfill our purpose, no mater what things look like right now."

I sighed. I wanted to believe the Captain, but a spiritual guru going to Las Vegas to win a bunch of money in order to pay off debt left by a drunken father was a little too much for me, even after all I had seen and experienced. The Captain sensed my skepticism and reminded me of something he had said earlier, "From the top of the temple to the bottom of the pit, Ray. The truly enlightened human must be able to freely live in either as duty calls."

Delia Fleet had given up hope. Her husband had not left the front bedroom even once in seven full days, and she could no longer bear to look in on him. She brought the children home from her mother's at night to sleep, but during the day they stayed at their grandmother's house away from their father.

Delia had begun to worry about what would become of them all. She almost couldn't bear the thought of Thurman being locked up in a mental ward, but she didn't know what else to do. The clock struck midnight, and as she got ready for bed she prepared herself to call the military hospital in the morning and ask them to begin the process of admitting her husband.

She sat on the bed brushing her hair and holding back tears when the bedroom door creaked open. Thurman stood motionless in the doorway. A week's worth of beard had overgrown the landscape of his face, and his clothes were rumpled and stained with sweat. He looked wildly disheveled, but she began to weep tears of relief at the sight of his face. He no longer had that otherworldly look that he had projected so strongly over the past week; his eyes had lost the fiery blaze that looked through this world and into another.

"Deddo, I came back," he croaked in a strained voice, "I could have stayed, but I came back. I—I wanted to help."

She ran to him and hugged him tightly, weeping and pulling him toward the bed. He looked so exhausted she was afraid he might have a heart attack. He kept attempting to explain what had happened to him over the past seven days in sincere but confused ramblings. Delia didn't know what he was talking about, nor did she want to know. She was simply thankful that she didn't see that look in his eyes anymore and she prayed to God that she would never see it again.

She hushed Thurman and brought him some food and water. He was able to sip the water, but he would eat no food. Finally she got him into bed, where he would sleep for the next twenty-eight hours. Delia wept tears of relief and stress and whispered in his ear as he fell into a dead, dreamless sleep, "I love you, Thurman Fleet, God help me. As much as you terrify me, I love you. I don't know if I will ever have peace living with you, but life will not be dull, that's for sure." She giggled uncontrollably for a time, and then the laughter resolved into muffled sobs—she didn't want to wake her husband.

The stress of the past week had weighed so heavily upon Delia that she was badly in need of rest and relief from responsibility herself. She fell into bed beside her husband and slept almost as soundly as he did.

She would wonder many times during their life together what she had done that God had seen fit to smite her by causing her to love this man so. His compulsive pursuits would make it impossible for either of them to live the normal, stable, relatively uneventful life that she longed for. Yet despite her discomfiture with his quests and obsessions, despite her longing for a life she knew she would never be able to have with him, Delia would always know deep down that she belonged with him, as if she was playing a part in a greater plan that involved them both.

CHAPTER SIX
FREAK

W e pulled onto the Las Vegas strip at around five on Saturday morning, and I was treated to a different kind of illumination: giant neon signs flashing *Stardust*, *Flamingo*, and *Frontier*. The Captain had me stop at a service station where I gassed up the car while he asked for directions. I noticed that he paid with his last twenty-dollar bill and got back a five and some change.

Back in the car, he said, "Okay, Ray, I think it's pretty simple. I think all we have to do is go straight down this street until we come to Flamingo Road."

"Uh-huh," I mumbled as I started down the street he had indicated, "then what?"

"You'll know what to do when we get there."

"Captain, how much money do you have left?" It was not so much a question as an accusation.

"Enough," he replied, looking out the window.

"Captain," I started, but he interrupted me before I could get into it with him.

"Ray, I think that's what we're looking for." I looked where he was pointing and saw the biggest hotel I had ever seen in my life. It looked like some huge L-shaped financial center that belonged in New York City or a government compound in Washington, D.C. It was kind of strange to see something like that out in the middle of a desert. The granite marquis said *MGM Grand*.

"What are we doing here?"

"This is our destination, Ray. Park right there."

I was exhausted after driving all night and in no mood for the Captain's shenanigans. "How do you propose that we pay for a place like this?"

"Love," was all he would say, to my great irritation.

I lugged our bags from the parking lot under the massive marquis and into the lobby. Although he had stayed awake all night while I drove, the Captain didn't seem tired at all. My ass was dragging and I was only seventeen.

Even at five-thirty in the morning the enormous hotel lobby was bursting with activity. Seemingly endless rows of slot machines whirled in giant slot rooms flanking the front desk. People came and went, oblivious to the fact that it was the crack of dawn.

The Captain went to the front desk and was greeted by a tall hotel clerk who didn't look much older than me. "Hello, sir, what can I do for you?"

"My grandson and I need a room for the night, young man. Something with two separate bedrooms."

"Yes sir. Our Marquee Suites are designed to give you twice the luxury appointments. A grand foyer separates two master suites, each lavishly comfortable. The entire suite is over 1500 square feet," the clerk recited from memory. "The Marquee Suites are $123.95 per night, and it looks like we do have one available on the sixth floor."

"That sounds fine, young man."

"And how would you like to secure the room, sir? We can secure it with a credit card, or you can go ahead and pay in advance with cash or traveler's checks."

This was what I had been waiting for. There was no way that the Captain's Star Trek mind-meld trick was going to work here. This was a Las Vegas casino, for crying out loud. Even a greenhorn like the young clerk we were dealing with would have seen just about every con in the book after just a few weeks on the job at a place like this.

The Captain began a story about us gambling with Ross Perot at another hotel. Even I had heard of Perot, the Texas billionaire who had just made headlines a couple of months before for being the biggest individual loser ever on the New York Stock Exchange. He lost $450 million in one day, which is a lot to just about anyone else, but the news had reported that Perot was still worth almost 2 billion. I had to admit that citing Perot was a good try, and given the Captain's accent, a somewhat plausible story, but I had zero confidence that the clerk was actually going to go for it.

The Captain continued his tale about meeting Perot the day before and staying up all night gambling with him. He told the clerk that he and Perot were friends from the Navy, and since we had been his guests, Mr. Perot had paid for our accommodations and gambling chips. He had been called away on an hour's notice to fly back to Dallas on his private jet, and he had suggested that we stay in Las Vegas one more day to see the fabulous brand new MGM Grand Hotel.

He went on and on, explaining to the clerk that we were having money wired in but that it wouldn't be here until this afternoon, and that we had been up all night with Mr. Perot and really needed to get some sleep. Then he began flattering the hotel and everyone in it by talking about how Mr. Perot insisted that we see it because it was one of the most impressive hotels in the world, employing only the best staff, and frequented by only the most discriminating customers. I waited for the clerk to call security and have us thrown out, but to my absolute amazement he gave the Captain a room key and had him sign the register. His eyes reflected a pleasant befuddlement, and I wondered if that was how I had looked when I agreed to work for the Captain for the summer.

We went to the elevator and when the doors closed I hissed, "How the hell did you get that guy to agree to that?"

"I didn't *get* him to do anything, Ray. Spirit directed me here because I needed to be here in order to serve a purpose for Life. The same Spirit that gave me the inclination to come here in the first place is inside that clerk too, don't you figure?" I nodded. "Spirit just talked to itself through me, and the outcome that was supposed to happen, happened. Nothing mysterious about that."

"Sure," I said dryly as the elevator doors opened on our floor, "nothing mysterious at all about that."

"Ray, when you live so that your individual life becomes indistinguishable from the universal Life, you will have everything you need. All the money in the world is yours, if you need it to serve Life. You will draw to yourself money, agreement, the right circumstances—whatever you need to fulfill your duty to Life. That is having an Open Garden. Life plants seeds into your garden, and they have no choice but to grow and flower."

By that time we were standing in front of our suite. The Captain unlocked the door, and I walked into a chamber that was more extravagant than I would have ever imagined. An oversize marble wet bar framed a foyer complete with a dining area that could seat six. A huge window stretching the length of the suite gave a panoramic view of the Vegas Strip. I took our bags into our respective rooms and checked out the bathrooms: Italian marble with complementary robes and slippers.

I went back into the foyer where the Captain sat in one of the lush recliners, peacefully smoking a cigarette. "Well, what now?"

The Captain squinted at me through the cloud of smoke he had blown up around himself. He spoke slowly, and I recognized the resonance of his voice as a portent to something unusual on the horizon. "We need a newspaper this morning. I would like for you to go downstairs and buy one. You need to do exactly as I say, do you understand?"

"Yes," I replied, noticing my voice rolling out with the fuzzy liquidity that let me know I had allowed myself to enter into the Captain's world again. I felt the sensation of lightness and time slowing down.

"I want you to go downstairs and get a copy of the *Los Angeles Times*. Here's a dollar. Take the elevator straight to the lobby. When you get off, turn right and walk straight ahead past all the slot machines to the far end of the hall. Buy the paper there—you should get two quarters in change. Take your change and my paper and walk back to the fourth row of slots and turn left. Go to the fourth slot on the left, put in the quarters, and pull the handle."

I nodded and left the room. As if in a pleasant daze, I did exactly as I had been instructed to do. I was jolted out of my state of mild somnolence by flashing lights and ringing bells; when I came to I realized I was standing in front of a winning slot machine that had just paid off the jackpot.

I frantically collected the quarters in one of the black plastic buckets that the casino provided for winners and raced back up to the room. I had left my key inside, so I banged on the door and when the Captain opened it I yelled, "Captain, look! I won the jackpot—a thousand dollars!"

He moved aside so that I could enter the room and in an almost bored tone said, "I know that Ray, but where is my newspaper? You forgot it at the slot machine."

"What?" I shouted incredulously. "You tell me a specific slot machine to play, I play it *one time* and win the jackpot, and all you can say is, *where's my newspaper?"*

He smiled a little and said, "You're right, Ray. I do have more to say. Go back downstairs and get my paper; if a job is worth starting it is worth finishing. While you're at it, convert those quarters to something less cumbersome—let's say half cash and half gambling chips. I will be sleeping when you return, and I encourage you do the same; we will wake up this afternoon to eat and gamble, so I suggest you get some rest."

I was speechless, so I simply nodded and turned to leave the room. He stopped me on my way out, "Ah, Ray, one more thing. You are, of course, free to do whatever you want with your own money that you brought with you. However, I don't recommend that you gamble this morning." I nodded again and started down to the lobby, this time taking the room key with me.

I picked up the paper, which was still sitting on top of the slot machine I had played, and I cashed in the quarters for a sizeable stack of chips and five one hundred dollar bills. I was about to return to the room when a commotion caught my eye at one of the blackjack tables. Apparently someone had won a big hand—there was a crowd gathered and they were all cheering and excited. I went over to watch.

Two men who looked like professional gamblers played against the dealer. The first one was about fifty—bald on top, overweight in a jolly kind of way, and a large gap between his two front teeth. He wore one of those clear green visors and chewed on an unlit cigar. The other guy was small, thin, and nervous looking. He had on a white suit and a pink, wide-collared shirt. He looked to be in his late twenties or early thirties.

Nervous-looking guy must have been the big winner; his stack of chips was larger than the other man's. I watched them play for about a half hour; they won some and lost some—no big pots. I guessed they were about even during that half hour.

Just as I was about to leave, the dealer laid out a hand and the guy in the green visor pushed forward a huge stack of chips. I decided to stay to see what happened. Nervous-looking guy ended up busting with the first hit, so he was out early. The dealer asked for bets again and green visor pushed another tall stack of chips onto the table; he had to have at least a thousand dollars on this one hand.

Since he increased his bet he had to take a hit, which was really risky—if he got any card higher than a four, he would lose. Everyone held their breath as the card was being turned over, and all at once the small crowd cheered when it turned out to be a three of clubs.

Watching the guy win such a big hand was so exciting that before I could think about what I was doing I had turned twenty of my dollars into a very small stack of chips and was sitting at a blackjack table playing another dealer. Four minutes later I was walking back to the room twenty dollars poorer wondering why I hadn't listened to the Captain's warning about gambling.

As I waited for the elevator door to open, I saw a boy and a girl through the lobby windows obviously hanging around the entrance to the casino. They were about nine or ten, somewhere around Dawn's age, and they looked dirty, scared, and too thin. One of the bellhops saw me looking at them and said, "Sad, isn't it?"

"What's their story?" I asked.

"Mom's an addict." He curled his lip in distaste.

"A drug addict?"

"No." He shook his head. "Those people don't hang out around here. No, she's a gambling freak. She gambled all the family's money away and Dad left. I don't know how she gets it—I don't really want to know, to tell you the truth." He wrinkled his nose. "But she scrapes together enough money to come play a few times a week. Stays for three, maybe four hours, just long enough to lose everything she's got. Goes out, finds more, and a day or two later she's back."

I was shocked. "What about her kids?"

"They mostly fend for themselves. I don't know where they sleep; they can't have a stable residence the way she gambles everything away. Sad. Working here I see it more often than you might think."

I rode the elevator up to the sixth floor thinking about those kids. By the time I got to the room I was a little depressed and more than a little tired. I fell onto the luxurious king-sized bed and into a heavy, dreamless sleep.

∞

Thurman Fleet sat on his front porch, rocking in the swan-armed Statesville Chair Company rocker that Delia had given him two years earlier. It had been four and a half months since he secluded himself in the front bedroom, and Delia was worried that he had suffered permanent damage. He had recovered physically from the week-long wandering in the wilderness of his mind, but for the second time in his young life he seemed soul sick.

Delia didn't know much about what had gone on in his consciousness during that week, nor did she want to know. She knew that he had struggled with sorting out reality from fantasy. She knew that he had emerged from his experience certain that the sights he had seen and the entities he had conversed with had been real, and that the longer he spent back in a normal conscious state the more he doubted his own mental stability. It seemed to Delia that Thurman hadn't been able to reconcile his spiritual experience with the mundane affairs of the physical world he found himself back in. He refused to return to work or school; he just sat on the front porch brooding and living off military disability.

She brought him a copy of the *San Antonio Light* like she always did in the morning, and left it with him on the porch while she started breakfast. She was inside mixing flour for biscuits when he came wandering into the kitchen holding the paper loosely in one hand. She saw him out of the corner of her eye and said, "Thurman?"

No answer. She took a better look at him and her lungs sucked in a quick burst of air. His face was intensely expressionless, like a corpse, and she could tell that he was somewhere else. Her mind panicked at the possibility that the four-and-a-half-month period since his episode was just a brief respite and another journey was starting.

"What is it Thurman? Are you all right?" She sat him down at the table, wet a towel, and rubbed his face with it. "*Thurman? Are you all right?*"

She almost wept with relief to see recognition dawn in his eyes and expression return to this face. "Y-yes, Deddo, I'm all right, just give me a minute."

While she waited for him to collect himself, it occurred to her that whatever triggered this latest brief episode might have something to do with the newspaper, so she picked it up off the floor where he had dropped it. The headline read: "*U.S. To Abandon the Gold Standard, Top Economists Say.*"

According to the article, the world's top economists were predicting that there would be a direct correlation between remaining on the gold standard and continuing to languish in a depressed economy. Apparently Italy had divorced its currency from the gold standard a year earlier, and their economy was already turning around. The UK was taking immediate steps to follow their lead. The article predicted that the United States would follow the trend and do the same, although it noted that President Hoover had been quoted as saying that he would save the U.S. from leaving the gold standard.

"It's just like we talked about," Thurman said to her as she finished the article.

"Who talked about, Thurman? What do you mean?"

"We planned it, Deddo. God and me. He asked me what I would do if I were in charge, and that's the first thing I told him." Thurman looked like he had recovered from the surprise; in fact, Delia now saw a strange glint in his eyes. Not the thousand-yard stare he had when he was in the middle of his hallucination, she thought, but not different enough for her comfort level.

"You're not making any sense, Thurman. What are you talking about?"

He looked thoughtful for a moment, as if deciding how much to tell her. "Deddo, when I was in that room I saw all kinds of things that I can't describe. Sometimes it seemed like I was experiencing the Power that created and sustains the entire universe naked and unfiltered, and I can't really describe what that was like; it was beyond any words or language."

He paused as if struggling to explain and finally went on, "But other times it seemed like my mind was filtering the experience; kind of creating a fantastic framework to allow me to get some kind of a mental handle on the whole thing. During those times I knew that my visions were like pouring pure consciousness through the filter of my inherited and acquired concepts, and I had the sense that the result of that filtering was fantasy, but it was the only way my mind could understand it."

She waited patiently while he paused again to think. Finally he continued, "During one of these visions, I had a conversation with God in which He asked me what I would do to change the world if I had all the power that He had. The answers kind of came out automatically, like I wasn't really the one doing the talking, but the first answer was that I would take all the gold and lock it up so that it wouldn't be accessible like it is now." He tapped the newspaper. "It's happening, just like God and I decided it should."

Delia didn't know what to say. She wasn't in any way convinced that the newspaper article validated Thurman's story, but he was obviously certain that it was a sign that his experience had been real. He just *knew* it, he said. He went on to describe the rest of his mental conversation with the Deity and the plans they had made to clean up society.

Delia didn't know it yet, but she would eventually become convinced that he had experienced something significant as well (exactly what she had no idea), because over the next eighteen months every single one of the plans Thurman described that morning over breakfast at their rented house at 719 Mason Street, San Antonio, Texas, would come true.

She would be shocked speechless to open up the paper one morning to the announcement that the newly inaugurated President Roosevelt was creating a peacetime army to be called the Civilian Conservation Corps. She would remember Thurman recounting how he had suggested to God that they should, "Get all the men without jobs together and put them into camps so that they could do some constructive work on the land."

She would ultimately come to recognize that Thurman's account of his vision predicted not only the creation of the Civilian Conservation Corps, but the National Youth Administration, the Civil Works Administration, the Federal Housing Administration, the Federal Emergency Relief Administration, and the Social Security Administration as well.

Eventually she would scan the newspaper each morning in anticipation looking for a story that would signal another prediction coming to pass.

But not today.

She had had all she could take for the time being. When he finished recounting his Divine meeting, she asked, "Thurman, where is this all going to end?"

He looked surprised and hurt at her cold tone. "What do you mean, Deddo? This is a good thing. It means I'm not a freak or a lunatic."

"Does it?" She held up a hand to cut off an answer. "Let me recap what you just told me and let's see if I heard you right: You had a vision in which you and God decided together in detail how to clean up society." Her voice grew increasingly shrill as she talked. "You went to Heaven, which had millions of miles of solid gold streets and St. Peter at the gate. God told you that you could either stay in Heaven or you could go back down to earth and be His agent in gathering up the Truth that has been fragmented among the world's various philosophies, religions, and sciences. You wanted to stay in Heaven, but you felt like you could help God by coming back to earth and taking on this task for Him, so St. Peter directed you to a cloud a million miles above the earth and nodded for you to jump. You were scared because the earth was so far below that cloud, but you didn't want St. Peter to know it, and he finally ended up making you mad enough that you went ahead and jumped. You landed in the front bedroom and your vision was over." She put her hands on her hips. "Now, is that about it? Because that's not freakish at all, is it?"

"Well, yes—but I told you it was fanta—"

"If it was fantasy, why are you acting as if it was real?" she shrieked. "If it was fantasy, why are you considering attempting to carry out this mission?"

"Deddo, please, calm down."

He moved to touch her arm and she recoiled. "Don't tell me to calm down, Thurman Fleet," she spat, "don't you *dare* tell me to calm down after what I've been through with you. You're either in constant danger in a war, or you're getting death sentences from doctors, or you're obsessing over healing, or you're having week-long visions in the bedroom telling God how to fix the world and jumping off a cloud a million miles above the earth. *How can I calm down?"*

They both looked at each other for a moment as the absurdity of her rant transmuted the energy of frustration into laughter. Then she allowed Thurman to hold her.

"Deddo, I know it sounds crazy," he said as he stroked her hair. "Don't you think I know how it sounds? That's why I haven't talked about it more before now. But I promise that as fantastic as my mind's interpretation of events was, there was something real and extraordinary about what I experienced. I tapped into something that lies at the core of reality, and this newspaper article confirms it, at least to me. I will figure it out, I promise."

Delia knew that her husband had meant that promise as a comforting statement, but to her it sounded more like a threat.

∞

I woke up from my nap to the sound of the Captain singing. I got up and leaned my shoulder against the door jam watching him putter around the room and singing some song that sounded like it was from the 1920s or 1930s, something about surrendering.

I clapped as he finished. Even though he had given no indication that he knew I had been watching and listening, he didn't seem surprised in the least.

"Good morning in the evening, Ray," he said with his usual cheerfulness. "How was your rest?"

"It was fine. What time is it?"

"Time to get ready to gamble." He was squinting again. "Although I think you've already tried that on your own, haven't you?"

I sighed. You couldn't keep anything from the crazy old man. "Yes, I tried."

"How did it go?"

"You know how it went," I said with mild irritation. "Why couldn't you let me win at blackjack? You let me win the slots with your money."

He paused for some time before answering. "Ray, I want you to ask me that question again after our gambling session tonight. I'll answer you then."

We showered, ate room service, dressed and started downstairs to the gambling tables. I remembered the children I had seen outside the lobby and told the Captain about them. He looked thoughtful, but said nothing.

We went through the lobby of the giant hotel past the slot machines and into the casino proper, where the real gambling was going on. There were people everywhere wearing tuxedos and skimpy cocktail dresses. I was anxious to see what the Captain was going to do, but my anticipation soon dwindled, as he did nothing at all. We just walked around looking at the various tables while he smoked a cigarette.

Suddenly he said, "Right there, Ray." I looked at where he was squinting and saw a roulette table.

"So is roulette your game, Captain?"

"Never played it before in my life," he said as he approached the table.

We watched for a few minutes. Apparently there were a whole bunch of different ways you could bet—inside bets, outside bets, you could bet on whether the color would come up red or black, or whether the number would be even or odd, or high or low. You could bet for any number in a column, different groups of numbers, or the grand bet of all: the single number bet. This one you had to get right on the money, so the odds were pretty long, but it paid out at 35 to 1.

He exchanged all his chips for special colored roulette chips and placed a single chip on a "split," which was the line between two numbers. If either of them came up, he would win at a healthy payout of 18 to 1. The slot machine victory was still fresh in my mind, and I held my breath as I watched the small white ball go around the wheel—around and around, until it finally fell into number 19. The roulette croupier announced the number, and I was reaching out my hands to collect the Captain's winnings when it dawned on me that he had lost the bet.

For the next hour and a half the Captain lost close to four hundred of the thousand dollars I had won in the slot machine. I kept waiting for something to happen, some crazy Captain magic, but he just kept making random bets and losing.

Finally I whispered in his ear, "What the hell are you doing? We better stop before we lose back all the money we won in the slots." He took a paper napkin, turned his back on me and hunched over it so that I couldn't see it and wrote something on it. He turned back to the table, placed an obviously completely random bet, and handed me the napkin as the ball was rolling around the wheel.

I opened it just as the ball was dropping into a number and the Captain was losing again. It said, *"Don't give in to the illusion, Ray. LOVE will find a way."* The words were enclosed in a giant heart the Captain had drawn.

I looked up to see him snickering at me and I threw the napkin down on the edge of the table, instantly angry. "Why are you doing this?" I demanded. "Right now we at least have enough money to pay for our room and get back to Boerne. If you keep on we won't have anything, not even our room fee." I lowered my voice to a hoarse whisper, "We'll probably get arrested."

"Hold on Ray," he said in a distracted tone as he placed another random bet. He turned back from the table and said, "Okay, what were you saying?"

"You know damn well what I'm saying! We need to keep what we still have left and get out of here before we get into trouble."

He squinted at me with his dark eyes and said slowly, "Ray, does a little baby get into trouble when he goes to town with his mother?"

"Jesus Christ, Captain, I'm not in any mood to play games!"

"I assure you son, I'm not playing any games." He looked at me with a stare that I felt penetrate to the core of my being, and he repeated his question, "Does the baby get into trouble with his mother watching him?"

"No," I sighed with irritation.

"I serve Life, the mother of All. I do her bidding and

right now she bids me to stand here betting on roulette. She will not allow us to get into trouble any more than the mother watching her baby will. She feeds me, guides me, and protects me just like the human mother does those things for her baby. Now sit still and in a moment she will tell me which number is coming up next, and I will place a bet with all the money we have."

He was so serious about something so crazy that it scared me. I didn't say anything, but I decided that if he really tried to bet all his money on one spin I would have to object. He played randomly for another fifteen minutes and then all of a sudden he turned to me with his squint full on and said, "The next spin is going to land on number 23."

Before I could say or do anything he had placed his entire remaining stack of chips on number 23 and to my great dismay, he actually pulled out his wallet and laid it on top of the pile of chips.

I grabbed his arm and spun him around, "Captain, please, you can't do that." I was going to say more, but instead I gave an internal sigh of relief as the croupier interrupted us and agreed with me.

"I'm sorry, sir," the croupier said, "but you can't bet your wallet; we don't have any idea how much money is in there."

"Please call the pit boss," the Captain responded curtly.

"Yes sir." The croupier motioned to a large dark-haired man in his fifties wearing a full tuxedo. When he saw the Captain's wallet laid on top of the stack of chips he asked, "Sir, what do you think you are doing?"

The Captain looked him in the eyes and responded, "I believe I am gambling."

At that the man's left upper lip curled in a very slight sneer. "I'm sorry sir, but we have to know how much you are going to bet, so please take your money out of your wallet."

He turned to walk away without waiting for agreement from the Captain; I suppose that he was used to having his orders carried out without question.

"*Sir!*" The pit boss stopped and turned around to face the Captain's crazy squint. "Sir, I do not know how much money is in my wallet, but I am willing to bet all the money that is in there that number 23 is going to come up next. That is called gambling, and is this not a house of gambling?"

By this time the minor spectacle had attracted a small crowd of onlookers. The pit boss looked at all the people gathered around our table, and then he searched the crowd for another man located about forty feet away from us who was apparently overseeing the entire room. The man gave the pit boss a small nod, and he turned to the croupier and said, "Take his bet."

Before I could talk the Captain out of his latest craziness, the croupier spun the wheel and dropped the ball. Almost every eye around that roulette table was watching that little white ball. I couldn't bear to watch the carnage so I stared at the floor until just before the ball slowed down enough to fall, at which point I felt someone looking at me. I looked up and the Captain was squinting right through me, ignoring the ball and everything else. Neither one of us actually saw the ball drop into slot number 23.

The whole small crowd of people erupted in celebration. They cheered and slapped us on the back, congratulating us and laughing with us. The Captain only smiled and took out the money from his wallet. The croupier counted it and wrote something on a piece of paper that he handed to me; he gave me detailed instructions about turning it in at the front desk to receive a cashier's check for the amount of the bet, and I folded it carefully and stuck it in my pocket.

I turned to where the Captain had been standing to give him the receipt, but he was gone. I looked all around the casino but he was nowhere to be found. I guessed he had gone back to our room, so I headed toward the lobby to catch the elevator back up to the sixth floor. On the way I took out the receipt and unfolded it; in the hubbub of actually winning the bet and then losing the Captain, I had forgotten to even look to see how much he had actually won. When I saw the amount I almost dropped the paper: $21,369.00. I folded it back up and stuffed it back into my pocket before anyone else could see it.

Rounding the corner to the main lobby, I spotted the Captain sitting with a woman in a couple of plush chairs near the front desk. Two familiar looking children sat beside her. It occurred to me that she must be the gambling freak of a mother that the bellhop told me about. I guessed her to be about thirty, attractive, very black hair, dark complexion; she looked like she might have some Latino blood in her. She wore too much makeup and her dress was a little too short for a mother of two small kids.

The Captain talked to her like he was chatting with an old friend. She smiled at me as I approached, but her blotched face and bloodshot eyes told me that she'd been crying. I guessed that the Captain didn't remember me telling him about the woman—if he had there was no way he would be so friendly with her.

"Ray, here you are," he beamed as I approached. "I'd like you to meet my new friend Clarissa."

She stuck her hand out for me to shake, but I ignored it. "Are these your children?" I demanded.

She let her hand drop and gave a guilty nod.

"Lady, what are you doing in a place like this with children—"

"Clarissa," the Captain boomed while staring a hole through me with the sternest look I had ever seen him affect, "please forgive this young man; he grew up an orphan in a brothel in New Orleans and no one has ever taught him any manners."

I was shocked speechless. How could he defend this sorry excuse for a mother? "Close your mouth, Ray. You're catching flies," the Captain said, as though nothing uncomfortable was going on.

I snapped my mouth shut and he continued on, just as casually, "Ray, I believe you have a receipt, don't you?"

I nodded dumbly.

"Well, take it to the front desk and redeem it please. Have them take the room fees off the top, give you eight hundred dollars in cash, make one cashier's check out to you for nineteen thousand dollars and the other to me with the remaining balance. Got all that?"

I nodded again and turned to go to the front desk. I looked back over my shoulder and saw the Captain talking with the woman and her children again as if they were blood relatives at Thanksgiving. I sure couldn't figure him out.

It took a good twenty minutes at the front desk to get everything sorted out financially and to have the checks issued properly. By the time I came back the Captain was gone and so was the woman, so I went up to the room. He sat at the dining table, calmly smoking a cigarette.

I put the cash and the cashier's checks on the table and sat down. Neither of us said anything for a while. Finally the Captain exhaled a cloud of smoke and said, "You have many things you'd like to ask me, don't you Ray?"

"Yes."

"Well, don't be shy. Better ask now because we're leaving in just a little while."

No matter how much time I spent around this man I couldn't predict what he was going to say or do next. "But Captain, we just got here and it's almost seven o'clock. Why can't we sleep and get up early and leave?"

"Are you sleepy?"

I thought about it. We'd only been up about four hours. I shook my head.

"Me either. I figure it's best if we go on." His eyes took on a familiar shine and he seemed to look past the room to something else. "Yes, everything will be just right if we go on soon." He looked out to lunch for a few more seconds and then seemed to pop back into the present moment. "So, Ray, what would you like to know?"

"How can you do things like you do?" I waved my hands around as I talked. "How can you predict a slot machine paying out and a roulette number coming up? How can you read my mind all the time? How can you get people to do all these things you want them to do?"

"You are mistaken, Ray," he responded calmly through a cloud of cigarette smoke. "I haven't done any of those things."

"Like hell you haven't! I saw you do *all* of those things. Don't back out on me now; you said I could ask you and I am asking. How?"

He shook his head. "Like I said, Ray, you are mistaken. *I* didn't do any of those things. Spirit did it. You just *thought* it was me."

I dismissed this statement with a wave of my hand. "Ah, just more bull."

"Nope, no bull. There *is* no *me*, Ray. That's what you don't get yet." He moved closer to me, and I could see a blazing intensity in his eyes. "There is no *you*, either, but the difference between the collection of urges, impulses, thoughts, concepts, and desires that we perceive to be *you* and the one we perceive to be *me* is that I know I don't exist as a discrete entity apart from all that is, and you do not."

He arranged and re-arranged the monogrammed napkins on the table. "There is only One. No matter how much you think there are separate entities in this universe, there is only One. Everything is simply the *I AM* principle in manifestation. I can't read anyone's mind, don't have any special roulette knowledge, nor can I make anyone do anything."

He stubbed out his cigarette in the ashtray on the table. "However, Spirit, or Energy, or Consciousness, or whatever name you wish to assign to the essential substance of the universe, can do all those things. It knows all, directs all, and IS all. It's like that question that you asked me about why I didn't let you win at blackjack. I didn't cause you to lose or me to win. I just listened to Life and acted. I knew you wouldn't win on your own because you had no reason to win for Life, and you don't have the right temperament for gambling for personal gain, that's all."

He looked thoughtful and added with a smile, "Not to mention the fact that you are too young to gamble legally, so if you had won something they would probably have just checked your I.D. and bounced you out anyway."

I raised a hand to get a word in edgewise. "I hear what you're saying, but my experience of events is that you always know what I am thinking. I don't know what others are thinking. I could play that roulette game for a hundred years straight and never be able to predict when a single number was going to hit like you just did. So how does that happen for you? What is it like? How do you know?"

He paused and finally took a deep breath. "Ray, after I had my illumination experience I thought I had gone crazy. I *knew* it had been real, but my mind told me that it couldn't be real. A few months after I came out of it, Life began to bring me signs that validated my experience and I understood that I hadn't gone crazy, but that I had stumbled into a new level of awareness. The awareness I had discovered was so different from my normal walking-around consciousness that it *seemed* crazy by comparison."

He pulled up another chair and propped a foot up on it. "But even after that validation my life wasn't very different than it was before. In fact, for a while I was probably a less effective human being than I was before the illumination because I had become aware of a possibility of Life that I didn't know how live up to. Do you remember what I told you about living up to the possibilities we become aware of?"

I nodded.

"Well, that goes for me, too. There has to be balance between our ideals and our actions. I started to search; I researched and read everything I could find that might possibly have to do with my experience, and I went back into chiropractic practice again. I began to understand how to connect with Spirit in order to bring about healing. I noticed that the more I lived for Life and the less I lived just to gratify my own limited and limiting desires, the more my perception increased. I began to perceive what other people were feeling, what might happen to them in the future, but mainly I began to perceive the perfection in and of Life. I started to realize what I AM by recognizing what I am not."

"What do you mean by that?"

He thought for a moment. "Once there was a famous artist who produced the most amazing sculptures the world had ever seen. People came from all over the world to see his works. A reporter asked him how he was able to produce such great art and he answered, 'I wait until I know what I want to sculpt and then I just chip away everything that doesn't look like that thing.' Understand?"

"I think so," I answered, "but I don't know how to do that."

"You do it the same way as the sculptor—by chipping away what you are not. For example, you start by realizing that you are not your body. Our compulsive self-identification with the body stems from limiting our consciousness to the illusion of space-time, as in, 'I am a being living in this time as opposed to that time, in this place as opposed to that place.' Then you realize that you are not your mind. The mind is nothing but the activity of the brain, subject to all the limiting concepts that we have inherited through evolution or have acquired during our lifetime. It loves conflict and problems, and its language is the language of the opposites. In reality, there is no such thing as this or that, you or me, right or left, hot or cold, right or wrong, but the mind forever perpetuates those illusions. Given some reflection it becomes self-evident that there can be no peace in the environment of the mind."

He got up and filled a plastic cup with water from the tap. "And that's the process. You just keep realizing what you are not. You start with the body, then the mind, then you realize that you are not your experiences, your thoughts, your desires, your concepts, your imaginings. Anything that is temporary, anything that changes, anything that comes and goes, is not what you really are."

"But how do you recognize these things?"

"By practicing your role as the observer," he smiled.

I laughed. "What the hell does that mean?"

"In Concept-Therapy we called it becoming the *thinker* apart from the thoughts, the *actor* apart from the action, the *feeler* apart from the feelings, the *willer* apart from the voluntary activities, and the *conscious subject* apart from the phenomena of the senses."

"Oh yeah, that clears it all up for me, thanks."

He chuckled heartily. "It takes practice to understand, Ray. It takes actually *applying* the idea, not just listening to me talk about it." His mouth was still curled in a smile, but his eyes were serious and intense. "It takes responding to a situation, or a thought, or a feeling differently than you would have before you became aware of the idea of Oneness. Just like anything else, talk is cheap. You can talk to yourself or someone else about it, but *acting* as though Life is One, that's what is actually going to produce change in your life."

He took a big swallow of water. "There is nowhere to go, nothing to attain, nothing to become. You are already home. You just haven't looked around to realize it yet. All you have to do is wake up from the illusion that is nothing more than the sum total of a trillion precepts gathered by your senses and cooked by your mind, and you will see that you *already are* the Real. Look. Investigate. Question what you think you know—what you most take for granted. You can't know what you are; what you are is by definition unknowable, but you can know what you are not, and by doing so you will melt into all that *IS* and find seamless, unfragmented Life with nothing to fear, worry about, desire, be jealous of, nothing to be angry or vain about, nothing to want or to be selfish or greedy about. You will know yourself to be Life, however indefinable that is to your mind."

I had no response to that, so we sat in silence for a while until finally he said, "Well, let's get moving."

As I packed my stuff I remembered the woman and her kids. "Captain," I called from my room, "what about that gambling freak? Why did you cut me off when I asked her about her kids?"

His voice struggled in from the den, sounding muffled and far away, "Ah, yes, I left that out a few minutes ago. Thanks for reminding me."

He didn't say anything else for several seconds, and I concluded that his silence meant that he planned to wait and answer me when we both got our stuff together and met in the den. I was bent over packing with my back to the bedroom door, so he scared the crap out of me when he screamed from right behind me, *"Criticism, Ray!* The worst thing you can ever engage in if you really want to know what you really are."

By the time I whirled around he was gone. I could hear him from the den chuckling softly at how badly I had jumped.

I finished packing and joined him in the den. "But

surely you don't think she was doing the right thing, do you?" I gave the room an idiot check to make sure we weren't leaving anything.

"There is no right or wrong, Ray, only action inspired by Life. I do think that her present actions are not supporting the constructive forces of Life, but understand that Life is a continual building up and tearing down process, just like the cells in your body. I hate to break it to you, but millions of cells in your body just died while we were standing here talking."

I rolled my eyes and he continued, "And, millions of new ones were just born. We all have a part to play in Life, and Life needs those that are destined to tear down as well as those that are destined to build." He grabbed the two checks from the table, stuffed them in a complementary MGM Hotel envelope, and added them to his suitcase. "The trick is knowing which path you are destined to walk and then walking it the best you can."

I was skeptical. "So Hitler was playing his part just like Buddha, or Jesus?"

"Yep. Understand too that Hitler experienced the fruits of his actions also. It's not like he got off without paying the price for the path he walked."

Now I was really skeptical. "What do you mean? Jesus hurt no one and was crucified. Hitler killed literally millions of innocent people and lived a longer life than Jesus. He even survived dozens of assassination attempts."

The Captain smiled a little. "Yes, his work wasn't done yet. He had to complete his task and Life wasn't going to let him go before it was finished."

"And what was that?" I was starting to get irritated now. "He hadn't killed enough people yet?"

"Ray, those who are destined to walk the path of unrighteousness have an important role too. They highlight human failings, inspire kindness, courage, and generosity, and give a contrasting context to goodness that otherwise wouldn't exist. That they do it by producing pain is only part of the human experience. They are like the pain in your butt that finally gets so bad that you go to the healer to change whatever you did to cause it. They inspire change when more constructive motivations won't."

He stubbed his final cigarette out in the hotel ashtray. "As for Jesus, a person like that doesn't fear life or death. An individual like Hitler is afraid of both. Jesus experienced heaven in all things, but Hitler's whole life was hellish. Trust me, outward appearances aside, Hitler related to the Law of Love so that he was a nail, not a hammer."

We walked out of the room to the elevator, and as we waited for it the Captain said, "I do need to let you know one thing about that woman, Ray."

"What?"

"She is the kind of person who isn't really destined to walk the path of unrighteousness. She just hasn't yet found the motivation to change her expression. You scolding her wouldn't have changed anything; it actually would have interfered with what is about to happen because she would have been able to use your hostility to rationalize her actions."

The elevator opened, and we got on and pressed the button for the lobby. "What is about to happen?" I asked a little nervously; something about the Captain's tone was foreboding.

"Well, she feels bad to a small extent about what she is doing to her children, but she hasn't allowed herself to really feel that pain yet. She keeps it at arm's length by rationalizing to herself that she is going to win big and provide for them in a way that she would never be able to by working a steady job."

We moved to the back of the elevator as more people got on. "See, although you criticize that woman and call her a freak, she's only doing outwardly what every human mind does inwardly all the time: we constantly chase pleasure and avoid pain. Over time we create a mask, made mostly of fear, to try to hide what we really feel. That mask is what we commonly refer to as our personality.

"We call other people freaks and perverts for the various ways that they attempt to fulfill their desires, but the urge to fulfill isn't the problem. In fact, it's the same great urge that motivates both constructive action and destructive action. The problem is that in cases like this woman's, the urge is unrefined and the person is deluded into believing that the false will satisfy. People only *think* that what they want is sex, or money, or excitement, or power, or even spiritual experiences, but what they really want is peace. They just aren't yet very aware of that possibility or what it means. In short, the problem isn't that we desire too much, it's that we settle for too little. We settle for one little distorted aspect of Life instead of aspiring to experience the whole thing."

There were three other people on the elevator with us, but the Captain talked to me as though the two of us were all by ourselves.

"Human consciousness revolves around the sense of self-awareness. What we used to call in CT the soul. We don't like for our idea of self to be threatened, either materially or morally. We have a great capacity for denial, hypocrisy, rationalization, and we will go to great lengths to hide our urges and indulgence of desires from ourselves and from others. This woman is no different than any of us in that regard."

The elevator opened in the lobby, and we picked up our suitcases and walked out to the front desk to check out.

I tried again. "So what is about to happen?"

"Oh yes, I almost forgot," he said. "I feel strongly that we will meet her again. In fact, unless I miss my guess, very soon. And I feel that something will happen that will end up being significant enough that it will become a life-changing experience for her."

I couldn't imagine what he was talking about, but I figured it would eventually become clear. We walked outside lugging our suitcases. It was almost completely dark, and we wandered for a few minutes trying to spot our car in a lot the size of an amusement park. We finally found the Captain's Olds, and I had opened the trunk and was loading our luggage when I felt someone beside me. A hoarse whisper behind my right ear said, "Don't move, kid." Something pressed hard into my ribs and the voice whispered again, "Do what I say and you won't get hurt."

I started to turn but my assailant jammed the gun into my side even harder. "Don't turn around. That's a gun in your ribs; don't make me use it. Just put your hands in the trunk and stay down and we'll all go home in one piece."

I could feel him move around behind me. "You too, old man," he barked. "Get over here and grab the bottom of this trunk."

The Captain leaned in and put his hands on the floor of the trunk beside me. I looked in his direction, but he wouldn't allow me to catch his eye. He just stared expressionlessly at the black fabric under his splayed fingers.

The voice behind us said, "Okay, a little birdie told me that you two did well at the gambling tables this afternoon. Don't move, just tell me where the money is."

The Captain's voice sounded strange and hollow in the trunk. "The money is in the wallet in my back pocket. Please take it and then leave us be."

I had the eight hundred dollars that the Captain had me cash out from the front desk in my wallet, but I stayed quiet. It occurred to me that the Captain must still have several hundred in his own wallet—the money that was in there when he placed his winning bet. The robber pulled out the Captain's wallet and said nothing while he went through it.

"Good for you, old man, you didn't lie. I'd hate to have to rough up an old man."

He tossed the empty wallet in the trunk beside us. "Okay, where are those cashier's checks?"

Before the Captain could tell the man where they were, however, a new voice spoke up. "Carlo, you idiot, we can't use those!" It was Clarissa, standing several feet away to the right of where we were.

"Shut up, bitch," the man spat in his hoarse whisper, "you know I can fake a driver's license, then I just go to the bank and open an account with these checks. According to you we're talking about real money, not nickel and dime shit this time."

"They'll just put a stop payment on the checks and have every bank in the area looking for us to walk in with them, you simpleton. You'll be arrested on the spot!"

It was easy to see who the mastermind of this operation was. The Captain's new friend had immediately contacted a thug accomplice and conspired to separate us from our newly acquired winnings. I wondered if the Captain felt as friendly toward her as he had an hour ago.

Just then, I heard a child's voice near Clarissa. "Mom, what are you doing over here? What's going on?"

"I thought I told you to stay in the lobby," Clarissa scolded. "Get back there right now!"

"But Mom, what's going on?"

"Don't worry about what's going on! Get back to that lobby right now or I'll smack you good!"

Small footsteps ran away from us for maybe ten steps, and then a car horn sounded, tires screeched, and all hell broke loose.

CHAPTER SEVEN
CONTROL

D r. Thurman Fleet started a new chiropractic practice
with his friend from The Texas Institute of Chiropractic
Sciences, Dr. Alonzo Woodman. They set up their office in
the first floor of Calvin's house with Calvin and his family
occupying the second floor, but the practice had already
outgrown it. Thurman's application of the healing principles
he had intuited during his illumination had drawn people from
all over the city. His methods were so effective that within six
months of opening, the clinic was serving an average of well
over a hundred patients a day, and Calvin's neighbors were
complaining about the traffic.

Now Thurman sat reading in the middle of his study.
Only the top of his head was visible above the stack of books
that surrounded him on all sides. Books were everywhere.
There were stacks in every room of the house except the
bathroom, and it had only been spared due to the threat that
a moist environment poses to paper. The storage shed in the
backyard was stacked full to the top with books, and piles of
books covered both the back and the front porch.

Thurman had begun maniacally acquiring them soon
after his "confirmation" showed up in the newspaper. Most
recently he had purchased fifteen thousand books from the
Fort Sam Houston Library, and he was consumed by the task
of looking through them for any information that might shed

some light on his strange shift in consciousness.

The old compulsion to understand had returned, worse than ever, and Thurman had become enslaved to the impulse to understand what had happened to him and what its significance might be. He had returned to chiropractic practice, an endeavor that served two purposes: it had provided needed income to pay for the research materials that he had been collecting at such a rapid rate, and it had served as a laboratory for him to experiment in. Although he didn't yet fully understand what he had tapped into, he had intuited early on in his quest that it would have particular significance for him in the healing arts. Healing had seemed so simple and clear to him during his illumination, and he had been working out and testing healing principles based upon his experience.

Thurman had settled into a routine of seeing patients during the day, and reading and researching at night. He divided his piles of books into categories, and he developed a technique for scanning books quickly for information that was valuable. He became so good at this that he could effectively scan a two hundred-page book in half an hour, underlining and bookmarking the pertinent sections. Somehow he seemed drawn to exactly the right passages.

Tonight he was reading a book that he'd recently discovered in a small batch he had bought wholesale from a metaphysical bookstore in San Antonio. He had been attracted to its title immediately: *Cosmic Consciousness*, by Richard Maurice Bucke, M.D., and he had been studying it in greater detail than his usual scanning method allowed.

There was a knock on the door of the study, and Calvin appeared before Thurman could answer. Calvin whistled. "Wow, Thurman. Delia told me last week that your whole house was getting filled up with books, but I never expected anything like this. How do you all move around in all of this?"

"Hm?" Thurman mumbled, engrossed in the book.

Calvin tried again, louder, "I say, *how do you all move around in all of this?*"

That broke Thurman's concentration and he looked up at Calvin and smiled. "We make do. The other day we lost little George in the stacks and it took half the morning to find him."

"How old is George now?"

"He's a big three and a half," Thurman said as he laid his book down. "Thurma is eleven, and Vivienne is fourteen, if you can believe it."

"They do grow up fast," Calvin agreed, before getting around to the reason for his visit. "Thurman, I think I may have a solution for the office. The Milam Building downtown will be ready for occupancy in a little over three months, and they have the entire second floor available."

"Three months!" Thurman snorted. "We need a new location *now*. We're already busting at the seams. I've got the fire marshal giving me hell about the building capacity, and the police are going to start writing us tickets due to traffic congestion. Isn't there anyplace else we could get into faster?"

Calvin shook his head. "Not anyplace big enough to handle the patient load in a convenient, central location with adequate parking. I suggest we go ahead and contract with the Milam building and lock up the whole second floor, and then make do until then. We may have to put patients on a waiting list."

Thurman thought for a moment and then shook his head, "No, we'll just extend our office hours until then. Take the second floor of the building. Woodie and I are already splitting the shifts, so we'll just start earlier and stay later. I'll open up at six a.m. and he can stay until ten p.m. We'll stay open on Saturdays and Sundays too. We can keep that up for just a few months, then we'll go back to regular office hours once we make the move."

Calvin had been acting as the clinic superintendent, so all clinic operations fell under his jurisdiction. It had been a challenging task to keep up with the rapid growth of the healing practice, and he was anxious to locate in a facility that they wouldn't outgrow so quickly.

Feeling relieved, he turned to the door, but Thurman stopped him. "Cal."

"Yes?"

"See if this sounds familiar to you." He picked up the book he'd been reading when Calvin had entered and quoted a few paragraphs. It was about a doctor who reported an experience similar to Thurman's illumination. Calvin listened patiently, albeit uncomfortably.

Thurman finally looked up at Calvin and said, "The experience the author describes here is almost exactly like my own. Not only that, but his theory is that such illumination experiences are evidence that the human race is developing the capacity to become aware of higher states of consciousness."

Calvin gave a nod and made a small, short humming sound that he hoped would convey affirmation without really having to commit himself. The truth is that he didn't really know what to make of Thurman when he started talking about these things. He had witnessed some startling things during Thurman's stay in the front bedroom, and he had to admit that the healing principles they had been using in the clinic had worked wonders with patients. Thurman had tried to explain to him how he worked with people on all levels: body, mind, soul, and spirit, in order to bring about health, but Calvin hadn't been able to grasp exactly what he meant by all of that. He had faith that Thurman knew what he was doing, but he had no desire to get involved in the details.

Thurman raised his chin and peered through the bottom of his bifocals. "The author theorizes that the founders of all the world religions had these spiritual experiences, and their attempts to convey them to others resulted in the collective hodgepodge of theories, fantasies, and misunderstandings we call religion. He also makes a good case that our collective capacity for true spiritual understanding is growing, so more and more individuals will be having these illuminations as time goes on. He says eventually the human race will no longer need fantasies and theories about our spirituality; we will have direct knowledge."

Calvin suffered in uncomfortable silence. He almost breathed an audible sigh of relief when Thurman changed the subject back to the clinic. "One more thing about the office, Cal. How are we coming on finding a medical doctor?"

As clinic superintendent of a chiropractic office, Calvin had been dealing with an unusual problem: as of the early 1940s, chiropractic hadn't been legalized in Texas yet. It wasn't illegal, either—there were no laws about it at all. Since there were no laws regulating it there were also no laws protecting it, and doctors of chiropractic had to be careful to ensure that no unscrupulous elements attempted to destroy their healing efforts by charging them with 'practicing medicine without a license.' Thurman's solution had been to employ a medical doctor to write prescriptions for the treatment, and Calvin had been charged with finding a willing M.D.

"I think I have one: old doc Barker. If I can keep him from drinking while at the clinic I think he'll work out fine."

"Excellent. Good work, Cal." Calvin turned to leave again and Thurman stopped him again. "Oh, Cal, you do remember that tomorrow is my meeting with Dr. Drake, don't you?"

Calvin slowed and looked back, "Tomorrow? I had forgotten." He smiled. "Are you ready?"

Thurman smirked. "Sure. Why wouldn't I be? Even as stubborn as Drake is, how can he deny the obvious?"

Calvin offered one cheerful parting reminder as he

turned yet again to leave. "Remember—never underestimate the power of obstinacy."

∞

Thurman walked into Dr. Drake's office for the first time since the professor had disciplined him for disrupting his class over a year ago. Drake sat behind his mahogany desk smoking his pipe, and he looked genuinely pleased to see Thurman. The two men shook hands, exchanged pleasantries, and sat down across the giant desk from each other.

Thurman began, "Dr. Drake, I have come to offer you and The Texas Institute of Chiropractic Sciences the opportunity to help me revolutionize our profession. I would like to share the principles I am putting to work in my clinic with other doctors. With your contacts and the endorsement of the college, we can teach doctors all over the country what I have discovered."

Drake sat back in his seat with a slightly bemused expression on his face. He paused for a long moment and finally responded, "Well, Fleet, I certainly appreciate you giving this opportunity to me and the college—"

"You're welcome, sir," Thurman interrupted sincerely.

Drake's expression of amusement deepened. "But I don't exactly know what to make of it. Let me get this straight, you want to teach doctors, right?"

Thurman nodded.

"And you want The Texas Institute of Chiropractic Sciences to endorse your teachings, and you want me to use my contacts to help you establish your audience?"

Thurman nodded again.

Drake took a large puff on his pipe and said, "So what is it we are going to be teaching these doctors? How to seclude themselves in a bedroom for a week? How to manage clever parlor tricks, make it seem like you are disappearing and reading people's minds? Is that what you want to teach?" Thurman was stunned. Dr. Drake had been there. He had *been there.* He couldn't deny what had happened, and yet that was exactly what he was doing.

Dr. Drake softened his tone. "Fleet, I know that what I saw you go through was real. I'm just trying to give you a different perspective. How do you think people who *weren't* there are going to react to your story? Did you ever think of that?" He puffed on his pipe again. "Do you have a curriculum? Do you have any substantiation for what you are going to be telling these doctors? Any research?"

Thurman shook his head and Dr. Drake laughed heartily. "Fleet, you are quite the hypocrite!"

He laughed so hard he couldn't talk for a moment. "You sat in my class and demanded proof of *everything.* If I said the sky was blue, you would stand up and yell *Icon* at me until I proved it, and now you want people to believe you went to some spiritual La-La Land in your own front bedroom and learned the secret of healing. You've got no proof or even an organized curriculum. Do you not see the humor in that, Fleet?" He chuckled some more.

Thurman recovered quickly and tried again, "I see your point, Dr. Drake, but healing is ultimately about results. I am getting tremendous results in my clinic and—"

"Are you documenting them?" Drake interrupted.

"Well, no, but—"

"*But nothing!*" Drake yelled. "You may know about healing, Fleet, but you don't know squirrel-squat about academia. If it isn't documented it doesn't exist, period. If what you are going to be talking to these doctors about it so damn revolutionary, you are going to have a hard enough time getting doctors to listen to you *with* research, but without it you have virtually no chance—really new ideas always have a hard time gaining acceptance, no matter how true they are."

Thurman said nothing; his former college president had a point and he knew it.

"And one more thing you obviously haven't considered," Drake said, "you aren't even a real doctor, Fleet." He pointed at Thurman with the stem of his pipe. "Jesus, why would anyone think you were anything other than a bug-eyed crackpot? You didn't even finish your degree."

Drake put down his pipe and held up both hands with fingers outstretched, "Finish your degree and document ten years worth of research; then you'll be in a position for someone to take you seriously."

"Ten years?"

"Oh, stop bellowing, Fleet. The Wright Brothers developed their ideas for ten years before they were granted a patent on the airplane. James Watt developed the steam engine for longer than that before he got his patent. If what you've got is so all-fired great, then give it some time. Develop it, and most importantly, organize it into a curriculum so that you can really communicate it to other people." Drake stood up and held out his hand. "Just because you understand it doesn't mean other people will. You have to give them some context for it."

Thurman knew his professor was right. He stood up, shook the outstretched hand, and turned to leave.

"Oh, and Fleet?" Drake said as his former problem student was almost out the door.

Thurman stuck his head back in around the door.

"If you are serious about this, I will see you in class. You will need your degree to be taken seriously."

Thurman exited without comment, leaving Dr. Drake to enjoy his pipe.

"He ran right out in front of me. There was…nothing… nothing I could do," the man repeated, his hands shaking and his tear-streaked face flashing alternately red and blue with the waves of light emanating from the bulbs crowning the police cruisers that had responded to the accident.

An EMT covered the small form on the stretcher with a sheet, and then he and the ambulance driver loaded the stretcher into the back of the ambulance. Their lights were off; there was no hurry.

Clarissa was calm now, having been sedated by the paramedics. She slumped drunkenly against the inside of the police car door, handcuffed, while someone from children's services asked her questions through the open window and informed her that they were placing her other child into foster care pending an investigation.

I sat next to the Captain, waiting on the police to question us about what had happened. My legs still felt weak. I had never witnessed something like this before, and I didn't really know how to handle it. I'd seen dead bodies before, but only at funeral homes already prepared for burial. I had never seen anyone actually die, much less a child. Right after it happened I felt like I couldn't breathe, like I was going to be sick, and the world seemed to fade sideways and out of focus. I remember thinking, "this is how Dawn must feel." The Captain had placed his hand on the back of my neck and told me to not try to breathe, but to *allow* breath to flow through me. He kept repeating this directive until I felt calm again.

Immediately after Clarissa's son was struck by the car Carlo had split——without checking to see if the kid was all right, without calling anyone for help, or even looking back, for that matter. Clarissa was hysterical. She picked up the boy's lifeless body and screamed, "Talk to me!" over and over, refusing to let anybody else touch him. A member of the hotel staff finally called the cops.

Sirens, lights, attempts at resuscitation, Police Line–Do Not Cross tape, weeping, Clarissa freaking out, an innocent child's blood staining the parking lot, and stinking Carlo probably still running. It was one depressing scene.

I saw them finish questioning the man who had hit the kid, and he sort of wandered over toward his car and looked at it like it had betrayed him or something. Like he couldn't imagine actually getting in it and starting it up and driving it anywhere ever again.

I turned to say something to the Captain, but he wasn't there anymore. I looked around and saw him approaching the driver. He touched the man on the shoulder, leaned in close to the guy's ear, and said something to him too low for anyone else to hear. The floodgates opened; the man stood there crying, hard, for about a minute, and then he seemed to collect himself. He shook the Captain's hand and got in his car to drive away.

"Name!" A uniformed cop barked in my left ear. I gave him the information he asked for, answered all his questions, told him what happened, and after what seemed to be an eternity he finally said, "Thank you for all your help Mr. Tolouthe. We'll find this guy Carlo; even though you two didn't get a good look at him I think the woman over there will be able to give us the information we need to pick him up. You should know, however, that there's not much chance we'll be able to get you guys your money back. We'll be in touch." I nodded dumbly and the cop walked away.

I looked around for the Captain again and found him squatting beside the police car where Clarissa sat. I inched closer. Clarissa was crying her head off, trying to talk to the Captain between sobs. "S-s-so…can you help me? Y-you s-s-said you used to teach about concepts and s-stuff. C-can you help me with this gambling a-a-ddiction?"

He was silent until she looked straight at him. "No, I don't think I can. I doubt anyone else can, either. Matter of fact, I think you might be in about as good a shape as you're ever going to be in." Then he got up and walked away.

I was stunned. Clarissa's face recoiled in that open sort of way that people do when they are truly shocked, then it screwed up in a tight mask of pain and she began to sob again. I didn't know what to say. I just turned and followed the Captain.

When we were finally able to get in the car and start the long drive back to Boerne I asked him first thing, "What was with what you said to Clarissa? I know you don't really think she is always going to be that way; you told me that she was due for a turning point in her life."

"Yes, this is, in fact, the turning point I was referring to."

"Well—what did you mean? Why did you basically tell her that there was no hope for her to turn herself around?"

"The Law of Kindness, Ray."

"What does that mean?" I didn't even try to hide my anger.

"The Law of Kindness dictates that sometimes it is appropriate to act gently toward a person needing help." He unfolded the road map. "And sometimes it is appropriate to kick them in the seat of the pants just about as hard as you can. Wisdom lights the way to the correct choice at any given time."

He studied the map for a moment and continued, "When we say someone has become addicted to something, all that has happened is that they have become trapped by their sense of separation from Life to the degree that they become myopic. Normal human consciousness is characterized by the desire to seek pleasure and avoid pain; ultimately it is the mechanism that creates the motivation for all the action that we take in this consciousness."

He turned away from the map and looked directly at me in order to make his next point. "However, our consciousness evolves when we realize that we gain more pleasure by realizing our connection with Life rather than maintaining our sense of separation. Once this principle gains ground in an individual, that person is drawn to greater and greater union with the One Life until he realizes his unity, transcends normal human consciousness, and rises above the opposites of pain and pleasure.

"If an individual does not realize the bigger picture and it doesn't dawn on him that connection will ultimately help him gain more pleasure and avoid more pain, he will channel all of his energy into seeking pleasure in some limited, fragmented area of life. It might be sex, alcohol, exercise, food, whatever, but it will not satisfy him because the seed of failure lies in his starting premise—separation and limitation. Such seeds can only grow bitter weeds. Even if a person is successful in gaining what he seeks, he or she will still suffer the pain and the fear of loss. If life is separate, anything can and ultimately will be lost, and that is the fatal seed that is planted. Follow me so far?"

"Yes, but what does that have to do with what you told that woman?" I was still shocked and a little indignant. "Her child just died, for Pete's sake. She's going to jail, which I suppose she deserves, but she's losing one child for good and another to Child Protective Services. She wants help overcoming her addiction, and you basically told her she has no hope. What does that have to do with seeking pleasure or avoiding pain?"

"A lot, actually," he answered patiently. "People in her position have learned to avoid responsibility; it's a big part of the separation mindset. Even when they 'hit bottom,' so to speak, and resolve to change, they are still almost always looking for someone else to place the responsibility of their recovery on—a therapist, a doctor, a treatment program—something other than themselves. That's one reason why recovery rates for addicts are as low as they are. What I took away from her was the hope that someone else could or would attempt to be responsible for her change. I feel that without hope of someone else helping her, she will rise to the challenge of helping herself. I understand that she has a long road ahead of her, but having to reach down inside herself is going to be much better for her than looking for someone else to fix her problem. Ultimately each soul must take its own steps."

We drove in silence for a minute and then I remembered the foreshadowing statements he had made earlier. "That's another thing I wanted to ask you: you *knew* this was going to happen?"

I glanced sideways and saw a very small tug at his lips. "Kind of."

"What the hell does kind of mean? Did you know or not?"

His voice sobered and he said, "I knew that she would somehow try to get our money, and I knew that in doing so she would suffer a great personal loss, something significant enough to shake her out of her self-hypnotic fixation with gambling."

"So you knew we might get *robbed*?"

"Yes, I knew that was a distinct possibility."

I sat for a moment feeling anger boil up inside me. I kept my voice even and calm, despite my anger. "Did it ever occur to you that I might have wanted to know that? Did it ever occur to you that I might have the right to know that there was an excellent chance that my life might be in danger?"

"Yes," was all he said.

I pinched off each word with icy precision. "Then why didn't you say something?"

He folded up the map, which seemed like it took forever, and finally answered, "Because you would have interfered."

I lost it. "*Because I would have interfered?* Yeah, you're *damn right* I would have interfered! I would have done something so that we wouldn't have a dead child that never hurt anyone and another going to foster care while their mom goes to jail!"

"Exactly," he said softly. "You would have interfered."

"I thought you were always talking about serving life and the power of love. How do you reconcile those things with letting an innocent child die?"

"I know you don't get this yet, Ray, but I did what Life inclined me to do. I am not in charge of what happened to that child, and neither are you. That's another one of the chains you must begin to break: the illusion of control. I don't control anything, and neither do you. We act according to our inclinations, but the outcome is always up to Life."

I shook my head. "Bullshit! That is nothing but a bullshit rationalization for excusing yourself for doing what you please. Talk about refusing responsibility! That's like all the holy-rollers who justify doing whatever they want by saying that God told them to do it. Or the people who excuse their sins by claiming that the Devil tempted them."

The Captain chuckled softly and nodded. "Yes, Ray. I see your point. You can't just believe every Tom, Dick, or Harry that tells you that they were divinely inspired to do this or that, can you?" His voice got serious. "You *can*, however, compare the words of such fellows with their actions and see if they compare favorably. The Bible says, *Ye shall know them by their fruits*. Well, you've seen some of my fruits. What do you think? In light of comparing my actions with my words, is what I say about inclinations logical or not?"

I said nothing and he went on, "I mean, it would be one thing if I claimed Life was guiding me and I had no better success or different outcomes than someone just winging it, but that hasn't been your experience with me, now has it?"

I chose to remain wrapped in the meager comfort of silence rather than admit defeat; my refusal to speak was the only resistance I had left. After a while I finally gave up and said, "I still don't get it. You *can* do some amazing things, I admit. So why couldn't you just hypnotize that woman to get her to stop gambling? Why was all that tragedy necessary?"

"Well, Ray, you're not going to like my answer. I know you're not going to like it because I've told you the same thing before, yet here we are dunking the same old doughnut. I couldn't hypnotize her because I can't hypnotize anyone. I've never hypnotized anyone in my life."

I let out a giant irritated sigh and he said, "Now wait a minute, hear me out. Remember that human beings are composite entities—the effect of consciousness acting upon consciousness. We are made up of sub-atomic particles, atoms, molecules, chemicals, cells, tissues, organs, systems, and each one of those groups of lower forms has its own expression of consciousness. The sum total of all those expressions of consciousness interacting with each other produces the physical body we have. The physical body's interaction with itself and its outside environment produces a slightly higher frequency of consciousness—what we might refer to as our mind. This part of us includes both the thoughts and emotions we become aware of."

He waited while I made a lane change. "When an individual is only aware of his physical and mental self, he is motivated only by the attractions and repulsions of the sum total of the lower forms that make up his body.

"However, human consciousness has within it an even higher connection; the seed of cosmic consciousness, the awareness of One Life. If that seed blooms and is tended to so that it continues to thrive and grow, the motivation changes for that individual from actions motivated by electro-chemical attractions, pursuits of pleasure, mental affinities, and emotional pacification to motivations that flow directly from the Spirit or Consciousness within. The individual no longer acts to satisfy a craving, complete an unbalanced chemical reaction, or solve a problem created by the mind, although those forces are indeed part of Life. He responds to a higher call, a complete formula that takes into account not just the individual in question, but all of Life. That formula very often comes to different conclusions because it takes into account an infinite number of variables."

I couldn't take any more. "Yeah, you've told me all this before, but I still don't understand how that means that you don't hypnotize people, and that you can't make any of the things happen that I've seen you make happen."

"I'm getting there, Ray. And then we're going to talk about the Law of Patience." I could hear a smirk in his voice. "Whether you are an individual who is only self-aware or whether you are aware of the cosmic, Life is really what acts. You think you are a noun and your actions are verbs; it's not so. You don't exist as a noun, a discrete entity, any more than a wave on the ocean exists as an entity separate from the ocean. You are a verb. A wave is only a particular motion of water, and you are only a particular function of Life.

"You don't really act because you don't really exist as a separate entity, and when you know this, truly *know* it, your experience will be very different than the person who is only self-aware. To that person it seems as though she is making completely independent choices and influencing a cause and effect scenario.

"The cosmic-aware individual, on the other hand, doesn't experience the illusion of independent choice. She doesn't feel a part of life in the sense that she is a separate entity among many other separate entities; she feels that she *is* Life. Not all of it, mind you, but more along the lines of a drop of water in the ocean. Such a drop can't truthfully say, *I am the whole ocean*, but it *can* truthfully say, *I am ocean*. The essence is the same. Notice that in both cases, Life is the only actor. It's just that the cosmic individual is aware of that fact and the self-aware individual is not."

He paused to check the map again. "Where was I?

Oh, yes—control. The illusion of control is like a blind man who thinks he can see because he imagines scenes behind his eyelids. When the rest of his senses tell him that the outside world doesn't match up with his imaginings, he feels fear because he is faced with the apparent conclusion that he is disconnected from the outside world. So do we feel fear when we identify with the desire for a certain outcome and that outcome does not manifest. We desire to control outcomes, and in that desire lies the seed of separation which blooms into the flowers of fear, worry, anger, jealousy, hypocrisy, selfishness, criticism, vanity, envy, greed, prejudice, and hate. Those flowers feed the illusion that traps us in human consciousness and keeps us out of the cosmic awareness."

I sighed, "So what is all this talk about 'learning how to live' if I am not the one living in the first place? If I have no control, how can I change anything about my life? Why should I even try?"

He nodded, "Yes. I said you couldn't control *outcomes*. However, there is an aspect of the idea of control that is very relevant to you. Pull off up there at that truck stop and let's see if we can't explore that aspect."

The car trailed a cloud of dust as we pulled into the dirt parking lot and parked by the side of the building. The sign on the roof said "Don's Truck Stop & Restaurant," and it definitely looked like it had seen better days. I went to the bathroom while the Captain went inside, and by the time I came out he was returning to the car with a small brown bag so I quickly stretched and got behind the wheel.

I was reaching for the ignition when he stopped me. "Look at this Ray, before you start the car." He reached into the paper bag and pulled out a small paperback dictionary.

"Don't leave home without it," I joked. "Better than Traveler's Checks."

"Well, not as good as the one I have at home," he smiled, "but it'll do in a pinch. It really helps to define your terms when exploring concepts. Here," he handed me the dictionary, "look up the definition of the word *control*."

He'd left his door partially open so I could read by the dome light, and I quickly flipped to the right section of the book. I read the first two definitions and immediately had a good idea of where the Captain was heading with all of this.

Con•trol
[k*uh*n-**trohl**]
verb, -trolled, trol•ling, noun

1. To have power over. To dominate.
2. To exercise restraint or direction over.

I read the first two definitions out loud and closed the book. This time the Captain didn't stop me or make me open it back up. He just closed his door and nodded for me to start the car. We drove in silence for a few minutes and he finally said, "So I guess that first definition is self-evident, yes?"

"Yes."

"We don't have the ability to dominate anything. We try like the blazes to do so, and we sometimes think we are doing so, but we really don't. Even in a situation in which one person uses violence or the threat of violence against another, the so-called victim still complies, albeit out of fear."

"Well, you can't really blame them, can you?" I asked.

"It's not about blame, Ray. We aren't assigning blame to anyone, we're just accurately assessing the situation."

He rolled his window back up a bit—it was getting cool outside. "When Gandhi began speaking in India about non-violent resistance he said, 'The British may kill me, but if they do, all they will have is my dead body. They will never have my obedience.' Complicity is a choice, and though it may be difficult, other choices are available."

"You make it sound so easy." I flipped my hand to demonstrate nonchalance. "What if someone was threatening to kill your family?"

"Assuming I was able to keep my balance I would act as I always do. I would act according to the inner inclinations that Life gives me to guide me."

"Even if it meant allowing harm to your family?"

"Yes. Theoretically, at least. In the practical world of everyday life, however, I don't think you would see a situation arise very often in which Right Action would be to allow family members to be harmed by outside aggression."

"What do you mean by *Right Action*?"

"Right Action means doing what Life tells you to in any given situation. It's potentially different for each person in each circumstance—what might be Right Action for one person might not be for another. It depends upon the Law of Duty. What do you think the Law of Duty means, Ray?"

I thought for a moment and answered, "It means fulfilling your obligations. Doing what you should."

He nodded. "Yes, that's how we normally use the term, but let me give you a different idea about duty."

He pointed at me. "You, Ray, are an absolutely unique expression of the Divine. There has never been another human being exactly like you, nor will there ever be another human being exactly like you. You have a unique combination of attributes, personality characteristics, talents, skills, abilities, limitations, and concepts. And so does every other person who has ever existed or will ever exist. That unique combination requires a unique path to reach happiness, peace, and fulfillment, and walking that path is your duty. Duty isn't doing something you don't want to do; it is doing something designed to bring you ultimate happiness—custom tailored just for you."

He paused and added, "It is worth noting that usually there are also unique challenges and obstacles to overcome in order to develop the capacity for an individual to fully manifest his or her duty. It's not a free ride."

I thought about that for a moment and asked, "So what does that have to do with the idea of control?"

He tapped the dictionary. "You remember that the first definition had to do with domination. Do you remember the key idea in the second?"

"Restraint?"

"Excellent, Ray! Are you always so smart or is it the Nevada night air?" He chuckled. "Yes, restraint. But what is being restrained and what is it being restrained from?"

"That I don't know, Captain."

"What runs all day without legs?"

"I don't know," I rolled my eyes. As a rule I hated riddles.

"Think, Ray! You can make it up or change it at will."

I reluctantly thought for a moment and sighed, "I still don't know."

"Yours must be on the fritz, then," he smiled and tapped his head with one finger, "because I'm obviously talking about the mind."

"But I distinctly recall you telling me that the mind doesn't even exist," I reminded him.

He nodded again, "Yes, very good Ray. I'm glad to see that my words are getting through to the gray matter between your ears." He paused for a moment to extract a cigarette from the pack he kept in his shirt pocket. "Do you remember me asking you on the way out here what this was?"

I nodded.

"And I told you that it didn't exist, right?"

I nodded again.

"Well, that ain't the whole truth."

At that I snorted audibly and the Captain cackled with delight at my disgust. "It does exist, and yet it doesn't at the same time."

"Will you please stop fooling around and tell me what the hell that means?" My half-whine, half-order made the Captain laugh even harder.

He finally finished laughing and dispensed with all signs of foolishness. "Ray," he whispered in a dramatic stage voice.

"What?"

"We still need to talk about that Law of Patience." Then he broke into another raucous peal of laughter that seemed like it would never end. I sincerely hoped he would pee his pants.

Eventually he calmed down and said, "If a thing exists at all, there is a *way* in which it exists. It may exist as a fantasy, a theory, or a fact. It has no objective existence because its existence depends upon an observer to give it reality."

"So the old, 'if a tree falls in a forest and no one is there to hear it, does it really make a sound' question?" I asked.

"Sort of," he answered. "It goes deeper than that, though. Quantum physics recognizes the role of the observer in manifesting what we call *reality*, which is nothing more than what our collective senses agree on. The physicists describe an infinite matrix of possibility in the form of waves of energy, which collapse into tangible forms when one of those possibilities is observed."

He lit his cigarette, inhaling and exhaling and totally fumigating the car with Pall Mall smoke. "But it doesn't have to be that technical. Remember my analogy about the dog and the music?"

"Yes."

"Well, that analogy seems simple because I used a comparison of perception between two relatively similar forms, but if you compare more dissimilar forms, or even contemplate how different forms affect the formless reservoir of pure potential, you begin to see that it is the same principle even when applied to manifested 'reality' itself. The observer *creates* reality."

I was lost. "Wait, wait, wait," I moaned. "Can we get back to whether the mind exists or not?"

"Sure. The mind exists to most people as a thing, which is to say that it exists as a fantasy. They feel that they have a mind, but they don't a have a mind any more than you have a digestion. Like you yourself, *mind* is a verb, not a noun."

I held up my hand for him to stop. "Wait, can you explain this fantasy/theory/fact thing?"

"Fantasy is an idea that shocks normal adult reason. Theory is something that is logical and reasonable, yet which cannot be proved or disproved, and fact is something that can be demonstrated or can be deduced from other demonstrable facts."

I still didn't get it. "Can you give me an example?"

"Do you believe in Santa Claus, Ray?"

"No." I shook my head.

"Why not?"

"Because there is no way that a fat old man could make and deliver toys to all the children of the world in one night. There is no such thing as flying reindeer or magic. It's obviously a fairy tale."

"Exactly," he said. "It violates normal human reason. However, the idea still exists as a fantasy, yes?"

"Okay..." I waited for the trap to spring.

"And it is even valuable as a fantasy. It exists as such for those whose reasoning capabilities cannot comprehend a more advanced idea, right?"

"Yes." I felt safe in this one. "It's for kids."

He nodded, "And it serves an important function for them. It prepares them for the more advanced and refined versions of the ideas of goodwill and unity that they will one day be able to comprehend. Religion is like that for adults."

He took another drag on his cigarette. "Now, Ray, have you ever been to Alaska?"

"Never."

"But do you believe it exists?"

"Yes."

"How do you know?" he asked.

"Well..." Here it was. The trap. "I guess I don't *know*. I believe it because reputable sources report it, and there isn't anything inherently illogical or suspicious about what they report."

"So you, of yourself, can't prove or disprove its existence yet you find it a logical theory, and so that is how it exists for you. If you ever went there yourself, it would cease to be a theory and it would become a fact. Understand?"

"I think so."

"Now, notice that depending upon the state of the consciousness of the observer, fantasy can change into theory or theory into fact. One hundred years ago the idea of going to the moon existed only as a fantasy to everyone alive at that time. It became a more logical theory as we made advances in materials, mathematics, communications, electronics, and physics, and when we did it, it became fact."

"Okay."

"The mind exists only as a function, but we think about it as though it is a tangible entity, don't we?"

"I guess so."

"Well, that is a fantastic conception. But fantasy eventually leads to theory, and theory to fact, so we can still gain a measure of understanding from contemplating even a fantastic aspect of something, in this case the idea of the mind."

With a puff of blue cigarette smoke he finished, "So, like Santa Claus, the mind exists, and yet it doesn't."

My head hurt and we had gotten so far off track I couldn't even remember why we had begun talking about the mind in the first place.

The Captain must have sensed my confusion. "Control, Ray. What are we really restraining? What is this mythical mind we are contemplating?"

"I don't know," I responded wearily. At this point I just wanted to get away from the Captain and go to sleep.

"Give it a shot, Ray. You might surprise yourself."

"Well, if the mind is a function, I would say that it could be defined as our most consistent mental habits."

"Hey, good definition!" the Captain beamed. "I would say you are right." He flicked his cigarette out the window.

"I would add a few observations as well," he said. "Because this function we call the mind stems from our human self-awareness, it has some characteristics that tend to hold true across the board—they're inherited habits, and they tend to be true for the whole race. The mind is addicted to opposites and problems. It loves conflict and craves contrast and separation. It ushers in all the negative emotions we have talked about, and it lives by limitation. Now, how can we tame such a beast? How can we apply this idea of control as restraint or influence?"

I passed a truck on the left. "I'm sure I don't know, Captain."

"The mind is a great servant, but a terrible master, Ray. We control it by not attempting to control it."

I sighed again. "Okay, so explain what that means."

"We instead control our attention, our observation. We use our powers of observation to choose and identify with an image, and we allow the image to take over. The mind goes along with the image. In this way we see the mind for what it is—an automatic function of what we have identified with. If you want to change your mind, all you have to do is change what you have identified with."

The picture wasn't getting any clearer just yet. "What do you mean *identify with*?" I asked.

"Well, Ray, I could look up the word in our dictionary, but I hardly think it necessary. Make the word a noun instead of a verb and tell me what that noun is."

I thought for a moment. "Identity."

"Exactly. Whether they know it or not, people are straining to discover their true identity. Of course, our true essential identity is the unknowable X, which we can't define or comprehend with the mind, so we try to fill in the blank with whatever illusion appeals to our search for pleasure or avoidance of pain."

He reached into the bag for a pack of crackers from the truck stop. "Some people identify with their age, or gender, or occupation. Some identify with their family, their accomplishments, or their past. Some identify with an illness, some with their physical body or personality characteristics, some with their mind, and some with a loved one. Whatever we truly identify with becomes one of our fundamental basic concepts, and each basic concept we have strictly dictates how the mind operates with regard to that identification— what thoughts it thinks and what emotions it induces relative to that basic idea. Understand?"

"I—I think so," I answered slowly. It was still a little fuzzy, but I thought I was beginning to get the idea.

"Let's try an example. Have you ever known someone who was really lucky? I mean someone who everything always seemed to turn up roses for?"

I nodded; Mr. Jim was like that. Mom used to joke that he could fall out of a boat and come up with a fish in his mouth.

"Now, whether that person knows it or not, he has identified with the idea of being lucky. Life simply responds by validating his identification."

I frowned. "What do you mean by that?"

"Well, remember that everything that is manifested in the physical is nothing more than a reflection of some idea that has been impressed onto the fabric of Universal Spirit, whether by mass consciousness or an individual. When you identify with an idea strongly it impresses it into the Spirit within you, and Spirit supports whatever idea you most strongly identify with. It will arrange your affairs to manifest *exactly* what that idea calls for."

He swallowed a peanut butter and cracker. "So your lucky friend has consciously or unconsciously identified himself with the idea of being lucky. He *feels* that he is lucky, deep down inside, maybe even so much so that he doesn't even realize it. Life responds by bringing to him experiences that validate that idea."

"So you're saying that if he felt unlucky, the opposite would happen?"

"Absolutely. He would have more bad luck than thirteen black cats. Universal Spirit doesn't judge like we do. It won't say to Itself, *I know Ray has impressed upon me that he is accident prone, but I know he doesn't really want that to be the case, so I am going to change his idea to one of him being safe at all times.* It won't do that, it will just give you what you have impressed upon it."

I frowned again, "Captain, that's a little hard to swallow. Do you mean that I can just say to myself, *I am lucky* and I will start to have good luck?"

"Well, you can't just *say* it to yourself a few times, you have to really convince yourself of it. You have to let go of your memories of past experiences to the contrary— that's a big part of the Law of Forgiveness. Memories have power over us only because we trust them as reality instead of recognizing them to be simply mental states that have no more reality than any other image we choose to pay attention to. You have to be the observer, the soul, the feeler apart from the feelings, and you have to choose to concentrate and vibrate upon an idea so strongly that you lose yourself in the process and *become* the idea. Then the mind will automatically think thoughts consistent with that idea, and the soul will automatically engage in actions consistent with that idea. There is no need to tame or repress it, just hitch it to the star you want it to follow instead of allowing it to determine its own course."

He held up one finger to emphasize a point, "But above all, don't make the mistake of thinking you *are* your mind, any more than you should make the mistake of assuming you are your body. Both are tools for you, the soul, to use. If you start thinking that you are your mind or your body, they will start using you."

The Captain suddenly grabbed the steering wheel, not threateningly or recklessly, but firmly, and said, "Ray, I've got the wheel and there are no other cars around. Keep steady pressure on the gas pedal and close your eyes."

I hesitated and he said, "Go on, it's all right. I'm going to keep my eyes open and I won't let us hit anything. Close your eyes."

I closed them and he said, "I want you to concentrate very carefully, Ray. Whatever you do, I do *not* want you to visualize an American flag. No-siree, do *not* see the red, white, and blue colors, or the stars and stripes, and whatever you do *please* don't imagine it fluttering on a flagpole in the breeze."

I began to giggle and opened my eyes. The Captain let go of the wheel and chuckled, "How did you do?"

"You know how I did. I saw exactly what you were describing."

He nodded. "Yeah, that's how the mind works. It can't deal with, 'Don't notice this,' or 'Don't experience that.' As soon as you tell it what not to experience, it has already experienced it. And your brain doesn't know the difference between signals coming in from your senses and signals you generated yourself from using your imagination, so it tells your body to experience it too, and your body does it. I could guide you through an image of eating a lemon, and if you were really listening to me your mouth would water like you just bit into a big, fat, juicy, Texas lemon."

I laughed. "Okay," I said, "but what does that have to do with control?"

"Well, most people attempt to control an undesirable situation by thinking about it," he answered, tapping his temple. "It is futile, of course, but it's what most people do."

"And you feel that it is better to *not* think?" I asked with one eyebrow raised.

"No, Ray, I feel that it is infinitely better to think about what you *do* want rather than what you *don't* want. Most people focus on the problem, so their brain never gets around to vibrating on the solution."

I considered that. "So, like the American flag example, if all I focus on is how much I don't want something or how much it stinks, I will keep drawing it to myself or creating it in my body?"

He nodded enthusiastically. "You got it, Ray. People do that all the time with health issues. Instead of just following the laws of the body and creating as much health as possible, which isn't complicated, they get all involved and identified with all manner of labels and complicated diagnoses for 'what's wrong.' They end up not giving any energy to feeding and expanding what's right within them because they focus everything they've got on 'what's wrong.' They do it with other issues too: money, success, relationships—but the popular favorite is health."

He finished his crackers and brushed the crumbs off his thighs. "Think about it like this: as we observed earlier, the mechanism of the mind turns around opposites. So it's like you have two flowers, one that you find beautiful and want to keep, and one that you feel is like an ugly weed and don't want. But you only have one watering can. Your attention is like watering the flower, so whichever flower you give the most attention to is the one you're going to get more of—literally. It will grow, and the other will wither. If you give all your attention to the ugly flower, be prepared to get more of it."

He rolled his window down and finished, "So, you can't control anything, really. You can guide your attention, and your attention will create your experience exactly in accordance with the ideas you identify with. If you focus on problems, you will create more problems. If you focus on simply living the life you want, with earnestness and enthusiasm, you will create more and more things that harmonize with that idea. And just as importantly, you can't get rid of anything you find undesirable in your life, but you can let it die of starvation by not giving it any attention. Eventually you will tire of identifying with illusory concepts altogether, and you will want to identify with your true reality, but we'll get to that later."

He turned on the radio and began to dial for a signal. "What I'm talking about is no secret, by the way; every wise person throughout the ages has said the same thing."

We drove for a while just listening to the radio. Eventually the Captain suggested we look for an all night diner, but nothing seemed to be open. I guess most of the diners and gas stations in sparsely populated areas closed down around sunset. We hadn't thought about eating as we went through Phoenix, and now we were in the middle of nowhere. The Captain said he supposed we could make it to Tucson, and he was just about to lean back and take a short nap when I saw a car stalled by the side of the road.

It was a beat up Ford Falcon, white, with the hood up and steam billowing out of the engine compartment. The Captain was squinting like crazy, so I knew something was up.

"Pull over, Ray," he said in a strange voice.

I did it, but I was starting to feel very uncomfortable about the whole thing.

Our car rolled to a stop and a man whose face I couldn't see leaned in the window on the Captain's side. His longish greasy black hair was tied back into a ponytail, and his clothes were dirty and sweat-stained. But it wasn't until he spoke that I knew why I had felt so uneasy.

"Good evening, gentlemen," he said in a voice that I had last heard whispering hoarsely into my ear.

"Hello, Carlo," the Captain said.

CHAPTER EIGHT
FREEDOM

D r. Thurman Fleet finished with the last patient of the morning, a woman who had come seeking help for anxiety and insomnia. To an onlooker the interaction would appear completely mundane, but there was infinitely more going on than the eye could see. The doctor *was* treating the patient physically by means of the hands-on adjustment he delivered, but that was only the most superficial layer of the treatment. He also gave frequent verbal suggestions designed to help her begin to mentally identify with the idea of being well instead of being pre-occupied with being sick. He knew that in order for any permanent healing to take place, the patient must begin to think, talk, and act healthy; otherwise she would soon re-create disease.

But that wasn't all. When he first set out to satisfy the compulsion to understand his illumination, Thurman had vividly remembered being able to feel emotions and receive vibratory impressions from other people while in that altered state of consciousness, and he had spent the last decade researching every detail he could remember about his experience and consciously recreating as much of it as he could. The initial illumination experience had been a deluge—an uncontrollable tidal wave that had threatened to drown him. In the ten years since, he had learned to connect with the same Source and work with the same elevated frequencies of energy, yet in a way that allowed him to control the flow and channel the energy into practical and constructive outlets.

His research and experimentation had led him to the conclusion that every human being possesses the potential to become aware of more than just the impressions delivered to the brain by the five outer senses and the thought patterns arising from the memories of such impressions. He had trained his perceptive abilities and had began to intuit unspoken and often subconscious mental and emotional disturbances that caused his patient's problems; sometimes he knew more about people's mental and emotional states than they knew about themselves.

Most importantly, he had learned to increase his own vibratory frequency to a level higher than his patients and to harmonize them with that higher vibration if they would allow it, thereby inducing the healing process.

He completed his last morning session, told the patient to come back in two days for another treatment, and retired to his private study to rest before the afternoon appointments began.

He was at his desk reading when Calvin stuck his head in after a brief knock on the partially open door. "Thurman, put down your newspaper and come check this one out." Without waiting for a response, he continued down the hall.

The doctor folded the paper and made his way to the consultation room where Calvin waited. "What is it, Cal?" "Can't one of the other doctors handle it?"

Calvin only smirked. "I think it would be better if you talked to this patient yourself." He handed Dr. Fleet the patient's chart. On his way out the door he said, "I'll send him right in."

It had been nine years and eight months since Thurman Fleet had received the challenge to test and document his ideas on healing. Since then he had cultivated the largest single medical practice of any kind in San Antonio, seeing hundreds

of patients a week and employing twelve doctors in addition
to himself and Dr. Woodman. He had patient testimonials
for everything from diabetes to chronic pain to cancer. He
couldn't imagine what this new patient might have going on
that he hadn't already seen.

He looked over the patient's chart while he waited for
him to enter the consultation room. It said the chief complaint
was indigestion, but provided no further detail. "Indigestion,"
he muttered to himself, "every fourth patient we see has
indigestion. What's so special about this case?"

A nurse entered with an uncomfortable-looking man
in his mid-fifties. He greeted Dr. Fleet with a nervous smile
and sat down, fidgeting with his hat in his lap.

"Well, sir, what can I help you with?" Dr. Fleet
asked.

"Um, well," the man started, then faltered.

"Sir," Dr. Fleet intervened, "I assure you that anything
you share with me will be confidential and handled completely
professionally."

The man nodded and continued to look embarrassed.
Finally he said, "Doctor, I will tell you what is going on, but
first you have to promise not to laugh."

"I promise."

"So you say, but I have been to four other doctors and
they all laughed at me."

"Well, I won't laugh. What seems to be the trouble?"

The man dropped his eyes. "Okay. I was driving out in
the country this past weekend, and I had the windows rolled
down, and there were grasshoppers flying out in the fields.
I opened my mouth to yawn and one of those grasshoppers
flew right in my mouth, and before I knew what I was doing
I had swallowed him whole."

Dr. Fleet nodded.

The man continued, "I didn't think much about it until
that night. Ever since I swallowed that grasshopper, the same

thing happens whenever I lie down to sleep: that little bugger tries to crawl up out of my stomach. I can feel him crawl up right to here," the man held his hand up to his Adam's apple, "and then he'll slip back down into my stomach. Pretty soon he'll get to crawling back up again, and back down he'll fall. It goes on all night long, until I can't get any sleep."

Dr. Fleet nodded again, "Yes sir, that must be quite an uncomfortable situation for you."

The man looked relieved. "Yes, doctor, it is." He hesitated. "So—you don't think I'm crazy, then?"

"Not at all." Dr. Fleet shook his head. "Sir, what did the other doctors you went to tell you about your situation?"

"They told me that it was all in my head, that there was no way that a grasshopper could survive in my stomach, so there was no way that he could be crawling up my esophagus."

Dr. Fleet nodded, "Yes, that is a common misconception, even among doctors."

The man looked surprised. "Really?"

"Absolutely. Let me tell you a true story." He leaned forward in his chair. "When I was a child we kids used to drink water with a wooden dipper from a rain-barrel. Bugs and other small things used to get in there but we didn't care; we'd drink it anyway. Anyway, there was a little girl who accidentally swallowed a young toad that had gotten in the water. No one thought much about it then, but eventually she began to have stomach pains, and finally she had to be operated on and have that toad removed from her stomach."

"Really?" the man asked doubtfully, as if he still wasn't entirely sure whether he was being made fun of again.

"As sure as I am sitting here right now," Dr. Fleet assured the man. "And here's the reason why: have you ever noticed that a dog will not eat a toad?"

The man thought for a moment and said, "Well, I never thought about it, but I guess you're right, they won't."

"You're darn right they won't, and with good reason. See, there's something about the skin of a toad and the exoskeleton of a grasshopper that prevents them from being subject to normal digestive enzymes. Whereas normal digestive juices would consume a piece of meat in a matter of hours, those animals can't be digested if swallowed whole, and most people, including most doctors, don't know that they are exceptions to the rule. If that grasshopper was still alive when you swallowed him, I have no doubt that he is doing exactly what you say he is doing."

"But what can we do to get it out? I'm not going to have to have surgery like that little girl, am I?"

"No sir." Dr. Fleet stood up. "We are going to normalize your digestive system so that it gets rid of that bug on its own." He walked over to a series of charts detailing each system of the human body. "See here, and here, and here, and here?" He pointed at the places in the spinal cord that gave rise to the nerves that innervated the entire digestive system.

"Yes, doctor."

"We are going to energize your digestive system so that it functions more vigorously by stimulating all these places in your spinal cord." He tapped the chart. "When we do that, your digestive system will increase the intensity of everything it does, including getting rid of what doesn't belong in it. Understand?"

The man nodded.

"It will probably take three or four sessions before it really gets cranked up, but when it does, you will vomit that grasshopper right out."

The man looked a little unsure, but he nodded and agreed just the same. "Well...all right doctor. When can we start?"

"We'll prep you for the treatment and get started right away."

They went through the session, and the man left

with instructions to return the following day for another treatment.

Thurman expected Calvin to follow up with him regarding their unusual patient, and he wasn't disappointed. He had scarcely been in back in his office for five minutes before there was a knock at the door and Calvin entered. "So you actually treated that man?"

Thurman nodded.

"Did he tell you what his indigestion was about, or did he just tell you that he had indigestion?"

"No, he told me all about the grasshopper."

Calvin looked thoroughly confused. "Thurman, you know just as well as I do that there is no way that any grasshopper could survive in that man's stomach, don't you? You know that it has already passed through the digestive tract by now."

"Yes, Calvin, I'm well aware of that."

Now Calvin was growing exasperated. "Well, then why in the blazes did you treat him? And what did you tell him?"

Thurman pushed back his chair and placed his hands, palm down, on the surface of the desk. "I treated him because he needed help. And I told him that his digestive system would get rid of the grasshopper."

"Well, why in the hell did you tell him that? You lied to that man!"

"I did no such thing," Thurman answered curtly. "You think I lied to him because we both know that he doesn't really have a physical, live grasshopper trying to crawl out of his stomach, don't you?"

Calvin nodded.

"Calvin, he's got something much worse than that going on. He has identified with the *idea* that there is a live grasshopper trying to get out of his stomach, and he has thought about it until it has become a fixed concept in his subconscious mind."

He stood up and pointed to a drawing he used to teach the other doctors in the clinic. It depicted a skinny, undersized stick figure with an enormous head, symbolic of the idea that what is going on inside the head is much more significant than what is going on in the body.

"Unless we diffuse that concept," he said as he pointed to the portion of the mind labeled *Subconscious*, "that man is going to suffer real physical symptoms even though there is no more physical grasshopper."

"Well why didn't you just explain to him that his body has already eliminated the bug?"

"Because four other doctors already tried that, Calvin. It didn't work. He is still identified with the concept. It obviously wasn't logical to him that the grasshopper was gone, so I used an idea that would be more logical to him to satisfy his concept."

"What do you mean it wasn't logical? Any doctor in the world would tell you the same thing!"

Thurman sighed. "And it would be logical to any doctor in the world, but it wasn't logical to our patient. It has to be logical *to him* in order to work."

Calvin was still visibly agitated. "Thurman, I know you're a fine doctor and you get great results with your healing. I see your patients every day in the clinic, and I have seen some pretty amazing healings here. But I just can't get behind this mind-body stuff. Why can't you just treat the patients and leave it at that?"

Thurman slowly walked around the desk and leaned against it right in front of Calvin. He said evenly, "Listen here, Calvin, I know that some of the things that I have talked to you about during our working relationship have been hard for you to swallow, but I need for you to listen to me now and listen good." He waited until Calvin met his eyes. "You were there when I experienced my, shall we say, alternate view of reality, were you not?"

Calvin nodded.

"Well, I have spent the past ten years researching my experience, and I am satisfied, based upon my personal experience, based upon my research, and based upon putting these ideas into practice and observing the results, that what any of us experience on the physical plane is only a reflection of what is going on in our mental, emotional, and spiritual lives. You may say that this patient's trouble is all in his head, and you'd be right so far as that goes."

He held up a finger to emphasize his point, "But the problem is that you don't take it far enough. Every patient we have ever had, every patient we have now, and every patient we ever *will* have, has the same trouble. I don't care if we call the specific manifestation cancer, back pain, depression, or rigor mortis of the bunghole. If there is a manifestation in the body, it is there because the person has identified with a destructive idea or emotion to the degree that the idea has manifested on the physical plane—*period!"*

He slammed his palm down on the desk behind him. "If we treat patients without acknowledging that and doing our best to work with *all* aspects of their being instead of only one of them, *then* we are lying, *then* we are denying reality, and *then* we are cheating our patients!"

Calvin sighed and nodded. He turned to leave and Thurman stopped him, "Cal," he said softly.

Calvin turned around with his eyebrows raised into a non-verbal question.

All the sternness was gone from Thurman's face, replaced by mischievous merriment. "Go out this afternoon and catch the biggest grasshopper you can find."

Three days later the patient returned for his final treatment. Thurman met him in the treatment room and asked him how it was going.

"Well doc, it's just like you said. I've been feeling more nauseated at times, which I understand is a normal reaction to the bug still being in my stomach, but I am so ready for you to get this thing out I don't know what to do! Every night it crawls up and slips back, up and back, up and back, damn near all night long. I've got to get some sleep!"

Dr. Fleet nodded. "No problem, Mr. Gardner. Today should do it, and you will be sleeping like a brick tonight. Now, you remember what is going to happen, don't you?"

The man nodded, "Yes, doc. We're going to go through a treatment just like we've been doing, but this time I am going to vomit after the treatment, and my body is going to eliminate that damned grasshopper once and for all."

"That's right. You'll probably vomit right after the treatment is finished, so I have had my nurse put a bucket on each side of the table; just aim for one of those if you need to, all right?"

"Yes sir, I'm ready."

Thurman adjusted the man's spine in the precise anatomical areas that corresponded with the organs of his digestive system, and the man regurgitated loudly and wetly into one of the buckets. Thurman handed him a towel to wipe off his face, and while the patient was using it he reached into his pocket and took out the grasshopper that Calvin had caught and threw it into the bucket along with the vomit.

When the man finished cleaning himself up Thurman showed him the grasshopper.

"Well, I'll be damned, doc, I told those other doctors that he was in there." He shook Thurman's hand repeatedly and gushed, "Thank you so much for your help and for listening to me when no other doctor would. I feel so much better already! Now I'll be able to get back to my old self again. Thanks doc!"

Thurman bade the man farewell, winked at Calvin and

motioned for him to follow him to his office.

He closed the door behind them and asked, "How many of those file boxes of testimonials do we have now?"

Calvin thought. "I'm not sure. Must be at least three or four hundred. They've taken over the back storage room completely."

Thurman nodded, "Good. I have finally finished a formal curriculum text for my first class, Calvin. It's time to re-visit old Dr. Drake."

Calvin chuckled. "Are you sure he's even going to remember you? You haven't talked to him since you graduated; that's been almost eight years, you know."

"He'll remember. He told me to research for ten years, which I have done, and to document the results, which he's about to get dumped on him."

"What do you mean?"

Thurman looked mischievous again. "Calvin, I want you to hire a dump truck and arrange to have all of those boxes moved from our storage room to the truck. At precisely ten o'clock tomorrow morning I want each and every one of those case studies dumped—not unloaded, mind you, dumped—on the lawn of the The Texas Institute of Chiropractic Sciences right in front of Dr. James R. Drake's private office window."

The office phone rang at 10:23 the following morning, and Calvin blatantly eavesdropped on the call. He couldn't hear much, mostly Dr. Drake delivering a screaming, largely unintelligible rant over the phone punctuated by Thurman's occasional short replies. Drake was shouting so loudly that Cal wondered if he might be sufficiently upset to have a stroke, but he snuck a furtive peak through the doorway and saw that Thurman was holding the phone receiver at arm's length while his former professor shouted. The absence of a skull to absorb the sound waves explained the impressive volume of Drake's voice.

After the storm subsided and Thurman hung up the phone, Calvin knocked on the partially open door and entered. Thurman sat calmly behind his desk, smiling and writing numbers on a yellow legal pad. He glanced up at Calvin and put down his slide rule.

"So, how'd it go with Drake?" Calvin asked, before he remembered that he shouldn't know that Drake had called yet. "I mean—I heard what I thought was his voice as I was passing by," he recovered, though he needn't have worried; Thurman couldn't have cared less.

Thurman's smile broadened, "So, you could hear the old man all the way out in the hall, eh?" Calvin nodded and smiled back. "Well," Thurman said, "he yelled at me for the case study prank, and for not acting professionally, and for just about anything else he could think of, and then he agreed that The Texas Institute of Chiropractic Sciences would sponsor my seminars to be taught to doctors all across the country."

Calvin's own smile bloomed across his face. "Hey, congratulations Thurman!" He reached across the desk to shake Thurman's hand. "What are you going to call the seminars?"

"Good question, Cal. I've given it a lot of thought. I'm going to call it *Concept-Therapy*."

Calvin gave no immediate reaction, so Thurman explained, "The word concept means, *a fixed idea*, and the word therapy means, *having healing qualities*. People get sick due to unhealthy ideas that they get attached to that end up getting fixed into their subconscious, and they heal by changing those concepts into healthy ones."

Calvin felt a little uneasy; he was genuinely happy for Thurman, but all this talk about concepts, the subconscious mind, and how people get sick because of ideas still made him uncomfortable. As with their conversation the day before, he deferred to Thurman on the subject, but he wasn't quite convinced himself.

Thurman seemed to sense his doubt and said, "Don't worry, Cal. I know this is a new idea for people, but when those doctors put it to the test they will see that it works."

When Calvin frowned, Thurman said, "What's the matter, Cal? You can tell me; whatever it is I won't be upset."

"Well, Thurman, I have watched you test these ideas for almost ten years, and I don't know that *I* believe you myself. I mean, I can't deny the results you get with your patients, but couldn't it just be the physical treatment you give them that makes them better? Is it really the most logical conclusion that somehow your thoughts, intentions, emotions—whatever you want to call it—are healing those people?"

Thurman thought for a moment and answered with a question, "Cal, what is your body made of?"

"Oh, I don't know, Thurman. Carbon, water—"

"Okay," Thurman interrupted, "so it's made of compounds and molecules, right?"

Calvin nodded.

"What are those things made of?"

Calvin scratched his head and said, "Atoms?"

Thurman nodded. "And what are those atoms made of?"

This time Calvin had no answer; he just held his hands out, palms up, and shrugged.

"Cal, everything is ultimately made of the same thing. Your arm and that desk are made of the same essential unknown substance, which science calls energy. Now, what is the difference between the two?"

Calvin raised his shoulders in another shrug.

"Vibration. The only difference between the energy that makes up your arm and the energy that makes up that desk is the differing resonant frequencies that the energy happens to be vibrating on at the moment, and vibration is manifested in patterns. Any pattern or combination or relationship of patterns can be understood as a language, like Morse code or music. Are you still with me?"

Calvin nodded slowly.

"The new physics demonstrated by Dr. Heisenberg a few years ago shows that any observer changes the observed. That energy responds to and changes its pattern of vibration according to the expectations of an observer. If this is true, and Dr. Heisenberg's principles have been tested several times so far, then why wouldn't a human observer be able to influence the patterns of vibration of his own or another human body? The latest ideas in science say the same thing I'm saying—what about it doesn't make sense to you?"

Calvin hesitated, then answered, "I guess because if all that were true, I could just imagine growing wings out of my back and flying to Dallas with them, and it would happen. I don't know about you, but I haven't had that kind of experience."

Thurman laughed. "Yes, I guess I see your point. But Cal, that's what I have discovered; that's what I want to teach these doctors. The metaphysical principles I am going to teach are true, *but you have to work with them in a certain way,* just like you have to follow certain protocols in designing an airplane to get it to fly."

He held out his arms to his side as though he were an airplane and asked, "What do you think would happen if I went out and collected a whole bunch of feathers, glued them to my arms, went up on the roof and jumped off?"

Calvin chuckled at the thought. "You'd fall."

"Sure I would. And why?"

"Because men weren't designed to fly like birds."

"Right! Another way to say it is that I would fall because I would be violating the laws of physics and aerodynamics, yes?"

Calvin nodded.

"So we could say that the particular aspect of the idea of human flight that I just described would be fantastic because it would violate law and reason, yes?"

Another nod.

"But human flight *is* possible," said Thurman. "There is an aspect of the idea of humans flying that is a *fact*. Human beings fly all over the world. *But we had to discover the laws involved and learn how to work in harmony with them—reasonably and realistically.* I promise you that it is the same with the metaphysical principles I am going to teach. The Wright Brothers proved that human flight was possible, and I am going to help prove these ideas."

He stood up and paced as he talked. "But before the Wright Brothers proved it was possible, they were ridiculed and their ideas were laughed at. They became aware of the idea, but they still had to learn how to work with the principles before their idea became a reality. They had to fail before they could succeed, and so humans must fail before they may succeed at anything new. Our understanding is limited right now, but it will grow, and our ability to use intention and vibration to create our images will increase, just like our understanding of aerodynamics was very limited in the beginning."

Calvin nodded. It was hard to resist Thurman when he was oiled up; he even found himself a little excited.

"So what are you figuring?"

"Just doing some planning about logistics, expenses, what to charge, things like that."

"Thurman," Calvin cocked his head to one side as the question occurred to him, "*when* are you going to do this?"

"Right away. I figure we could schedule the first class for—"

Calvin raised his hands to interrupt. "No, I mean, when are you going to have time for this? This clinic is the busiest clinic in San Antonio, and you are the head doctor.

How will you do both? We almost fell apart when you left for California, you know."

The year before Thurman had spent an eight-month sabbatical in California researching hypnosis. He had simply packed up his family and moved them into a rented house in Los Angeles while he consulted with experts in the field. Calvin had nearly gone crazy trying to hold the clinic together without him.

Thurman smiled and replied, "Ah, Calvin, I guess I might as well tell you. Keep it between me and you, though, all right? I haven't talked to Woodie yet."

Calvin nodded in agreement.

"I have plans for this idea that go well beyond teaching a few classes. I have plans for an entire teaching center, a metaphysical university."

He spread his hands to convey expansiveness. "You see, Cal, these principles I am going to teach are the result of what I experienced in that bedroom ten years ago. During that time I experienced them viscerally, intuitively, but for the most part, unconsciously. It has taken me ten years to take those principles from my subconscious and put them into my conscious mind so that I can actually convey them to other people. I have a particular interest in how they apply to healing, but their usefulness extends way beyond that application. I foresee a time in which people of all different professions and backgrounds will want to learn what we are going to offer, and they will need a school, a campus to go to in order to get the needed instruction. I want to begin to build that place."

Calvin was shocked. "What will you do about the clinic?"

Thurman shrugged. "I'll ask Dr. Woodman to take it over."

Calvin understood his sister's concerns regarding her husband. It seemed as though Thurman was incapable of sticking with something and allowing real stability: here he was again, about to give up the lucrative healing practice that he had spent an entire decade building. Calvin congratulated him again and left the office, wondering what would become of this new venture.

And Calvin was indeed correct in his assessment. Thurman was again being urged by that mysterious compulsion that he could no more ignore than he could ignore the impulse to breathe. It was driving him again, but this time he knew what he needed to do. His destination was no longer hidden, and he was ready to begin a long journey that would end in fulfilling the responsibility of passing on the principles gleaned from his experience and its significance.

The revelations he had intuited during his illumination had bubbled up from the depths of his subconscious mind and gradually found a place of awareness in his conscious mind, and an inherent set of instructions seemed to accompany them. He knew that he was to develop a series of classes designed to evolve consciousness. They would be designed to take people living in normal human awareness and gradually, safely, and gently lead them into moving their consciousness into the next phase: cosmic consciousness. He would start a national organization dedicated to bringing people together around this goal of elevating consciousness, and he would find a physical home for this organization.

He understood that this was to be his task, and he sat at his desk continuing to solve the logistics necessary to manifest the idea, recording the details on his yellow legal pad.

∞

Carlo leaned with both forearms on the Captain's window.

"Haven't we met somewhere before?" He waved his

gun in the window in a figure-eight pattern, as if he wanted us to admire it. "Damn, now whattaya figure the chances are of us running into each other like this?"

The Captain kept his voice steady. "Listen, son, you're in enough trouble already; do you really want to give the police something else to charge you with?"

"Shut up, old man!" Carlo spat viciously on the ground. "What are they going to charge me with? I'm already in for felony murder; that right there gets me the damn 'lectric chair." He cocked his gun and aimed it at the Captain's forehead. "So there is *nothing* they can threaten me with that they aren't already going to do to me anyway. I got nothing to lose and my life to gain."

"Wait a minute." My voice shook a lot more than I wanted it to. "Calm down, man. You haven't murdered anyone. That kid died in an accident."

Carlo un-cocked the gun, dropped it from the Captain's face, and feigned impressed surprise. "Wow, kid, you must be some kind of lawyer, huh?" He shook the Captain by the shoulder. "Tell him how it works, old man."

The Captain answered while looking at Carlo, "Ray, if someone dies during the commission of a felony, the perpetrator is held responsible for the death, even if it is an accident. If the death is in any way a result of the crime, the perpetrator is charged with felony murder, which carries the same penalty as first degree murder in Texas."

"That's right, old man, and you knew that all along. I had a cellmate in for felony murder once, and I know how it works." He gave the Captain a particularly violent shove and growled, "So no more trying to reason with me. I ain't no reasonable man."

Carlo opened the passenger door and waved for the Captain to step out. He told me to throw him the keys, which I did, and he waved me out too.

He looked like he was trying to decide what to do. He

just stood there, pondering the situation, as we leaned against the trunk of the Captain's car.

"Why not just continue with your getaway?" the Captain suggested. "After all, you still have our car."

Carlo thought about it. "Nope. I'm going to Mexico, and I ain't coming back. I need all the money I can get, and you guys still have those big, fat gambling checks."

"Take the checks and leave us be," the Captain answered. "We'll sign them over to you."

Carlo peered at him with his dark, stupid-looking eyes. "Yeah, you'd like that wouldn't you old man? I leave you two here and the first car that comes by picks you up. The first phone you come to, you call the state cops, and they call every damn bank between here and Mexico—there would be plenty of time, too—the banks won't open for almost ten hours. I'd never be able to cash them checks, and you know it."

He seemed to come to a conclusion. He took the keys, opened the trunk, pointed the gun at me and said, "All right kid, get in."

My heart skipped a beat. The Captain started to say something, but Carlo cut him off. "Old man, I told you to *shut up!* Kid, get in that trunk, *NOW!*"

The Captain nodded and said, "It'll be all right Ray. You'll be able to breathe."

I climbed into the trunk slowly. "Okay now," Carlo said, " here's what's going to happen. We're probably an hour or two from Tucson, so we're going to hole up there for the night while we wait for the banks to open up in the morning. Kid, you gotta ride in the trunk so's I won't be outnumbered in the car. Don't freak out, you hear? And stay quiet. It's only going to be for a little while, and if you was to draw undue attention to yourself I might get nervous with this gun here, you dig?"

I got all the way in the trunk while he backed away from it and retrieved a small bag out of his own car, all the while keeping the gun trained on the Captain.

"I'll tie you two up for the night once we get to a motel." He waved the gun in a wide arc at us. "And in the morning, we're all going to walk in the first bank in Tucson that looks like they can handle the deal and we're gonna cash them checks." He licked his lips like a starving man contemplating a steak. "Once I have the money I'll tie you guys up again back at the hotel, and then I am off to Mexico with the cash."

He raised his eyebrows. "Everybody got it? Now here's the important part: I'm always gonna be holding this gun on one of you. If either of you so much as blinks the wrong way, I'll dust both of you. Don't test me or you'll end up leaking. Do exactly what I say, when I say, and everybody'll have a happy ending. Understand?"

We nodded and he waved for the Captain to close the trunk. I was engulfed in a musty, muffled darkness—the inside of the trunk smelled like rubber and gasoline. I could hear Carlo instructing the Captain to drive, but once he started the engine and pulled out on the road I couldn't clearly make out much of what they were saying.

I did hear the Captain say, "You realize they aren't going to cash those whole checks, right? Banks don't just hand people twenty thousand dollars in cash and let them walk out the door with it."

Carlo gave some irritated-sounding reply that I couldn't make out, and then there was no more conversation, just the sound of the V-8 engine pulling and the road passing underneath the car.

I had nothing to do and no distractions, and after a while my mind began to wander. I began to think about what Carlo had said, about how he had promised to leave us at the motel once he had the money. It sounded plausible enough, and I can't really explain it, but I knew without a doubt that he was lying. I could *feel* that he didn't want any witnesses in case he was caught.

I know it might sound crazy, but the stress of the night's events, the rhythmic vibration of the car, and the fact that I could only lie down in the dark without being able to see or hear anything affected me like a drug. I actually dozed off and began to dream.

In the dream I was nine years old again, but this time I found myself looking up at a clear blue sky instead of the white ceiling of a church. I was standing at home plate waiting for the pitcher to wind up and deliver the ball, and I was literally scared stiff.

I knew right away where I was. During baseball practice as a kid, I was relaxed and had no problem hitting and catching the ball. There was no pressure to perform on the practice field. But games were a whole different story. The pitch would come in, and I wouldn't be able to decide if it was going to be a good pitch to swing at or not. I was terrified of making a mistake, so my muscles would tense so badly that I couldn't move, let alone swing at the ball.

My desire to please my father had been terrible. He coached my little league team, and I felt like everything I did had to be perfect. Of course the more I worried about it the less perfect it turned out. Even at nine years old I realized that I was sabotaging myself, but I couldn't figure out how to break the cycle.

The pitcher in my dream had his hat pulled down so low that I couldn't see his face. He was a southpaw, and he began an elaborate wind-up that looked slightly awkward and strangely exotic at the same time, like left-handed deliveries often did. Just as he was about to release the ball, my bat shrunk to the size of a small stick. I was clutching it so hard my knuckles were squeezed white and bloodless. The pitcher threw the ball, and it rocketed past me so fast I couldn't even see it—I just heard it explode into the catcher's mitt with a sound like a cherry-bomb. *"Strike one!"* the umpire yelled.

I stepped out of the batter's box and looked over to the dugout. My father smirked at me, hanging drunkenly onto the chain link fence and slurring, *"Come on, RRRaay, t-tee offf on one!"*

My heart pounded in my chest, but I got back in the batter's box again and faced the pitcher, who was no longer nine years old. He loomed over the pitcher's mound, over six feet tall. He wound up, and just as he was about to release the ball, I caught a glimpse of his face and gasped—it was Carlo's face.

"Teeee off on one, RRRaaay," my father slurred again from the dugout.

The ball buzzed past me again as a faint blur. It popped the catcher's mitt like a sharp taunt without my bat ever leaving my shoulders, and the umpire screamed, *"Strike two!"*

I backed out of the box again and looked away from my father into the stands. They were completely empty, but I could hear voices shouting out advice from all directions:

"Choke up on the bat!"

"Watch for a curveball!"

"Bunt and try to leg it out!"

And my father again from the dugout, *"T-teeee offff, RRRaayy!"*

I caught a glimpse of the umpire and was startled to recognize the Captain's face behind the black mask. He looked at me, lifted up his umpire's mask, and said, "Come on, batter, let's play ball."

I got in the box with my heart pounding again, and I could *feel* the umpire-Captain calming me down. It was as though I could hear his voice inside my head thinking, "Calm down, Ray. Fear is not going to help you right now. The answer isn't in the stands, and it's not with your father, either."

The Carlo-pitcher viciously scraped the dirt along the

rubber and glared at me from the mound. I looked down at my bat. It was still too skinny to be an effective baseball bat, and it had also now transformed into an odd shape, almost like a boomerang with one side much longer than the other. The bat's transformation seemed significant, but I had no time to ponder it; Carlo was beginning his wind-up.

The umpire-Captain thought, "Ray, you have everything you need. Let go of all your fears, doubts, attachments, and desires, and you will find yourself free. You won't have to worry about anything, because you won't be the one doing anything—you will be free to act as Life inclines you. Life will act through you. Let it go, and be free."

"Let it go."

"Let it all go."

I closed my eyes and focused on letting go of everything I had been holding on to, and I felt the tension in my muscles flow out like water running down a drain. I no longer cared about pleasing anyone. I no longer feared striking out, or making a mistake and doing the wrong thing. The outcome no longer mattered. I was playing the role of the batter, and I decided that hit or miss, I was going to play my part to the best of my ability. If Life had decreed that my part was to strike out, I would do it with all my might.

The Carlo-pitcher heaved the ball toward the plate. Though it was still moving like a blur of white lightning, I trusted my inclinations, stepped forward, and swung as hard as I could, bringing the bat around in a smooth, quick arc. The impact of the bat on the ball vibrated solidly through my hands and I looked up to see the ball moving up and out as if it had been shot from a cannon. I watched in wonder as it cleared the left field fence by fifty feet.

As I trotted around the bases I looked toward home plate where the umpire-Captain was watching me and nodding, and I felt him reverberating inside my head again saying, "That's good, Ray. When it's time to act, don't hesitate, don't doubt.

Just follow your inclinations and *act*."

"*Act—*"

"*Act—*"

And then I woke up inside the trunk. The gravity of my situation fell back down on me like an avalanche. I was still trapped inside the Captain's Oldsmobile, kidnapped by a robber who probably intended to kill us after stealing our money. A flash flood of fear rushed back into my chest and through my veins.

I closed my eyes again and tried to calm down, struggling to re-connect with the feelings of euphoria and peace that the dream brought. I thought about how it felt to hit that ball, to trust that it was going to work out okay, even though I had struck out so many times before, even though I was a nine-year-old boy facing a full grown man, and even though my bat was just a silly little stick shaped like a strange boomerang.

My bat.

My mind struggled to comprehend the significance of the bat like a dog with an itch it can't reach. I knew there was something important about it, but I couldn't figure out what it was. The shape. Something about the shape. I took a deep breath. My bat in the dream wasn't a boomerang. I felt another rush of adrenaline. It was shaped like a tire iron.

I scrabbled along both sides of the trunk, my fingers searching for the metal shaft, in case it was in one of those storage depressions that they build into trunks, but no luck. Next, I rolled my body back as far into the trunk as possible so that I could lift up the carpet and check it out. I was just about to give up when I felt the cold, hard texture under my fingers. It was wedged under one corner of the spare, so it took me a few minutes to maneuver it out, but I finally got it. I tucked the straight end into the inside of my left sock and covered up the other end with my bell-bottoms.

By that time I was sweating. The stale air in the trunk

didn't help. I tried to dry my hands off on my clothes and control my breathing. I had no idea how long I had been asleep or how close we might be to Tucson, but I wasn't in suspense long; after a few more miles the car slowed, turned onto a crunchy surface that I assumed was gravel, drove a hundred yards or so, and stopped.

The Captain killed the engine and I heard Carlo telling him to get out of the car and to let me out. Someone keyed the lock, the lid of the trunk opened, and I could see a clear, dark sky with millions of stars shining overhead. My lungs sucked in the night air greedily. I was plenty scared about what might happen next, but for a brief moment I was happy just to feel some fresh air.

Carlo's voice came from out of my line of sight to the left. "Kid, come on out."

I climbed up and sort of stumbled out of the trunk. I felt stiff from being in such a cramped space for so long. We were on a dark dirt road located on top of a mesa that overlooked Tucson. The Captain stood to my right, and I joined him in facing Carlo.

"All right," Carlo said, "we're now maybe fifteen minutes from Tucson. I can't just pull the kid outta the trunk in the middle of a parking lot, so congratulations kid, you get to ride the rest of the way in the car."

"*But,*" he brandished his gun again, as if he was afraid we might have forgotten about it, "I want to remind both of you that if you get any funny ideas you'll find yourself leaking out of a very large and ugly hole. Kid, you ride in the front. Old man, you drive, and know that I'll have both of you covered from the back seat."

Carlo leaned forward with his forearms on the back of the front seat, gun barrel pointing at me. We drove towards the city lights. Carlo told us to be on the lookout for a motel with a vacancy, but before we spotted one I recognized the lights of an all night diner in the distance and my stomach really began to rumble. We hadn't eaten since before we went gambling the afternoon before.

"Excuse me, sir," even as the words came out of my mouth I wondered why I was being so polite to someone who was probably planning to shoot me, "is there any way we could stop and get something to eat? I really need to use the bathroom, too."

Carlo looked like he was going to refuse, but just as he was about to speak, the Captain said, "Mister, it's a good idea. I am slightly diabetic, and if I go too long without eating I risk passing out. Wouldn't be good for that to happen as we are checking into a motel, or worse, when we get to the bank."

Carlo looked suspicious and started to speak, but the Captain interrupted again and said, "Something like that could blow the whole deal. If an old man passes out in public it's going to draw an ambulance for sure and maybe the police, too. And wherever it is we end up staying tonight, I doubt they're going to have room service."

Carlo said nothing; he just looked like he was struggling to comprehend whether the Captain was making a valid point or whether he was trying to fool him somehow.

"Listen," continued the Captain, "I'm telling you the truth. I know that the smoother this thing goes, the better chance my friend and I have of walking away safely."

Finally Carlo answered, "All right, old man, but I'm warning you: we go in together, we go to the bathroom together, we eat together, and we leave together. If either one of you tries to run, to warn someone, or just so much as twitches, I'll blow a hole in you both."

By this time we had already passed the restaurant, so the Captain swung us back around and we backtracked to Ron's Roadside Diner. There were only two other cars in the parking lot, and we could see three customers through the big front window.

When we got out, Carlo positioned himself behind us. I was scared that he would see the tire iron; even covered with wide bellbottoms I was sure it was visible, but it was dark and he didn't notice. He had his left hand in his jeans pocket gripping the snubnose, and he reminded us as we approached the door, "Gentlemen, my hand is on the trigger right here in my pocket. Let's all be on our best behavior."

We sat down and a waitress came right over. The big clock on the wall over the pickup window said it was fifteen minutes past four. We'd been on the road for longer than I thought. We all ordered breakfast, and when the waitress left Carlo said, "Okay, let's all go to the bathroom."

Carlo stood guard while the Captain and I used the urinal and then he had us lock ourselves in the stall while he went himself. We returned to the table just as the waitress brought our food.

Carlo sat on one side of the booth and the Captain and I on the other. She served our plates and poured coffee, and she was just about to return to the kitchen when the Captain began to strike up a conversation with her.

"Excuse me, miss, but do you know if there is a motel near here?" He smiled. "We're on our way back to Texas, and we need to find a place to get some rest."

The waitress was a small blonde probably in her late twenties. She answered right away, "Yes, sir, there is a motel about five miles down this highway toward town, but I don't know if you really want to stay there."

Carlo's jaw tightened. He frowned, but the Captain ignored him and went right on chatting up the waitress, grinning like a mule eating briars. "Oh really? Why not?"

She wrinkled her nose. "Well, it looks old and run down. I've never been inside it, but I drive past it every night on the way to work and it just looks trashy."

Carlo leaned a bit to his right so that he partially

inserted himself between the waitress and the Captain and glared at him with a molten anger that I was sure would melt the sugar he was pouring on and shut him up, but it didn't.

"Well, thank you so much for the tip," the Captain gushed.

She smiled and turned to leave, but the Captain engaged her again. "Miss, do you work here every night, or do you work some days, too?" He sipped his coffee and kept his eyes on her, still ignoring Carlo.

Carlo's hand disappeared under the table toward his gun. The menthol echo of adrenaline reverberated through my body, and I began to feel tingly and distant.

Just then the Captain delivered a sharp kick to my shin that shot a fresh wave of liquid fear coursing through my veins. This was it, and the Captain was calling on me to participate in whatever was coming next.

I wanted anything but that. If I could have frozen that moment in time and contemplated the choice of either acting in that moment or just letting Carlo kill me without having to act, I swear I don't know which I would have preferred.

Carlo slowly began to raise his arm from under the table. I was stiff with fear, but just as his hand cleared the table with the gun my mind *did* freeze the event, at least in my own consciousness. All of a sudden I was back in the dream I had in the trunk. I felt myself letting go of the fear and I saw myself hitting the ball again, all in a split second of actual time.

While my mind overrode my current physical circumstances and instead replayed my dream, my body had already begun to act in the moment. I reached down and pulled out the tire iron from my sock. Carlo was so focused on the Captain that he never saw me.

As he raised the gun, the Captain, still grinning merrily, doused Carlo's face with his hot coffee with a quick flick of the wrist.

The big man let out a guttural moan of rage and pain. He clutched the gun in his left hand and buried his face in the crook of his right elbow. The waitress screamed, dropped her tray, and fled.

Without any conscious thought I stood up and swung the tire iron as hard as I could, feeling the bones in Carlo's left wrist shatter. The gun clattered to the floor and I kicked it out into the aisle.

Carlo's moan became a sharp scream; he let go of his face, which was now splotched red from the coffee, cradled his left wrist with his right arm, and rocked back and forth on the bench in pain.

The Captain picked up the gun and held it on Carlo. *"Miss, please call the police,"* he yelled, eyes on Carlo.

"Don't worry, mister," the cook shouted from the back, *"we're dialing right now."*

And we stood there, gun on Carlo, until the state police showed up. For the second time in eight hours we answered what seemed like an endless stream of police questions. By the time we got to the trashy motel, I was so tired and stressed I felt like nothing was real, like I was floating.

I called Mom to check in, just like I had when we first got to Las Vegas and again right before we left, and I couldn't tell her about any of this stuff. Pretending everything was normal over the phone just increased the surreal feeling.

I hung up and looked over at the Captain sacked out on his side of the room. Wizened-crazy-old-guru-superman or not, he was already asleep. I lay down on the bed fully clothed; my exhaustion immediately drew a comforting blanket of darkness over me, and I knew no more.

CHAPTER NINE
DESIRE

A man stood on-stage in a large conference room lustily singing the Star Spangled Banner. Another man crawled around on the floor, barking like a dog. Another sat in a wooden chair, baiting an imaginary hook and fishing for imaginary fish in an imaginary pond. A fourth greedily sniffed an ammonia-doused handkerchief as though it were Parisian perfume.

An audience of about sixty doctors watched the on-stage participants, and Thurman Fleet stood at the back of the conference room watching the doctors' expressions, which ranged from looks of amusement to fear to consternation.

Thurman was used to the range of reactions. He had spent the first six years of his Concept-Therapy campaign travelling and teaching classes wherever he could find an interested audience. He had built up a sizeable following of doctors who recognized the value in his instruction, and who endeavored to study the principles they had been taught. From those dedicated students he had trained several more teachers to mirror his own instruction. This particular seminar's co-instructors, Dr. Conrad Schenk and Reverend E.L. Crump, were two of the best instructors he had trained so far.

Almost ten years ago he had bought over three hundred acres of land in Boerne, Texas, and established a teaching and healing center to serve as the permanent home for the

Concept-Therapy Institute. He had named the place the Aum-Sat-Tat ranch, a name he had taken from the Bhagavad Gita. Now students travelled to the ranch to hear him teach.

One man shook his head in disgust, rose from his seat, and stormed toward the conference room exit. As he passed by, Thurman caught his eye and asked, "What's the problem, doctor?"

The man stopped, drew himself up to his full height, thrust out his chest and raised his chin up in the air. "I should say the problem is obvious! Is this a healing conference or a carnie side-show?" Face scarlet, he pointed his finger at the seminar leader. "Your advertisement said that if we weren't fully satisfied we could get our money back. Well, I want my money back *now!*"

Unabashed, Thurman agreed to refund the price of the seminar immediately. "First," he added, "I would like to ask you a few questions—would that be all right?"

The man seemed to be caught off guard a bit by Thurman's complete lack of resistance in agreeing to his refund request. "Well—I guess so," he muttered, but he sounded suspicious.

"Doctor, other than these hypnotic demonstrations, how did you like the seminar so far?"

The man stroked his chin. He looked uncomfortable. "I thought it was fine, doctor. Your explanation of healing is the best I've ever heard."

He paused, and quickly added, "But this hypnosis thing is going too far. It's not right, and it's not natural, and above all, it's not *dignified.*"

"Yes, I see," Thurman nodded. "Doctor, are you sincerely interested in helping your patients to the best of your ability?"

"I should say so!" The man puffed his chest out even more.

Thurman nodded again. "Yes, I thought so. You seem

very sincere."

Thurman paused and deftly moved around so that he stood shoulder to shoulder with the man instead of opposing him. "Well, doctor, I have no problem walking right over to that registration table and finding your tuition check and tearing it up right now; if you don't want to be here I don't want you here. However, I want to ask you to think about one thing first."

"What's that?"

"The vast majority of your patients are people who have identified with ideas—just ideas—until those ideas have begun to manifest problems in their bodies. We know for a fact that mental and emotional distress causes by far the greatest portion of illness in the developed world, yes?"

The doctor nodded.

"Well, your patients are just like those people on that stage right now. They may be locked into a destructive marriage, or they may hate their job, or they may have some other circumstance in their life that makes them feel trapped, despondent, or hopeless. Someone may have given them the idea that they are sick. Those negative emotional states or ideas of disease get repeated until they become lodged in the subconscious mind, and then they manifest in the patients' bodies as illnesses or they attract the necessary physical circumstances to produce accidents or other misfortunes. Are you with me so far?"

The doctor nodded again.

"Well, here's the thing: we know how this process works. We are demonstrating it for you on stage for instructional purposes. Yes, it's through the use of some silly demonstrations, but we have to use some means of conveying the idea to you doctors. If you don't understand what is going on when patients come to your office, how will you be able to address them on any level but the most superficial?"

The doctor still didn't look convinced. Thurman said,

"Doctor, if you will permit me to make one more point, I will go immediately to retrieve your check and return it to you if that is still what you desire. Is it a deal?"

He hesitated slightly. "Yes."

"Doctor, you look pretty up to date to me. And after all, it's 1959. Do you perform surgery in your practice?"

The man's face reddened again. "I should say not! Why would I do that?"

"Well, did you participate in dissection lab when you were in chiropractic school?"

He nodded. "Of course; you know that we all had to dissect cadavers in order to graduate—you had to as well."

"Yes," Thurman agreed, "I did. Now, all I am asking you to do is participate in an exercise designed to instruct, just like cadaver lab. Dissection didn't mean that you were preparing to do surgery, and participating in these exercises doesn't mean that you should plan on performing hypnosis in your office. But you will gain a much better understanding of how people get sick and how you can better help them get well if you learn what we are teaching by these demonstrations."

Thurman stretched out his hand and spread it in an arc to indicate the masses. His eyes were focused beyond the room, as though he were seeing a vast ocean of humanity, and he said, "If you understand what we are teaching here, your healing efforts will be multiplied a thousand fold. You will be the healer of the future—the doctor who understands how to work with a patient's body, mind, and soul."

Thurman watched the doctor return to his seat. The teacher knew his student didn't really comprehend the lesson he had just been given, but as long as he *felt* that it was all right, the ideas would take hold in his subconscious mind.

Thurman went to the front stage and concluded the demonstration by releasing the participants from their assigned roles and bringing them all back to their normal waking consciousness. Then he addressed the seminar audience.

"Gentlemen and ladies, what you have just witnessed is a microcosm of human life. Each of you will have a chance to participate in at least some of the activities we will be engaging in over the course of this seminar, and I encourage you to make use of those opportunities. Let's start with a question and answer session about the hypnosis demonstration you have just witnessed."

A woman in the front row raised her hand and said, "I know that you explained it before, but would you please tell us again what the significance is of hypnosis in healing?"

"Yes ma'am." He smiled. "Before I do that, let me ask you, do you remember the first part of the class when we talked about energy, and vibration, and how thoughts and ideas are actual vibrations of energy?"

The woman nodded. "Yes."

"Good. As you will recall, the physical plane, which is obviously the plane that our physical body occupies, is the crudest plane of which we are aware, and it is always reactive—that is to say, it doesn't *cause* anything in and of itself; it is the *result* of higher vibratory causes. Remember that?"

Another nod.

"Okay, what that means is that if someone gets sick, it is not a random occurrence. If someone attracts an accident, it is not a random occurrence. There is no such thing as a random occurrence. In fact, everything, everyone, and every event is related through the law of vibration. We're just not usually aware of that fact."

He referred to a chart depicting the conscious and subconscious mind. It featured an oversized circle head on a stick body with a line dividing the upper and lower halves of the circle.

Thurman pointed at the top half of the circle and said, "You will all remember that this represents our conscious mind. This is the portion of our awareness that we think drives

- 231 -

our decisions and creates our lives, but it doesn't."

He pointed to the bottom half of the circle, "This portion of what we call the mind is the subconscious, meaning that it represents the mental processes we are not generally aware of, and believe it or not, this portion of the mind has the greatest impact not only on your decisions and your life, but your body as well."

He moved forward toward the front of the stage to address the woman who had asked the question. "We are using these demonstrations because in hypnosis the hypnotist bypasses the conscious mind of the subject; the ideas he or she suggests go straight to the subject's subconscious. The phenomena that you see are the effects of concepts on that portion of the mind.

"And the ultimate significance," he waved his hand at the stage where moments before his hypnotized subjects had cavorted, "is that what we call hypnosis is not a special state of consciousness at all. We are all hypnotized to certain ideas, sometimes individually, sometimes collectively. The ideas we are hypnotized to, or we might say, *identified with,* end up defining our experience of reality. They end up producing phenomena in the body, inducing emotional states, and creating the perceptions of our entire life experiences. People get sick when they identify with certain ideas, and breaking their concentration on those ideas and getting them to concentrate on the opposite ideas brings healing."

A man in the fourth row held up his hand and asked, "Can you elaborate on the subconscious having the greatest impact on the body?"

"Certainly," Thurman nodded. "Would you mind participating in a demonstration to illustrate the principle?"

"Fine with me."

"All right then, come on up here to the stage."

Thurman continued to speak as the man made his way forward. "When you think about it, it is really self-evident that your subconscious is primarily in charge of the body. As an example, did you eat lunch today?"

The man nodded as he climbed the stage steps.

"Well, then," Thurman addressed the audience and spread his hands, "could you tell us the exact chemicals in the exact amounts you will use to digest that meal?"

By this time the man was standing on stage beside Thurman. He looked quizzical. "The *exact* amounts?"

"Of course. We don't want you to get indigestion, now, do we?" The audience snickered.

The man thought and said, "No one can answer that question. The amounts of enzymes and chemicals needed to digest a certain amount of food might be different each time you eat depending on a host of factors."

"*No one* can solve that puzzle?" Thurman asked in a tone of feigned surprise.

The man shook his head.

"Well then how do we digest our food if no one knows how to do it?" Silence from the audience. The participant shrugged.

Thurman laughed. "The fact that we haven't all starved to death or succumbed to fatal indigestion means that obviously we *do* know, we just don't *know* that we know."

He pointed to his chart again. "That knowledge or information is down *here* in the subconscious, not up here in the conscious. And when you think about it, almost all of your biological processes are the same way. Your conscious mind has no idea how many beats per minute your heart needs to beat, or how much thyroxin you need at any given time, or how to digest your food. But you *do* know those things, you just aren't aware of them."

He turned to the audience member. "Now, sir, are you ready to experience this principle?"

The man nodded enthusiastically.

"Are you willing to feel a little uncomfortable in order

to have the experience? I promise I won't leave you that way."

Another nod, though not quite as enthusiastic.

"I want you to sit right here in this chair and just listen to me." The man did as instructed, and Thurman retrieved a small wastebasket from under the podium and placed it next to where he was sitting.

"Now, since we were just talking about digestion let's use that as our example. Is your digestion working pretty well?"

"Yes."

"No nausea or vomiting?"

"No, no problems."

"Okay, just listen to my voice. I want you to imagine that when you got up this morning you ate some raw oysters and pickles, and a little later on you went past the hotel restaurant, and even though you were full of oysters you decided to go in and eat again. They were serving fried pork chops, and you had two very large and greasy ones. Then you went outside to walk those pork chops off, and passed a hot dog vendor who served you a Coney Island with the greasiest chili you had ever eaten."

The man squirmed in his seat. Apparently oblivious to the audience, he held his stomach with his hands and affected a disgusted expression.

Thurman went on, "And then you came in here and I gave you a glass of milk, and the glass hadn't been cleaned well and there were little chunks of lard in it. And then when I brought you up here on stage I made you drink two big spoonfuls of castor oil. Now, you are feeling quite nauseous, aren't you?"

"Y-yes," the man gagged.

"Well, go ahead and vomit, you'll feel better."

The man regurgitated for several seconds into the wastebasket and Thurman finally said, "I am going to count to three and when I do, you will no longer feel nauseated. You will in fact feel refreshed and very comfortable. One—two—three."

Instantly, the man stopped vomiting and sat up with a look of wonderment on his face. After giving him a few seconds to compose himself, Thurman asked him to describe his experience to the audience.

He addressed the doctors in attendance, "I could hear Dr. Fleet talking to me, but it wasn't like I was consciously trying to carry out his orders. My body just automatically did what he was describing, and the very instant he counted to three the sensations disappeared."

The man started back to his seat and another man from the audience yelled out, "Now wait a minute. How do we know that wasn't just a put-on? All you did was talk about a relatively unpalatable combination of food and the man started to feel sick. What's so amazing about that?"

Thurman invited the skeptic up to see for himself. He took him through a similar demonstration, giving him the idea that he had gas and wouldn't be able to stop belching until he had taken exactly three sips from a certain glass of water. The exercise went exactly as described, and that man became a believer. Some in the audience were still skeptical, however.

"So you're telling us that these principles work all the time, no matter who the person is?" a man in the front row asked.

"Yes, if the subject has placed faith in the operator and they are en rapport," Thurman replied. "They have to agree to work together."

The previous skeptic spoke up. "But I didn't agree. I didn't even believe it was true, and yet everything you said happened. Why did I not have to agree for it to work?"

Thurman pointed at his chart again. "This great reservoir we call the subconscious mind contains all kinds of concepts, ideas, and knowledge. It contains the biological information we discussed earlier that we all have but are not aware of, but it is much more than that.

"In your subconscious mind is a higher level of connection to Life itself." He drew an imaginary circle around the chart with his finger. "Science tells us that we are all connected, we just don't perceive it in normal conscious states. I have done a great deal of work to bring that connection from my subconscious mind to my conscious mind, which any of you can do as well. As a matter of fact, that's what this whole course of instruction is designed to give you the tools to do.

"In any case," he pointed at the man who had asked the question, "you did agree, you just agreed subconsciously. If you hadn't, it wouldn't have worked."

Another man raised his hand and said, "I don't believe that I can just tell another person that something is going to happen and have his or her body do it."

"In fact, doctor, that is *exactly* what happens each time you treat a patient and tell them how their body is going to change as a result of the treatment." Thurman scratched his chin. "Like most people, you are strongly identified with the body, and so you think the primary healing element is the physical treatment you give, but it isn't."

Thurman let that sink in for a moment. "It is the intention, the *vibration* of the idea of health that causes the change. The physical treatment merely mirrors the idea and makes it logical to a mind primarily identified with the body."

"Vibration is amplified by emotion, concentration, and expectation. When you, as the doctor, with enthusiasm and confidence, expect positive changes to take place in your patient, they will. And if they don't, it's usually because the patient doesn't truly wish to heal or is in some other way unable or unwilling to cooperate."

After an extensive Q & A session, Thurman ended the class for the night and called a quick meeting with his co-instructors to go over the next day's itinerary. The meeting was just winding up when four uninvited guests walked in. They were familiar faces, men who had been involved with the Concept-Therapy Institute for anywhere from several months to over a year. What they all had in common was that they had been agitating for some time for Thurman to restructure the institute he had founded.

"Good evening, gentlemen," one of the men beamed. "I hope you had a splendid class tonight."

"We did," Reverend Crump replied, "thank you, Mr. Albright."

"What can we do for you gentlemen?" Thurman asked.

The four men sat. "We wanted to talk to you about the direction of the institute," said Albright, obviously the ringleader.

"The proper direction depends entirely upon where you want to go," Thurman replied, squinting behind his glasses. He had, of course, been given all sorts of advice over the years about how he should proceed with his work and usually a polite acceptance of another opinion ended the matter. These particular men, though, were dead-set on forcing a change within the institute.

The man at Albright's left smiled. "Now, Dr. Fleet, don't be like that. We all just want what is best for this organization. I'm sure you can appreciate that, can't you?"

"Mr. Thomas, I always appreciate sincerity." Thurman smiled in his own way, paused, and continued, "when it's truly sincere."

The second man's smile faltered a little at that, but he pressed on, "Doctor, I understand that you are going to open up the classes to laypeople, that you are no longer going to be teaching just those in the healing arts anymore. Is that true?"

Thurman nodded. "Yes, I believe that we have reached a point at which many people who do not have a professional interest in healing can nevertheless benefit from our teaching. Next month we will be opening our first class to anyone who is interested."

Albright grinned from ear to ear. "Then now is the perfect time."

Reverend Crump piped up, "Now is *always* the perfect time, sir. In fact, it's the only time that exists." He laughed his signature belly laugh and Fleet and Schenk joined in.

Albright seemed to be getting irritated, but he held onto his smile like a jealous toddler clinging to a toy that he didn't really want in order to prevent anyone else from playing with it. "Gentlemen, let's be frank with each other," he tried, "we have discussed the issue of re-formatting the Concept-Therapy Institute before, and now seems like the perfect time to do it. Allowing laypeople to take classes is going to increase the potential market exponentially. If you re-structured this school as a religion instead of an educational organization, think of how many more people you could positively influence."

"Positively influence?" Thurman's face took on a completely sober countenance; the laughter of the previous moment had disappeared like morning fog burning off of a Texas pond. "Sir, tell me how much religion has positively influenced people over the ages. The worst wars we have ever fought have featured religion as either the reason for the war itself, or the primary justification for its continuation. It divides people, confuses people, justifies base action, sets up a power differential that exploits people, and separates people from the true reality of their situation as human beings."

Mr. Thomas affected an expression of feigned surprise. "Dr. Fleet, I never realized that you were so against religion. You certainly quote enough religious texts to support your teaching. And even the name of this ranch was taken from a religious holy book, was it not?"

"Yes, I quote the texts," Thurman replied with a squint,

"I try to teach what they really mean instead of what they have been taught by religious institutions to mean."

He took his time lighting a cigarette. "Nor am I against religion. Mass consciousness has always needed external gods, and it still does for those who are not ready to understand the higher truth that the Divine is within. There are still many people for whom their religion is the highest ideal they are capable of aspiring to, and for them it is invaluable.

"However," his squint deepened, "*this* organization is for people who can accept a new truth and think for themselves. *This* organization is for people who are ready to learn the laws of their being and do their best to follow them without needing a priest or other intercessor to shift responsibility to. *This* organization is not for exploitive purposes, nor will it traffic in the politics of fear or guilt or manipulation. It will exist for the simple purpose of teaching people who and what they really are and how they can live up to that idea, *or it will not exist at all!"*

Thomas retreated to frustrated silence, but Albright wasn't giving up yet. He tried again with another sly smile, "Dr. Fleet, have you considered that this work of yours is bigger than you? That it goes beyond your own desires for it? Think about the advantages of shifting to religious status; the tax-exempt status alone would solve many of the financial difficulties you have around here."

His eyes took on a greedy gleam. "You could establish churches in major cities and have ordained clergy or certified teachers, if you prefer, to tend the congregations there. That would take some more financial burden off of your shoulders, and don't you think that people would be well served by having a local teacher to guide them in everyday life instead of just being able to take a class every now and then? Churches use that model because it *works*, Dr. Fleet. It spreads the word, gets people involved, fosters stability, and helps them live better lives."

Thurman snorted, "And it doesn't hurt the clergy's bank account or community standing either, does it Mr. Albright?"

Albright sputtered with obvious righteous indignation, "Well, if you think that my own personal benefit is my motivation—"

"Your motivations are your own business," Thurman interrupted. "Investigating your true desires is your responsibility, not mine. However, I *will* share with you something about my own motivations for this institute."

He paused. "You gentlemen have heard about how this work came to be, yes?"

They nodded.

"Well, my experience during that illumination was hard to describe in words, but I can tell you that when I set an intention to assist Life in evolving consciousness I was shown a vision in which it seemed like Truth had been fragmented and scattered in our world today. Parts of it remained intact within several religions and philosophies, but it was mixed up with fantasies and theories that confused people. I felt that it was my job to recognize as much of that coherent Truth as possible and put it together in a course of study that people living in today's world could digest, if they were so inclined."

Albright interrupted, "Dr. Fleet, that is exactly why it would be so much more powerful to turn what you have into a religion of Universal Truths. It could be the One Great Religion that all people could relate to. Don't you see the advantage of that?"

"What I see about religion is this," Thurman replied with flint in his tone, "religion starts out as a bridge between humankind and our Source. It's a way to connect that makes sense to the people in the time and culture in which it is born, and as long as it remains pure it is constructive and helpful.

But sooner or later the connection becomes an institution, and the bridge crumbles.

"Institutions have hierarchies and bureaucracies. Those factors shift the responsibility and freedom of working out an individual's spiritual path from that individual to another entity. It might be a church or a hierarchy of just one leader and one follower, but whether it happens to be a church, a priest, savior, or guru, the intercessory entity inherently promotes the idea of separation from Deity instead of connection. What starts as a bridge inevitably becomes a stumbling block."

Thurman punctuated his statements by tapping his fingers on the table. "Now, if there is one thing I gleaned from my experience, it is that spiritual realization must necessarily be a do-it-yourself-proposition because the Divine is within you already. Spiritual evolution is a process of learning to see the reality of what you already are instead of the illusions you have previously accepted. It means facing your own mirages, staring them down and being willing to see the Truth in yourself. While someone might be able to offer a measure of guidance or help, the journey is an inherently personal process."

He held up a finger to emphasize his next point, "*And there will be no gurus in this work.* Not me, not Crump or Schenk, and not any of you men. Just like there is nothing magical or mysterious about someone who has studied higher mathematical principles, there is nothing mysterious or magical about those who teach this work. Anything we can do or can know, so can anyone else who is willing to learn the principles involved and put them into practice in their lives. Turning this into a religion would necessarily mean putting me and some of you up on a pedestal, and I will never allow that."

Albright smiled another slick smile. "But Dr. Fleet, you are already on a pedestal. As much as you say others can do what you can do, it isn't true, at least not yet. All of us have seen you do amazing things—healings, intuiting information about us, attracting needed circumstances or money. Your students already hold you up high, sir. You might as well use that status to everyone's advantage."

Thurman looked thoughtful for several moments and then smiled back, "Gentlemen, you have opened my eyes to something here today. I think you are right. I *am* on a pedestal whether I want to be or not, and I should act accordingly. In fact, I invite you gentlemen to our class session tomorrow afternoon, and you will see a completely different approach than the one I have been using."

The men could hardly believe it; they glanced at each other with surprised jubilance.

"Tomorrow we will begin our class session at two o'clock." Thurman nodded to himself. "I will be spending the majority of the morning preparing for an entirely new presentation that you won't want to miss, so be on time."

They all shook hands and retired for the evening with some of those present feeling the thrill of an unexpected triumph and some feeling the bewilderment of a blindsided betrayal.

The following morning an expensively clad man ordered a cab from his hotel in downtown San Antonio and instructed the driver to take him to the Aum-Sat-Tat ranch in Boerne, despite the driver's protests that the trip was going to cost a small fortune. Money was no problem for this forty-three-year-old millionaire. During an apprenticeship while still in college, he had discovered that he possessed considerable talent in financial matters, most specifically futures markets, and he had exploited that talent diligently. During the end of the depression years he had held his own quite well in the badly damaged market, and ever since it had recovered he had prospered beyond all expectations.

He had flown in from Los Angeles the day before, having heard about Dr. Fleet's healing results from a doctor who had studied the methods but who had so far been unable to affect a cure for the man's condition.

His cab arrived at the ranch at about ten o'clock. The man instructed the taxi driver to wait and to keep the meter running, and he went into the main building to find the miraculous Dr. Fleet that he had heard so much about.

A tall, attractive woman with red hair greeted him in the main office; she told him that Dr. Fleet was in the cafeteria and gave him directions. As he made his way through the grounds of the ranch, he noticed a tree house such as one might construct for children, except this one was adult-sized and it sat in the branches of an oak tree with a sign nailed to the tree that read, *"The Roost of the Gusta-Gust."*

As he approached the cafeteria he saw a bright red structure about the size of a tool shed. *Hell Mart #1—Worry House* was painted in large letters across the side wall. It had a large open window in the front, not unlike a concession stand at a high school ballgame, and he surmised that the idea was that those on the ranch who wished to engage in the emotion of worry were to do so only in this designated structure.

The cafeteria was empty except for a middle-aged, grey-haired workman in white overalls doing some painting. The visitor approached the painter and asked, "Excuse me, can you tell me where I can find Dr. Fleet?"

The man rubbed his neatly trimmed mustache, leaving a smear of paint on it. "Yes, he's here." He put down his paintbrush and disappeared behind a wall where a sign said *Restrooms*. The man thought that Dr. Fleet must be in the bathroom and the workman must be going to get him, when to his surprise the same man immediately emerged from behind the partial wall, stuck out his hand, and said, "Hello, I'm Dr. Fleet."

The man laughed at the joke, but he was starting to

wonder about the eccentricities of this healer. They shook hands, and the man introduced himself as Jeffrey Abrams. "I've travelled from Los Angeles to your ranch to seek help with migraine headaches. They started about ten years ago and they've gotten progressively worse." Dr. Fleet listened intently, squinting at the man the whole time he was talking.

Finally the man finished his explanation and his new doctor asked, "And Dr. Lupkes in Los Angeles performed your treatment exactly as we taught him and you still have had no results?"

"That's correct."

"Well, in some cases we have to use our secret weapon. Are you willing to go to some extreme lengths to solve your situation?"

"I will do anything you tell me to do, doctor. I have got to get relief from this condition, once and for all."

Thurman got a pencil and a piece of paper and began to draw a map of the ranch. "Now," he said, "we do have a secret healing weapon here on the ranch, but you must promise that you will never tell anyone about it; I'm sure you understand that we can't have people overrunning the property trying to get to it, yes?"

"Certainly doctor, I understand." The man was growing more and more excited. "I will never tell anyone."

"We call it *Iron Springs,* and it's somewhat like the healing pool in Lourdes, France, where the water has mysterious healing qualities when bathed in. Follow this map and it will take you to it. I must also warn you that it is located on a secluded portion of the property, and you will have to go through some pretty rough terrain to get to it."

Now Abrams was almost twitching to get started. "That's all right, doctor. I will go through whatever I have to in order to solve this problem."

"Are you sure?" Thurman asked. "It looks like you have on some pretty expensive clothes today, and that part of the property is pretty dicey."

"Doctor, I make enough money that these clothes are not my main concern," the man assured him, not quite able to hide his pleasure at the fact that the doctor had noticed his expensive tastes. "I'd like to visit Iron Springs immediately."

"All right," Thurman replied, "I'll still be here painting when you return. Let me know how it goes."

The man told his taxi driver to stay put and began to follow the map across the property. The doctor hadn't been joking. The terrain was rocky and dusty, and about halfway to the designated spot it began to rain. Not a drizzle, but a Texas gully-washer that seemingly arose out of nowhere and beat rain down as if the sky held a grudge against the earth.

By the time the man reached the area labeled on his pencil-drawn map he was covered in mud up his shins. His suit was ripped in a half dozen places from the underbrush, and he was soaked to the skin. He approached the area labeled on the map and saw a sign that read *Iron Springs*, pointing to a small trail. He followed the path for perhaps fifty yards, rounded a curve, and found himself looking at an old, rusted iron bedspring with a bottle of dirty water sitting on top of it.

The man was livid; he retraced his steps and covered the ground back to the cafeteria twice as fast as he had on his way to the Springs. He burst through the door, shouting as he went. Dr. Fleet was still painting in his white coveralls.

"Listen doctor, I don't know what game you're playing here, but I don't appreciate it!"

Thurman turned around to face the man. He looked bewildered. "Was my map not correct, sir? Did you not find the Springs?"

The man's face reddened and he growled, "I found a set of rusty bedsprings and a bottle of rainwater."

Thurman smiled and nodded. "Yes, that's it. Remember

now, it's a secret. We can't let it get out." He winked at the man and turned back to his painting.

Abrams couldn't have imagined becoming any angrier than he had been already, but this response pushed his capacity for rage to new heights. "Let *what* get out? That you're a charlatan? A liar? A crazy old idiot?"

"I'm sorry, is there a problem? Did I do something wrong?"

"Sir, do you have any idea what I went through to get to your 'Iron Springs?' This suit is torn to rags; it was custom tailored for me in London. These shoes are Italian, also custom made, and they're ruined."

Thurman nodded his head. "Yes, I was afraid you might get a little wet with that downpour. It really rained, didn't it? Like a cow pissing on a flat rock!" He smiled and winked again, all the while cheerfully continuing to paint.

"Would you mind telling me where you get off treating someone like that? I came to you for help; you're supposed to be a healer, dammit! I came all the way from—*just what in the goddamn hell do you think you are doing?*"

Thurman had turned abruptly and, entirely without warning, slopped several generous strokes of white acrylic on the astonished man's clothes. He locked his gaze onto the new patient's eyes and asked, "Who are you?"

The man immediately felt a little drunk, like he was floating and a little off-center. He answered in a voice that seemed to be operating in slow motion, "Ah, you know who I am. I-I told you my n-name is Jeffrey Abrams."

Thurman shook his head, his eyes boring straight into the man's brain. "No, I didn't ask what your name is, I asked *who are you?*"

The man felt a fresh wave of befuddlement wash over him. His blood seemed to be pulsing in waves like the ocean, and his brain seemed to be pendulating between two extremes. His mind felt like it was vacillating between staggering like a drunk and peacefully resting on solid ground. He felt that he was on the verge of reaching some previously unimagined level of clarity.

"I d-don't know what you mean," he slurred.

"You have put too much energy into acquiring things," Thurman told him in a low voice that rolled into the younger man's mind like a fuzzy tumbleweed on fire, "in an attempt to justify yourself."

He balanced the paintbrush on the bucket. "There is nothing wrong with money or fancy clothes or nice cars, but you need to connect with the idea that you are sufficient unto yourself. Acquiring those things does not impart value to you. *Focus on who you can become* rather than what you can acquire, and you will have no more difficulties. You are much more than the clothes that you wear or the cars you drive. You are significant for what you *are*, not for what you have. *You are Consciousness. Connect with what you really are.*"

"Yes, doctor," the man whispered. He returned to the cab, where his disheveled appearance startled the taxi driver. It was almost three weeks later when it occurred to him that he hadn't had a single headache since he visited Aum-Sat-Tat ranch. He would remain headache free for the rest of his life, aware that his trip to the strange healer provided the necessary impetus for the change, yet not able to quite remember exactly what had happened or how the doctor had affected that change.

As he put away his painting utensils, Thurman reflected on the interaction with Mr. Abrams. This was exactly the sort of thing that so fascinated people, yet it was completely natural to him. People were impressed because they were still acting from a sense of limited self-knowledge, meaning that they were only aware of the thoughts and emotions that rattled around in their conscious minds, and this awareness represented such a small portion of the total knowledge they possessed that it made something like what just happened with this visitor seem miraculous.

Thurman had struggled to explain to people over the years what it was like to live the way he did. He still had all of the random thoughts, emotions, desires, personality quirks, and preferences that he had always had. The difference was that those parts of him had gradually over the years ceased to be the prime motivator of his actions, at least not with regard to any significant circumstances. They had been dethroned and replaced by pure impulses borne of a deeper connection with Life, flashing up from his subconscious mind, cutting through the clutter and confusion of his conscious mind's chattering.

Many times that connection supplied him with answers before questions had even been asked. He simply *knew* what the right thing to do was in any particular circumstance; he didn't guess, or reason it out, he just knew. He might not know *why* a certain act was the right thing to do, and to his conscious mind it might seem strange or even cruel, like sending that recent visitor on a snipe hunt across the ranch, but he had discovered that if he just went with the impulse, Life would take care of the outcome. In this case, Thurman's odd behavior had been just the thing to put his visitor slightly off-balance, bypass his defense mechanisms of vanity and criticism, and open him up so that a new idea could be vibrated directly into his subconscious.

Right now, Thurman had another impulse to follow. He retired to his private office to prepare himself for an entirely new afternoon class.

I woke up with twilight peeking through the dusty curtains of the cheap motel the waitress had told us about. It had still been dark when we both collapsed onto the musty twin mattresses. I found my watch, which didn't help much—I now knew it was 6:12, but I couldn't tell if it was sunrise or sunset. I looked over at the Captain's bed, which I was only slightly surprised to find empty. No matter what happened, he always responded more vigorously than I did—he was already up and gone while I was just struggling out of bed.

Just then the outside door opened and the Captain came in carrying a brown bag with splotchy grease stains decorating the bottom like shiny black clouds.

"Rise and shine," he bellowed.

"Uuuhhhgg," I groaned eloquently, "is it morning or night?"

This amused the Captain. "It is evening. Time to get up, eat some chow, and get back home. I don't know what you told your mother when you checked in with her the other night, but if we don't get home soon she's going to get suspicious."

"So we're going to drive all night again?"

The Captain gave me a cheery nod.

I groaned again. "Are you sure you're not some kind of vampire? My sleep cycle is going to be wrecked by the time we finally get home."

We ate burgers from the diner we had terrorized the night before without conversation, cleaned up, showered, and hit the road again for the last leg of our Las Vegas Crazy Tour, 1974.

We hadn't gone far when the Captain said, "Ray, you did very well in that diner last night. Tell me about it from your perspective."

I told him about having fallen asleep in the trunk and about my dream. I told him that when he started distracting Carlo in the diner, and I realized that I was going to have to participate that it seemed so scary at first that I thought my heart would stop beating, but at the height of my terror the dream pulled me back into the moment, and I simply acted without doubt or fear.

He nodded. "Yes, that's what I was talking about at my house and on our way out here. Those actions were authentic. They didn't originate in your mind, they came from beyond it. What do you think your dream meant?"

"What do you mean?"

"Dreams are almost always significant messages from your subconscious," he replied from the passenger seat. "Things that you have been repressing or have been too mentally busy to become aware of consciously. Your conscious mind can only be aware of a few things at any given time, and we generally choose to be aware of illusory things that we have identified with. What really runs our lives, informs our decisions, and stimulates our actions lives in the subconscious, the portion of our knowledge we generally are not aware of."

"If it's knowledge that I possess, how can I not be aware of it?" I asked.

"Most of your life takes place without you being aware of it. Are you aware of what your liver is doing right now?"

I shook my head.

"And yet it is operating with perfect knowledge. Did you know that no scientist in the world could take those hamburgers we just ate and convert them into lung tissue? Yet we all know how to do it—we do it all the time. We think we don't know because the conscious mind isn't the part of us that knows, and therein lies our great problem."

"What?"

"We think that what our conscious minds know is the pinnacle of knowledge. In reality, our conscious minds are severely limited, hopelessly confused, and weak as water. It's like putting chopsticks up against Rachmaninoff; there's no comparison."

"So what part of us is comparable to Rachmaninoff in your analogy?"

"Hell Ray, you have more wisdom in your big toe—literally—than all the deep conscious thoughts you've ever had. Remember my example from a few minutes ago? If we had to depend upon our conscious minds to digest our food, we'd all starve; no one would be able to figure out how to do it."

He rolled down the window a bit. "Your biological body contains within it the wisdom of countless eons of experience. Every challenge we give it, it still tries to do its best to adapt and help us, while we, in our infinite stupidity and arrogance, think we know what it should be doing and how it should be doing it."

He shifted in his seat. "But the body is only one part of you, and an illusory part at that. Ray, the part of you that is real is something that can't be defined by the mind or described by words, and so it is something that most people are not aware of. Physical and mental illusions tend to hook our attention. We identify with them, and they jam up our minds while the real wisdom in our subconscious tries desperately to get us to notice. Down there you have a complete connection with Life. Your questions are answered, your ideals are realized, and your perfect actions are scripted. Dreams are one way we allow some wisdom to bubble to the surface."

"Well, I did get the idea to search for the tire iron from the dream."

"Yes, and a great help that was. But the rest of that dream was even more significant, don't you think?"

"I suppose," I answered slowly, "and I guess I have a vague idea of what it might mean, but I don't really know how to interpret the specifics."

"Ray, I would say that your subconscious wisdom was alerting you to some deep-seated feelings of inadequacy, probably acquired early in life as a concept absorbed from your father. I would guess that he has the tendency to indulge in severe criticism of both himself and others, and I would say you probably learned the same habit from him."

I nodded.

"But the great thing about your dream is that you freed yourself from those feelings of fear and inadequacy. Or rather," he amended, "you allowed *Life* to free you. Remember when you told me about hearing all those voices from the stands, but there were no people sitting there?"

"Yes."

"That represented your mind; an entity completely without substance but nevertheless incessant. Your father represented the false ideals you have tried to live up to in the past. But again, the important part was that you claimed your freedom from all of those things, you let go of attachments to false fears and false ideals, you connected with the real part of you, and you let Life flow through you unrestrained. You broke the self-imposed chains of weakness and experienced the strength of connecting with Life." He smiled. "Felt good, didn't it?"

I returned the smile and nodded. It really *had* felt good, like I had returned a shoulder to its proper place that had been dislocated for so long I had stopped noticing it.

"The more you connect with that process, the more freedom you will experience. Real freedom."

He paused and asked, "Speaking of which, what is your concept of freedom? What does freedom really mean?"

I answered automatically, without thinking about it, "Being able to do whatever you want."

The Captain kind of snorted at that. He asked, "So if Clarissa back there in Las Vegas somehow got hold of unlimited funds for gambling, would she be free?"

I hadn't thought of it like that. "I...I guess not."

"Well, why not? She could do whatever she wanted, and all she wants to do is gamble."

"She would still be enslaved by her addiction."

He nodded. "Quite right. We are all enslaved by our

desires, our attachment to outcomes. Freedom isn't doing what you want, it's detachment from wanting at all."

I didn't know if I quite bought that idea. "So we should cease striving for anything? Just laze around and meditate?"

He looked at me as though I had just asked him if he thought it would be a good idea for me to start fulfilling my entire nutritional requirements by ingesting belly-button lint. "Of course not." I could almost feel him roll his eyes at me in the dark. "Your inclinations, your talents, and your true feelings—based upon connection rather than separation—will lead you to the proper endeavors for you according to the Law of Duty. And you had better engage in those endeavors with all the appropriate enthusiasm and passion.

"We have covered this before, remember?" he continued. "You won't completely get rid of your emotions, your mind, or your desires, and you won't end up walking around like a zombie. You will always have those things, but you needn't remain *attached* to them, or *identified* with them. You needn't indulge them, or above all, allow yourself to be bullied by them."

"So how do I become unattached?" I asked. "How do I just stop wanting things? It seems like a nearly universal part of being a human being. Everybody wants something, don't they?"

"Ray, if old Carlo back there had a dollar, and I asked if I could have it, what do you think he'd say?"

I chuckled, "Do you really want me to tell you?"

I could hear the smile in his voice as he answered, "No, I guess we both know what he would be likely to say, don't we? What about this: what if he had a dollar and I told him I would *trade* him the dollar for a twenty. Then what do you think he would say?"

"Well, as long as he really believed you, I guess he would say 'sure.'"

The Captain nodded, "Quite right. *If* he had faith that

it would really happen, as you so astutely pointed out. That's exactly how all our desires work, Ray. If you perceive that there is more value in an alternative, you have no problem giving up what you previously clung to, right?"

"I guess so."

"So we run around trying to gratify our egos and protect our limited lives, *until* we realize that there is a truly better alternative. Then leaving those attachments behind becomes automatic and easy, like Carlo choosing twenty dollars instead of clinging to one."

I slowed down for a Buick turning left. "So the trick is to realize that there is a better alternative?"

"Yep, you got it," he nodded crisply. "Realizing that what you have been clinging to is illusory and worthless, and becoming aware that there is a real alternative."

I paused. "That's it? That's the big secret?"

"That's it."

"Don't you think that's pretty self-evident? It's not very profound."

The Captain chuckled. "Profundity is a trick of the mind, Ray."

He paused and then asked in an ultra-serious, foreboding tone, "Ray—how do you keep from being burned by the fire?"

I had no idea what he was talking about.

"Come on Ray," he shouted with an urgency that almost scared me, *"this is important! How do you keep from being burned by the fire?"*

"I don't know!"

"Don't stick your hand in it, dumb-butt," he drawled calmly, his previous urgency and intensity vanishing in a wink.

I felt my face turn red with anger, and the Captain, obviously enjoying my shocked silence, began laughing uproariously.

"How's that for being profound?" he managed through waves of laughter, "It doesn't have to be obscure or profound to be true!"

Finally, he exhausted his mirth and got serious again.

"Ray, attaining that realization may be very simple, but it isn't easy—not at first, anyway. It requires constant attention to the reality of you and Life. It means disciplining yourself to act according to that reality. Every time you act as though life is a separate and random series of events and that you are cut off from it and that you have to protect yourself from it, you declare to the Spirit within you that your limited and separated perception is the truth. You reinforce the sense of separation. And whatever statements you make to Spirit with the most consistency and feeling will become your experience. If your overriding message to the Spirit within is that you are a seamless part of Life, having nothing apart from it to protect, hide, compete for, fear, worry about, or covet, you will create an entirely different experience for yourself. Spirit will produce an entirely different reality for you."

He paused and added, "Sometimes it takes time and other times it is relatively quick; it depends upon how earnestly you impress the idea. But if you are sincere," his voice took on an almost wistful tone, "you will blend with Life and make a connection that will change everything for you. But you must recognize your One True Desire. Once you see it for what it really is, following it becomes much easier."

"True desire?"

The Captain nodded. "All the carnal desires we get attached to are really nothing more than limited substitutes for the One True Desire. We desire Unity. We desire the Peace that comes with losing our limited selves to blend into the universe of unlimited Life. We *think* we desire pleasure because we are stuck in the confusion of the world of opposites, and we chase pleasure and avoid pain with the utmost passion, but what we really desire is to realize that pleasure is a dead end."

I thought for a moment and then asked, "Do you mean that it is wrong to pursue things that make you happy? Are you saying that we should practice total renunciation?"

"Yes and no. First, understand that pleasure does not make you happy. Pleasure and pain are the same. You can only experience one to the degree that you experience the other, because every pleasure you experience is sandwiched between two pains—the pain of not yet having what you desire, and the pain of losing it, or of fearing losing it, once you have it.

"True happiness is the natural state of being that we lose touch with once our minds begin to classify things into categories of good and bad, and we start to chase the one and avoid the other. Happiness is a simple state arising automatically from the realization that you are one with Life."

"But you still enjoy things, right?" I countered. "I see you do things that seem to bring you pleasure."

"Pleasures for the body, pleasures for the mind, yes, but the difference is that I am under no illusions that I *am* my body or my mind. I don't get attached to their pleasures, and if indulging in those pleasures interferes with my service to Life, I can forgo them."

"Really?" I smirked, "What about those?" I pointed to his cigarettes. "How easily could you give those up?"

He smiled, "Some things might be more challenging than others, but yes, I could give them up if they were interfering with my service."

I drove for a moment more and sensed a change from the passenger seat. I didn't see the Captain's expression clearly, but I sensed vulnerability in him that I hadn't experienced before. He said softly, "There was one loss that, still...even now..."

And for a long time he would say no more.

∞

The audience of doctors waited anxiously for the afternoon session to begin. They had travelled from various areas of the country to learn about Dr. Thurman Fleet's methods, and so far they had not been disappointed by what they had seen and heard. The man seemed to have an amazing ability to correlate different areas of science such as biology, physics, and psychology with theology, metaphysics, and philosophy, and the result was a practical system of healing that they felt could increase their efforts exponentially. Not to mention the seemingly amazing demonstrations he had shown them to illustrate the power of thoughts and emotions to influence the body.

There were four additional participants in the audience for the afternoon session. The four men who had apparently convinced Thurman that he needed to alter the format of the Concept-Therapy Institute occupied four seats in the center of the front row.

When the clock showed seven minutes after two the participants began to get restless. Dr. Fleet had started every other lesson so far exactly on time. They were asking each other if the start time was correct when Thurman entered the back door and staggered up the aisle to the podium.

He was dressed in a white choir robe and crowned with a ridiculous rhinestone studded tiara. Around his neck hung a cheap gold metal ladies' chain belt from which dangled a gaudy buckle that served as an icon, like the Pope wearing an oversized crucifix around his neck.

He stumbled up the steps and settled himself behind the podium. The audience whispered like wind sweeping through tall grass, and a few nervous titters peppered the murmurs from the crowd. The four would-be evangelists sat transfixed by the spectacle.

Thurman straightened himself, poked out his chest,

and with his chin raised regally, belched wetly toward the back of the auditorium. The aspiring ministers on the front row turned scarlet, then purple as they realized that the man they wished to elevate to prophet status was so drunk he was close to losing consciousness.

"Scuse me, everybody," Dr. Fleet slurred, placing his hand daintily over his mouth. A few giggles floated up from the back of the room.

"*Now,*" he yelled in the abrupt manner of loud drunks, swaying precariously from side to side, "I want to talk to you people about *G-O-D*. You all know what that spells, don'tcha? There are some people around here who think that I ought to act like I know something about old God that you don't know. They think that I need to make myself a priest, or a prophet, or some bullshit, and act like I have a spiritual position of advantage over you folks. They think I ought to make this course of instruction into a religion, and have churches, and have you folks make donations and tithe to the church."

He stepped on the side of his choir robe and fell over sideways, knocking over the podium and flinging off his tiara. Several people rushed to help him up.

"Thank you, you're very kind," his words slurred toward his helpers on a cloud of alcoholic fumes. "Where did meh Pope hat go? Oh, thank you, nice lady." Once the helpers had him and the podium upright again, he continued his soliloquy.

"Ah-right, where was I?...*Oh yes!*" he shouted again at full drunken volume, holding up a finger for emphasis. "I was sayin' that I will get drunk like this every damn day if I have to, *but you will not worship me!* This work is about freedom from that kind of crap. Jesus said that the kingdom of Heaven is within, and I agree with him. What you are all looking for is within you. I don't have it, I can't give it to you, and my only job is to help you in whatever small way I can to find it within yourself."

He straightened up his robe and his tiara with solemn dignity. "Now, my co-instructors will take over the rest of the class for the afternoon. They are quite c-capable and knowledgeable about the material we are presenting."

After a drunken, time-compressed pause, he stuttered, "I realize that my behavior today is ir-ir-irregalar, although I assure you that it is ne'ssary, and I would like to offer anyone who wants a refund a full return on the p-price of the seminar. Thank you, and I would ask that you 'scuse me now." He stumbled off the stage and lurched out the back door, losing his tiara one last time and declining to retrieve it. The rise and fall of the new prophet was complete.

Delia Fleet sat sideways in a green recliner, heels under her rump, hand propping up her head as her elbow rested on the arm of the chair. Her husband lay on the couch of the small cabin they occupied at the ranch, nursing a vicious hangover. "Thurman, I don't understand you. I love you, but I will be tarred and feathered if I understand you. Tell me again why you felt you had to do this."

"I just did." He groaned as he shifted the ice bag on his head. "I had to get the point across with actions. I tried to get it across with words, but they wouldn't listen."

"Well who cares what they think, anyway?" Delia asked. "You're the leader of this entire organization; why couldn't you just tell them to get the hell out of here?"

Thurman sighed, "If it wasn't them, it would be someone else. I had to put a stop to it or it would have just gone on and on."

He put down the ice bag, paused for a long minute, and said, "Deddo, I don't know if I can do this. I don't know if I can see it through."

Delia said solidly, "One thing I know about you, Thurman, is that you can do anything you set your mind to doing. I've seen that happen enough times to know that for sure."

Her voice took on a softer tone and she continued, "But *why?* What is it that you're trying to see through? What on earth is your end goal?"

He sat in silence for almost a full minute. When he finally answered, his voice was sad. "Deddo, that is a very good question. When I set out to do this I thought all I would have to do was start teaching about these things and people would understand and respond en mass. I thought it would spark a revolution in healing, in philosophy, and in people just living better lives.

"And it has," he rubbed his temples and grimaced, "for those individuals who have really understood what we are teaching. But there has been so much misunderstanding along the way, so much has been distorted, and there have been so many superstitions that have blocked people from accepting it, that the group we can put in that category is relatively small. I guess mass consciousness is simply not ready for the facts yet. Fantasies, most assuredly, and theories, yes, to some degree, but not facts. Not yet, anyway. Seems like half the people I have taught think I am the devil, and the other half want to make me a god. I will have to remain content to be the one who plants the seeds, not the one who reaps the harvest."

Delia listened with sympathy. She had, of course, witnessed her husband's efforts first-hand throughout the past decade, and she knew of his disappointment and frustration. She had watched him spend years building up a national following of thousands of enthusiastic students, only to have eight out of every ten drop out of the classes when he began to use hypnosis to illustrate the principles he was teaching. It seemed that people could tolerate talking about such things, but demonstrating them was out of the question, and inevitably those demonstrations drew charges of Satanism. She was, of course, also well acquainted with the financial challenges he had faced with the institute property. And now, she thought, he is getting stinking drunk in order to dissuade other students from trying to force him to be some kind of evangelist or avatar. "Can you be content with that role?" she asked.

He smiled, "What choice do I have? I have been hypnotized to this idea for almost thirty years now. Wanting it to succeed has been my greatest desire." He sighed and chuckled at the same time. "Desire gets to you after a while, doesn't it? It's a potent intoxicant." He looked thoughtful, seemed to come to a conclusion, and said softly, "Yes, I will go on with it, but I do need a different focus."

"What do you mean?" Delia asked. She hoped it wouldn't involve moving again.

He shifted the ice bag to the other side of his head. "Well, I've been operating under the assumption that there would be some kind of critical mass reached, at which point the mass mind would be ready for this sort of teaching. People wouldn't try to worship it, steal it and water it down, or be afraid of it; they would just accept it and study it on a mass scale." He drank a quick swallow of water from a glass on the coffee table and added, "But that isn't going to happen while either one of us is still alive.

"So," he finished, "I need to start preparing for this institute and this teaching to go on after I'm gone. I need to be finding and training the new generation of Concept-Therapy teachers. I need to finish the entire curriculum of study, and then I need to get out of the way and let it move on without me."

Delia shifted in her seat. "Are you sure you're going to be able to do that?" There was an undercurrent in her tone that he recognized and understood.

"Yes," he nodded, "I will always be involved to some degree, and I will always be promoting these principles, but

I will have to step aside to allow the movement to continue. I have no choice."

He reached over, took her hand, and addressed what she didn't verbalize in her last question. "Deddo, I know that this whole trip has been a long, hard ride for you. I know that this is not the life you would have chosen for us, and I'm sorry."

Thurman's voice wavered as he continued, "I owe you so much," he whispered. "You have always been understanding when most women would have left me for mad. I want you to know that I do realize what I have put you through, and I appreciate it more than you can imagine."

Delia knelt on the floor beside the couch and put her arms around her husband. "Well, Thurman, while your great desire has been teaching others about Concept-Therapy, my great desire has been being with you. I guess whatever Power gives us our desires arranges everything pretty well so that it all fits together, huh?"

He smiled through tears, hugged her back, and agreed.

CHAPTER TEN
FADE

We made it back to Boerne early Monday evening. I took the Captain's bags into his house and was about to get mine and go home when he stopped me. He pointed to Mom's car in the driveway. "Ray, I better go with you to talk to your mother." He zipped open his bag and brought out the MGM hotel envelope.

I was so tired and still trying to process everything I had been through since Friday morning that I had forgotten about figuring out how to explain it to Mom. It seemed like we had been gone for years. When I stopped and thought about everything that had happened since we left, I wasn't surprised that I felt that way.

I agreed with the Captain and we both went into the house, me carrying my bag, the Captain holding a hat that he had grabbed on the way out the door. Dawn was plopped in front of the TV watching a re-run of *The Monkees*.

"*Ray*," she yelled, as she shot up from the couch to give me a hug. "*Mom,*" she shouted in the general direction of the kitchen, "*Ray's back!*"

Mom emerged from the kitchen wiping flour off her hands. Either fried chicken or pork chops; after eating all that diner and motel food either one sounded great to me.

We hugged, and I quickly shoved my bag in my room. Mom asked the Captain about his "sick friend."

"Oh, I think he'll recover," he replied with a grin.

"Well, I hope so," Mom said, as she led us all into the kitchen. "I'm sure he was happy to have a visitor in a time of need."

"Yes ma'am," he nodded.

The conversation hit a small lull, and the Captain took advantage of it. "Ma'am, I need to confess something to you, and I won't blame you if you get mad at me for it."

Mom raised her eyebrows. "What's that Dr. Fleet?"

He shuffled his feet and fidgeted with his hat like he was a kid confessing a school rules violation. "Well, ma'am, while we were out there visiting my friend, I had Raymond take me to a hotel in Las Vegas that had a casino. I have never been much of a gambler, but I had always wanted to go and see what it was like."

Mom conspicuously raised her right eyebrow even higher, but she didn't interrupt.

"Anyway," he continued, "I know I shouldn't have, but I placed a bet for him at the roulette table."

"You did what?" She wasn't exactly in a rage, but her voice did have a bit of a sharp edge to it.

"I know ma'am. I know I shouldn't have, but he had been so nice to me, driving me all the way out there, and he was too young to gamble anyway, so I didn't worry about him gambling all his money away or anything, and he just wanted to try his luck. So I told him one bet only, and I bet with my money so that if he lost it wouldn't cost him anything. I considered it a bonus for his work for me."

The Captain continued to fidget with his head down in shame, but he changed the tone by pulling back his lips in a little guilty, schoolboy grin and looking up at Mom all doe-eyed. "Well ma'am, I guess he had beginner's luck, because his number came up, and he won."

Dawn interrupted, "Ray, you won a bet?"

Mom couldn't take it any more. She brushed Dawn off

and said, "Dr. Fleet, I do appreciate you giving Ray a job this summer, and I am truly grateful for the way you've helped Dawn, but I have to tell you that I really am disappointed by this."

He hung his head again. "I know ma'am; I know I shouldn't have, and I really am sorry."

"And the worst part is that he won," Mom went on. "Now he probably expects to win every time he lays down a bet. That's how people become gambling addicts," she added crisply, hands on her hips.

"Yes ma'am," the Captain said, still wringing his hat and studying his shoes.

I tried to help. "Mom, believe me, I have no desire to gamble ever again. As much as anything else I just wanted to see how the game worked, and now I know. Also, we met a true gambling addict at the hotel we stayed at, and trust me, I don't care if I ever see another casino ever in my life."

She seemed to calm down some at this. The Captain noticed too, and he seized the opportunity. "Ma'am, the money that Raymond won is his to keep; that was the deal. I know it's gambling money, but I'm sure you can put it to good use."

He pulled out the cashier's check and handed it to Mom. She didn't look at it right away; she was watching the Captain's hangdog manner and already starting to melt—I guess she figured she'd punished him enough with her disapproval. Finally, she took the check out of the envelope and glanced at it, then did a double-take. "Is...is this correct?" she asked in a voice that sounded like she had been sucking air out of helium balloons like we used to do when we were little kids.

"Yes ma'am," the Captain replied. "It's a lot of money, and Raymond won it fair and square."

Mom began to cry, and Dawn started going crazy to see the check. "How much is it, Mom?" she whined, "Mooooom, how much is it?"

"I'll tell you later, Dawnie," I directed. Mad at being left out, she turned her back on all of us and went back to *The Monkees*.

Mom sat down in the nearest kitchen chair, leaned her elbows on the table, and whispered, "Thank you." I knew she was thanking God, and it occurred to me that she must have been praying for days for an answer to our dilemma.

The Captain muttered, "Well, ma'am, we've had a long trip, and I guess I'll go home and get some rest."

I walked him to the door, and he motioned for me to come outside so we could talk privately.

When the door closed he half-whispered, "Raymond, we've had quite an adventure, haven't we?"

I chuckled softly. "You can say that again."

"Well, the real adventure is going to start soon, so you had better take a few days off before we get back to work. Rest up the remainder of this week and we'll get back to it a week from today, the usual time, okay?"

I nodded.

He turned to leave and then spun back abruptly. "Oh, Raymond?"

"Yes?"

He pulled the envelope from his pocket again. "Here's your overtime pay; probably better if you don't mention it to your mom." He handed me the eight one hundred dollar bills that I had cashed out for him from the casino winnings.

"Captain, that's too much," I protested.

"Too much for what?" he asked with a gleam in his eye. "Trust me Raymond, we both earned a little abundance this weekend. And besides," he mumbled cryptically, "very soon I will have no use for it anyway."

I didn't know what he meant by that, but before I could ask he blurted out something else I had forgotten about. "Also, remember that I should be getting back that money that Carlo stole as well. He had every penny of it on him when he was arrested, and as soon as the police don't need it for evidence anymore they will send it to me."

"Won't that take a while?" I asked.

He raised his eyebrows and replied, "Unless I miss my guess, with as much evidence as he has stacked up on him, old Carlo will plead out to avoid a trial, so they might be done with that money by the end of this week. It won't be long. Well, goodnight Ray, and have a good week."

I watched him make his way back to his house against the backdrop of the twilight—as he got farther away his personal features disappeared and he became just a silhouette with a cigarette. That visual effect and his unexplained comment left me with the feeling that I wouldn't be seeing the Captain for much longer, which rebelled against my sense of the man. I knew he was old, but he seemed almost impossibly vibrant, and I had come to think of him as a timeless fixture of nature, like Mt. Everest or the Redwood forest. His death seemed as out of the question as the moon falling out of the sky. I shook it off and chalked it up to the circumstances and being so tired.

I spent the rest of the week enjoying doing nothing. The Captain was right, as usual; I really needed some time to recover from everything we had experienced during the weekend. I lounged around during the day watching the Nixon Watergate scandal develop, read from a couple of books, and hung out with Griffin at night after the *Sani-Freeze* shut down for the day. He asked me about the Las Vegas trip, and I put him off. I really liked Griffin, but half the time I didn't believe what was happening with the Captain myself; there was no way I was going to ask Griffin to believe everything that happened during that crazy weekend, so I left out a good bit of our adventures and glossed over the rest.

One strange thing was that the Captain's car was gone most of the week. He seemed to be getting up and leaving early and not returning until late, which was a big departure from his usual routine of tending his garden most of the day and running the occasional errand. I wondered what he was so busy doing, but I reminded myself that, even though it seemed like I had known the man forever, I had only made his acquaintance a couple of months ago; I had no idea what his activities were like over any significant period of time.

I also noticed right away that Mom's demeanor became entirely different, like she had been relieved of a very heavy weight. In addition to having the debt problem solved, she told me she had learned from Mr. Jim that Dad had entered a rehabilitation facility to dry out, which explained why we hadn't heard from him in a while. I don't think she held out any possibility of reconciliation, but it was obvious that she still cared about him and wanted him to get healthy.

Dawn continued to improve, but she still had some issues. She had let go of many of the compulsive behaviors she used to engage in, but she had also picked up a new one recently. She began to fear germs, and she washed her hands over and over.

It was kind of hard to believe, but by the time I returned to the Captain's house on Monday morning the intense impressions of the weekend had faded quite a bit. I still remembered everything that had happened, but it didn't seem as real. My mind had started to play games with me, and I was wondering if winning that money had only been a coincidence. As usual, the Captain addressed those musings right away.

"*Ray, come on in,*" he called from the den when I opened the back door.

As I made my way through the kitchen I noticed that there was no coffee brewing. When I got to the den I found the Captain sitting in his green recliner, as usual, but something seemed very different. I couldn't put my finger on it, but something had changed.

"So, Ray, how have you been percolating?" He winked as I sat down on the couch.

I wasn't sure what he meant. "All right, I guess," I muttered.

"Well, you had to cram a lot into your consciousness in a short period of time. Don't worry if it seems to fade into the background. It will sink into your subconscious and bubble around a bit, but it will be there when you need it. Which brings me to our final project: distribution."

"What are we distributing?"

"My possessions," he answered casually.

Then it hit me. I hadn't been able to identify what was different about the Captain's house, but I realized that our voices sounded especially bright and harsh, the way voices sounded in a house without anything in it to absorb sound. I looked down the hall and saw that there were a few boxes stacked in it. Beyond the hall I could see the Captain's living room, bare. All the furniture was gone. He hadn't touched the den yet, but I got the feeling that the rest of the house was empty.

"Why?" I asked, dismayed. "Are you moving somewhere?"

He gave the slightest hint of a smile and answered softly, "Not exactly. There is really no 'where' to go, Ray, but if you want to talk about it like that you could say that I am going home."

"To your original bithplace?"

He spoke softly again, almost wistfully, "No, Ray. *Home.*"

The tone of his voice reverberated deep within my chest, and I knew what he meant. My eyes started to fill up, and I asked, "Why? Are you sick?"

He chuckled. "Because one's physical body must be sick in order for one to wish to be free of it? No, actually, I don't have any terminal disease process going on. No brain tumor, or lung cancer, nothing that has taken me over. I am just finished with my work, and it is time to leave this physical realm behind and move on to something else."

"Just like that? You're just not going to live anymore?"

"Well, isn't that what happens with all of us?" he asked as he lit a cigarette. "Whether we are aware of it or not, we fulfill the purpose for which we existed in the first place, and when we no longer need our physical expression, we are relieved of it. Most people are not in touch with the Power that assigns their purpose, so they aren't aware of it when their purpose has been fulfilled. Life provides them with some so-called accident or illness when it is time for their body and mind to die, and they resist it because they assume it is not in the plan."

I was angry. "So you are just going to leave everyone you know behind when you don't even have to? Your family? Kids, grandchildren, friends? Don't you care about anyone?" *Don't you care about me,* I wanted to scream.

"Ray, of course I care about others," he said gently. "The only real regret I have as I look back on my life is that I feel that I neglected my family and put them through some hard times so that I could develop this idea."

He rose from his chair and picked a carefully framed but obviously old and faded sepia photograph off the mantle. He stood there looking at it for a long time, and as he put it back he wiped away a single tear. Finally he said, "This is me and my wife, Delia, when we weren't too much older than you. For over half a century we lived a love affair that most people only dream about. She died just a few years ago, and I was genuinely surprised by how much it hurt."

I remembered what he had said in the car coming back from Las Vegas. "Is that the loss you mentioned before?" I asked softly.

He nodded. "I had thought I was past being so attached

to anything or anyone in this illusionary aspect of Life, but I was wrong. When she died, I felt the sting of every harsh word we ever spoke between us, every broken promise of every vacation we never took, all those times that I moved the family around and wrecked the stability she craved. I felt them all like daggers through my heart.

"But," he added in a brighter tone, "life goes on. Not just my little illusion of life, but *Life* goes on. As much as my mind and body have been genuinely attached to illusions, they are still illusions."

I was indignant again. "Are you saying that your wife of all those years was nothing more than an illusion?"

He smiled. "Ray, Ray, Ray, we've been over this, remember? There is an aspect of everything that is real, and an aspect of everything that is false. The false is the transitory, the ever-changing, the mind and body—all the temporary aspects. The real is the unchanging, permanent, timeless aspect. That aspect of her is, was, and will ever be Real."

He held up a finger and added, "But here's the thing— the Real part of her is the same part of me that is Real. And you. And those plants out in the garden. And everything that exists or has ever existed. It is the Source, the primordial energy that gives rise to every other form of energy. We're like a bamboo forest with a common root system. Seen above the ground bamboo looks like a forest of completely separate plants, but if you look beneath the surface you see that the individual shoots are just different stalks off the same plant.

"It is literally impossible for me to lose it or be separated from it, so the only part of my wife that I lost was the false part anyway. The only part of me that you will lose is the illusionary aspect of me. The real part will always be with you because it *is* you, in essence, at the deepest level. The body that dies and returns to dust and the mind that evaporates when the body disintegrates are illusions anyway; just functions of energy, like waves on the ocean. The essence—the water—is what is real, not the movements that we call waves."

I sighed. "So what about my training? You said you were going to help me learn how to live so that I wouldn't get into trouble. What's going to happen to me? And Dawn?" I added.

"I'm way ahead of you, Ray." He motioned to a large cardboard box by the other end of the couch. "Bring that box over here."

I retrieved it and placed it on his lap. He looked over the flaps at me and said, "Raymond, I have shown you many things to validate the principles that are written about in these books. I have paved the way in your consciousness for these ideas to take hold and flower. I have prepared the soil; now it will be up to you to continue to plant the seeds and tend the fruits."

"You're going to leave me with nothing but a bunch of books?" I asked, not without sarcasm.

"Books are just collections of ideas. These are the texts from every class I taught. You will need to study them diligently, and you will need to find a teacher who can challenge you and help you understand the ideas presented in the texts. Just don't be in too much of a hurry."

"What do you mean?"

"I used to teach students who would get excited about the classes and try to take all of them within just a few months. They were using the Law of Greed—not for material things, but for spiritual understanding. What you will see, is that the way to progress up this path is to study the principles and then spend some time and effort putting them into practice. Those people who wanted the knowledge instantly wanted the results without putting in the effort, and it doesn't work that way. You make progress in this sort of endeavor when you face challenges and respond to them differently, when you choose to believe that you are neither your mind nor your body, and when you choose to *act* as though Life is One. It takes time and the opportunity to face challenges in order to really apply the principles."

I didn't know what to say, so I just sat there.

The Captain broke the silence, "Helping your sister is going to be a good opportunity for you, Ray, although you might not realize it now. You will get to practice two of the most important elements of your training: listening for direction and getting yourself out of the way."

"What does that mean? Direction from who?"

"Spirit, of course. Or Life, if you prefer. Or whatever else you want to call it. It's about being able to perceive the correct thing to do or say in any given situation and then acting on it without intellectualizing it, doubting it, or being afraid of it. You will help your sister overcome her compulsions by doing that, but in order to be able to hear what needs to be done you must get yourself out of the way. Otherwise, all you will be able to hear is your own mind frantically seeking pleasure and avoiding pain."

"How do I do that?" I asked.

"When you are around her, consciously let go of any impulse or thought that arises as a result of your own desires, whether those desires be for her or for you. Set an intention to respond only to thoughts or impulses that feel like your inclination in that diner back there in Arizona. You've experienced it, so you know what it feels like. Mentally examine your interactions after the fact and honestly analyze your actions. Recognize when you have fooled yourself and acted from the standpoint of personal desire. It will take practice, but you will get the hang of it if you're diligent."

He put the box down on the floor and took something out of it. "Here, take this," he mumbled as he handed me a small blue book with gold lettering that said *Rays of the Dawn*. I thumbed through it and saw many of the laws that the Captain had been mentioning to me in passing, such as the *Law of Patience*, the *Law of Greed*, the *Law of Duty*.

He pointed at the book, "Everything I wrote and all the classes I created were for the purpose of helping people understand what is in that little book. It is written on many different levels, so to the uninitiated it appears to be a nice book but perhaps not terribly deep. As you understand more about the principles involved, you begin to see deeper layers in the writing. It will be the ultimate key to help you learn to use the principles you'll be studying."

I didn't know what else to say. It felt surreal; I couldn't believe I was sitting here talking about him dying like we would talk about when we were going to break for lunch.

Finally I blurted out, "You aren't going to kill yourself, are you? I mean, if you don't have a fatal disease and you are healthy, you can't just drop dead, can you?"

He chuckled. "Have you ever seen an old couple where one partner dies and the other who was, by all appearances, completely healthy also dies within a short period of time? When it is time to transition, Life provides you with a way to do it, just like it tells your body how to do everything else. When it is time to digest your food, Spirit tells your body how to do it. Dying is a natural physical process that is built in, just like digestion or birthing a baby. When it is time, it makes the necessary changes."

He leaned forward in his chair for emphasis. "We want to hold onto our bodies, so we assume that something must be wrong with death, but it is a great opportunity to realize something very important: everything that Spirit makes involves a dual principle of tearing something down in order to build something else up. In order to make one thing, another has to be unmade."

He paused, then added, "One of our very best teachers ever, a Mr. Bill McKeown, always reminded his students that when their lives seemed to be falling apart, as happens with all of us from time to time, it is merely a preparation for something new. If you fight it or try to cling to the old order, you will inevitably experience pain, and you may very well interfere with what Spirit is trying to build for you. Rejoice when you feel everything crumbling away, because your nature as a human being is one of being relentlessly creative, like the Phoenix rising time and time again from the ashes of the old. Do not mourn for the old; let it burn so that the new can rise."

Again I was at a loss for words. We sat there for a while until I could no longer stand the silence. "So what now?"

He slapped his thighs and sprung up off the chair, "Now we get to the task of distribution!"

We spent the day organizing his things into different piles: one to go to the Concept-Therapy Institute, one to go to his son, George, another for his oldest daughter, and so on. He had me put all the things in boxes and neatly label each one. He took all of his important legal documents and placed them in labeled manila envelopes on top of the box marked for his grandson, Warren McKenney, who was a lawyer and would be the trustee of his estate.

He told me that for the past several days he'd been arranging his affairs so that there would be no loose ends for anyone else to have to tie up—that's why he had been up so early and gone so much this past week. He had already contracted with a real estate agent to sell his house, he had put in with the utility companies to turn off his utilities at the end of the month, he had made funeral arrangements—he had done everything necessary to ensure that his departure would not inconvenience anyone else.

Finally we were done. I looked around, searching for something else to prolong the job. As much as the Captain had taught me that I should let go of attachments, I was resisting letting go of him with every fiber of my being. I felt like I had stumbled on a mysterious and not quite believable treasure, like a time portal or the fountain of youth, and before I had a chance to really understand it or share it, it was going to disappear. It would be a while before I would be able to look back and see how selfish my impulse had been; for the moment all I could think about was not having this crazy, extraordinary, maddening, enigmatic, unbelievable genius hiding in plain sight next door to me any more.

The Captain would leave quietly and, as always, with impeccable judgment. To avoid any prolonged goodbyes he would lead me to believe that he would be around for a few more days, but then depart that night almost immediately after I left. I would feel angry and betrayed at first, my emotions eventually giving way to an understanding of the Captain's wisdom. Over time I would dig out the books he gave me and begin to read them. After some more time went by I would began to really work with them, finding a teacher and doing the work necessary to make some spiritual progress, and after even more time went by I would start to try to live up to the charge he gave me, trying to pass on what I had discovered.

The Captain had a way of cutting right through the clutter of your mind and planting an idea directly into your consciousness. It might sit there dormant for years, I was to discover, but it was there, and when conditions were right, that idea would begin to manifest. The last thing he ever taught me was such an idea, and it was disguised by being sandwiched between a series of casual offhand comments.

I was getting ready to go home that evening, and the Captain went into the kitchen and came back with a couple of beers. He handed one to me and we sat on a couple of packed boxes and drank, talking about nothing in particular. "Ray, I want you to remember two things." He looked at me with his squint, and I felt the trapdoor to my subconscious open up wide. "If you will remember just these two things you won't get lost, you won't lose your way, and you won't get confused; not for very long anyway. Will you remember?"

"Yes," I warbled in my liquid voice, "I will remember."

"Good. First of all, remember that the secret of Life is that nothing you aspire to can fulfill its ultimate purpose for you unless you are willing to pass it on. You have to keep the energy flowing, so whatever comes to you, your intention must be to pass it on back into the flow of Life. Understand?"

"Yes," I heard myself coo, although the truth is that I really wouldn't understand until much later.

"Good. The other thing is this: no matter what happens, whatever circumstances you find yourself in, you don't want to take it too seriously. Love is a hammer, and it's always building. Whenever you find yourself playing the part of the nail—feeling sad, or frustrated, or hopeless—all you have to do is realign yourself with the energy of Love, and you will experience harmony instead of chaos. As this alignment becomes a permanent habit, you'll become a clear channel for Love—a Temple builder, playing your part to build the cathedral of Life. Got it?"

"Yes."

"All right," he spoke sharply, bringing me back into my normal consciousness.

We talked for a while longer, finished our beers, and I went home.

It was the last time I ever saw him alive.

Epilogue
Light

Thurman Fleet watched Ray return to his house through his bedroom window. Once satisfied that the boy was safe inside his own house and would not return, he took a shower, put on clean clothes, and lay down on his bed. He thought about his long life—he was almost 80 years old—and he remembered the pleasures he had experienced while in his physical body. He thought about Delia and the life they had enjoyed together, his children and grandchildren, the institute he had founded, and the people he had worked with. He had lived a rather extraordinary life, he supposed.

And yet, for over forty years he had craved something beyond the limited experience of his body and his mind. He had tasted a more expanded awareness at a relatively early age, and for the balance of his life he was unable to forget that expansion. Like the mythical man-eating tiger that, once having tasted human flesh could not be satisfied with anything less, Thurman had longed to return to that sublime state. No matter what task he might have been dutifully performing for Life, in the back of his awareness he had always been looking forward to permanently shifting from his life into Life.

Now that the moment was upon him his mind did conjure up some fear, but it was overpowered by his longing to experience the freedom of shedding the limits of his consciousness once and for all. He allowed his eyes to close, and he began drifting toward that destination.

He began to retrace his steps as he had come into this limited state of human awareness, like the Prodigal Son returning home. His body responded automatically to the impulse, and it began all the necessary physiological changes. Without the will to cling to corporeal life, the process was rapid and painless. As his physical body began to shut down, his higher senses began opening up, wider and wider with each passing moment.

Without a fully functioning brain to resonate with thought waves, he was no longer aware of the neurologically generated impulses we call thoughts, nor did he receive sensory impressions from his five outer faculties. Other, higher faculties that he had discovered and developed to some degree while in the body began to increase their activity exponentially. He found that his awareness was increasingly no longer limited to space and time, nor any opposites, and the collection of mental impulses known as his mind was willingly and gratefully abandoned.

His heightened extra-sensory faculties, rapidly rushing to maturity, began to deliver sensations of exquisite beauty and ecstasy. He was aware of something like music, though infinitely sweeter. It was as if a million stringed instruments manifested the universal embodiment of pure music, producing melodies that dwarfed any symphony he had ever heard, while a celestial choir wove harmonies of the most paradisiacal beatitude.

The boundaries of his awareness continued to crumble as he discovered an infinitely expanded palette of color, and his euphoria mushroomed as universes of exalted hues bathed his being in infinitely benevolent vibrations of Love.

It became increasingly inaccurate to describe Thurman as *he*, as the portion of Consciousness previously preoccupied with that tangled web of limitations, language, contradictions, emotions, and concepts called Thurman Fleet was steadily shedding all definitions of individuality. Every physical, emotional, conceptual, and mental filter that had compressed, limited, and distorted Consciousness into the sentience of a human mind and body was being lifted, and all that remained was the unbroken Universal Consciousness.

His delectation would increase to the point that he could no longer imagine it rising any higher, and suddenly another boundary would be shattered or another limitation lifted and the rhapsody would rise even higher. He began to feel ultimate freedom, increasingly unbound and without limits. All colors, all frequencies, all melodies and harmonies, rhythms and rests, sensations, vibrations, began to reveal themselves to him in a context of complete and utter perfection, and then he rose even higher in consciousness, and the spaces separating color from color or rest from rhythm collapsed in a final resolution of absolute unity, and the exalted divine bliss washed over him, through him; he was flooded with the incredibly benevolent vibration that it *was* him.

Oh, the freedom…

The joy…

Like a canvas on which a living portrait was painted, his awareness was being transferred back into the Witness of All—the Supreme Observer. All limitations—space, time, desires, beginnings and ends, fears, worries, physical identifications, mental opposites, were perceived for what they had always been—illusions dancing across the immovable, unchangeable screen upon which they were projected. He was melting peacefully back into the One Energy of All.

Oh, the peace—the absolute peace…

He was briefly aware of the *I AM*—the principle of pure Universal being, and that awareness gave way to simply *AM*, without even a subject to experience the being. Finally he was relieved of all sense of subject and object, time and space, and being or not being. The relative darkness of limitation was dwarfed by the infinite Universal Light that penetrates, animates, creates, and sustains All, and Consciousness once again dissolved completely into the pure, ecstatic, Primordial Energy.

The unbelievable, unending, and unbound ecstasy…

The End

The Power of You!

The purpose of this note is to invite you to join an online community of people interested in helping each other learn, develop, evolve, and heal.

You are powerful, and the process of living is interactive. You have a combination of talents, abilities, experiences, and skills that no one else can exactly duplicate. The online community is a place where others can appreciate your unique perspective. **Your voice is needed, please let it be heard.**

You may be able to change or influence someone else's life in a way that you can't imagine. Here's how:

♦ Log onto www.hurstpeacock.com and actively participate in the online community. Get involved! Someone may need to hear exactly what you have to say, exactly the way only you can say it.

♦ Use email, Facebook, Twitter, Myspace, etc., to invite and encourage your friends to join the online community and become active participants.

♦ Tell others about this book! If you benefited from the experience, you have received. In order to maintain balance, you must return the energy to Life. Give copies as gifts. Donate copies to libraries. Take advantage of the bulk discount on the website and buy several copies for resale, fund-raising, or educational purposes.

As of this printing, I am relying solely on word-of-mouth to let people know about this book and the online community. This is because I believe mass consciousness is evolving very quickly and power structures are shifting. Knowledge is going to increasingly become exchanged between people without first being edited or controlled by corporate or government filters. The Internet gives us all a powerful global voice, but it is up to us to speak.

I believe in the **Power of You**.

If you believe in the message, please pass it on.

Thanks,

Hurst Peacock